DISCARD

Notes from the Garden

Notes from the Garden

Reflections and Observations
of an Organic Gardener

HENRY HOMEYER

With block prints by Josh Yunger

University Press of New England
HANOVER AND LONDON

University Press of New England, One Court St., Lebanon, NH 03766

Text © 2002 by Henry Homeyer

Block prints © 2002 by Josh Yunger

Line art on pages 9, 26, and 137 © 2002 by Susan Berry

Line art on page 240 © 2002 by Jim Phelps

Printed in the United States of America

5 4 3 2 1

The photograph on page 40 is reproduced by
permission of the Valley News, Lebanon, NH.

The photograph on page 80 is reproduced courtesy of
Contact Press, New York, NY. Photograph © 2000
Annie Leibovitz/Contact
Courtesy of the artist.

Library of Congress Cataloging-in-Publication Data

Homeyer, Henry A.

Notes from the garden : reflections and observations of an organic
gardener / Henry Homeyer ; with block prints by Josh Yunger.

p.   cm.

ISBN 1–58465–109–1 (cloth : alk. paper)

1. Gardening—New Hampshire—Anecdotes.   2. Organic gardening—New
Hampshire—Anecdotes.   3. Gardeners—New Hampshire—Anecdotes.   4.
Homeyer, Henry A.   I. Title.

SB453.2.N4 H66 2002

635'.0484'09742—dc21

2002004177

This book is dedicated to my grandfather, John Lenat, who taught me to love gardening, to respect the earth and all living things. He was an organic gardener long before it was fashionable to be one, and taught me the value of a good compost pile.

John Lenat, circa 1950, in the garden

❧

Contents

I have always been a gardener. Some of my earliest memories are scenes from my grandfather's garden. I am an organic gardener, and although I have now studied the science of it, I grew up with compost and manure, not 10-10-10 and insecticides. I didn't know that most Americans consider chemicals necessary for gardening. I cannot remember a time when I was not interested in dirt and plants and growing things.

It was only when I owned my own land that I began to learn the "whys" of organic gardening, and many of the "hows." I knew I didn't want to poison my stream, or ingest any toxins with my vegetables. I also didn't want to kill the predatory wasps that help to keep down populations of cabbage loopers, nor exterminate any of the other beneficial bugs. And I have learned why my organically nourished soil outperforms soils "fed" with chemical fertilizers.

I was blessed with a piece of land alongside a stream, with good, moist alluvial soil. But I recognized that I could not expect that soil to perform well unless I treated it with respect, adding organic matter and minerals to replace those that time, weather, and my harvests removed. I began to read about gardening, to talk to other gardeners, and to try different techniques to see what helped give me better production for my precious tomatoes. Before long, I was a "serious" gardener.

I went through the University of New Hampshire Extension Services Master Gardening Program. I attended workshops, and took classes wherever I could. Gardening became an obsession, and finally a livelihood. I became a professional gardener, designing and installing gardens for others. Meanwhile, I continued to try out new techniques and new plants at home.

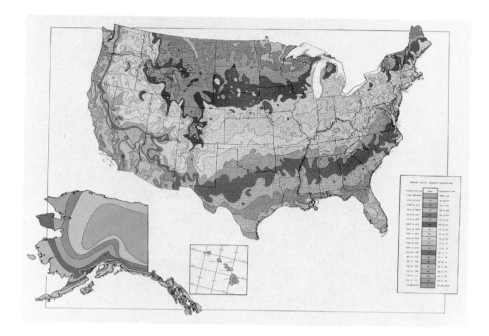

One day in the late fall I was driving down the road when it occurred to me that most people don't properly put their gardens to bed at the end of the season. They just stop gardening and hunker down for the winter. Having once been an elementary school teacher, I have never quite gotten over my impulse to teach. So I called my local newspaper, the *Valley News* in West Lebanon, New Hampshire, and offered to write an article about what to do for your gardens in the fall, and the idea was accepted.

I loved writing that first gardening article, and before long I was writing a regular gardening column. I still love writing an article every week. I love seeing people on the street who read my columns, and who have feedback for me.

This book is a collection of articles that I wrote over the past three years for my newspaper column, *Notes from the Garden*. It is written in 12 chapters, starting in March, which is when most of us start thinking seriously about the upcoming growing season.

Each article has one or more little icons above its title to give you an idea of what that article is about. The old-fashioned wooden wheelbarrow is used for articles of general gardening interest. To-

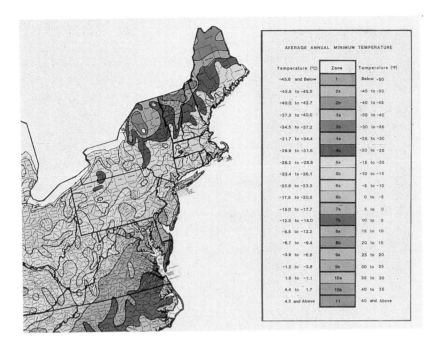

AVERAGE ANNUAL MINIMUM TEMPERATURE

Temperature (°C)	Zone	Temperature (°F)
-45.6 and Below	1	Below -50
-42.8 to -45.5	2a	-45 to -50
-40.0 to -42.7	2b	-40 to -45
-37.3 to -40.0	3a	-35 to -40
-34.5 to -37.2	3b	-30 to -35
-31.7 to -34.4	4a	-25 to -30
-28.9 to -31.6	4b	-20 to -25
-26.2 to -28.8	5a	-15 to -20
-23.4 to -26.1	5b	-10 to -15
-20.6 to -23.3	6a	-5 to -10
-17.8 to -20.5	6b	0 to -5
-15.0 to -17.7	7a	5 to 0
-12.3 to -15.0	7b	10 to 5
-9.5 to -12.2	8a	15 to 10
-6.7 to -9.4	8b	20 to 15
-3.9 to -6.6	9a	25 to 20
-1.2 to -3.8	9b	30 to 25
1.6 to -1.1	10a	35 to 30
4.4 to 1.7	10b	40 to 35
4.5 and Above	11	40 and Above

matoes or potatoes indicate a vegetable article; the flowers are for flowers. A tiny pair of pruners or a miniature shovel indicates pruning or digging is involved; a little rake is for articles about lawns. The skull and crossbones is used just once, in an article about pesticides. The ladybug indicates that insects are discussed. A frying pan is for food preparation.

I have touched on many topics: growing vegetables and flowers, planting and pruning trees, preserving the bounty, scaring away the critters who want a piece of the action, and lots more. Part of my joy in writing the column was always the excitement of learning new approaches, new techniques myself. And of course, I love sharing what I learn with others.

I love talking to other gardeners. I always learn something when I talk to a serious gardener. I have included an interview with an interesting gardener in each chapter. Most are organic gardeners, although I had to include Joe Mooney, former groundskeeper at Fenway Park, despite his decidedly nonorganic use of chemicals. I had to include him because he is such an interesting character, and because he was my first—and toughest—interview.

This book is based on my experiences in New Hampshire and Vermont. My own gardens are in USDA Zone 4, which means that the lowest temperature most years is between −20 and −30°F. I have survived Zone 3 winters here, of −30 to −40°F on occasion, and work in one garden near the Connecticut River in Vermont that I consider a Zone 5 garden, −10 to −20°F. This book is relevant to all those areas. Folks in warmer climes will experience spring earlier than we do, but the plants I mention are generally happy from here to the mid-Atlantic states, and west to the Rockies. I consider myself a New Englander, and throughout the book I refer to New England situations, but I hope readers elsewhere will not feel left out.

Doing a little gardening is a dangerous thing. You may *think* you can just dabble in it. But watch out; before you know it, gardening will become a passion that rules your life. It has for me, and I wouldn't change that a bit.

H. H.

Acknowledgments

Although I have been a writer all my life, it never occurred to me that I might one day make my living by writing. Karen Woodbury, my best friend and partner in all things, believed that I could, and she encouraged and supported me while I figured out how to do so. My most sincere appreciation goes to Karen, for believing in me and helping me to make a career change.

Many people helped me to learn about gardening. Thanks to Dave and Patty Talbot, whose course gave me the confidence to set out as a garden designer. Thanks to Pamelia Smith, whose course at Vermont Technical College taught me that shrubs can be wonderful, not just those evergreen blobs I grew up with. The University of New Hampshire Extension Service Master Gardening Program was a wonderful opportunity to learn and to become acquainted with experts in many fields.

My gardening buddies have been great teachers and friends, and I thank them all. I particularly thank Jamie Miller, Liz Blum, Alicia Jenks, and Doris LeVarn. Alicia has been a loyal reader of the manuscript as it developed, offering ideas and feedback. Thanks, too, to Barbara Barnes, my friend and mentor these past thirty-four years. Garden designer Ruth Anne Mitchell, who is also my big sister, has been a constant source of ideas and feedback, a good friend, and a loyal supporter. Thank you.

My appreciation goes out to all the readers of my newspaper column. Many have written or e-mailed me with questions, comments, ideas, and support. Without their feedback and appreciation I might have run out of steam.

Although I didn't turn my stepson, Josh Yunger, into a gardener, his artwork for the column, and now the book, have given me great pleasure.

Thanks go out to my first gardening customers, Joan Eckert and Hilary Pridgen, who each hired me as soon as I decided I was ready to hang out my shingle as a garden designer.

Special thanks to Richard Abel at University Press of New England for seeing the possibility of a book based on the newspaper column, and for providing feedback as I put the book together.

And finally thanks to Anne Adams of the Valley News, who bought my first column, and who has put up with me ever since!

Notes from the Garden

Chapter 1

March

On the Virtues of Organic Gardening

My grandfather, John Lenat (1885–1967), was an organic gardener. A tailor by trade, his greatest passion was gardening. He came from the old country, Germany, before the First World War and eventually settled in Spencer, Massachusetts. As my mother was growing up they kept a cow, had some chickens, and grew much of their food, particularly in lean times. By the time I came along the animals were gone, but Grampy grew enough vegetables not only for himself, but for neighbors, friends, and even the checkout clerks at the local A&P grocery store. His tomatoes and cucumbers were famous for their taste and abundance.

As a young child I never thought much about why my grand-father's vegetable garden was so amazing. I remember the excitement of going to the local chicken farmer to get manure, which we dumped into an old wooden barrel that was mostly full of water. My job was to stir the concoction each evening to make a "tea" for his tomatoes. He always had a huge compost pile that was full of earthworms. And around his house there were always copies of a funky little magazine called *Organic Gardening and Farming*, which he saved for years.

Later, long after Grampy had gone to the great garden in the sky, I started reading *Organic Gardening* magazine for myself and became convinced that organic gardening is a better, healthier, way to grow things. And although my grandfather never preached organic gardening to others, forgive me if I do.

Organic vegetables have become widely available at grocery stores, and most of us prefer to buy organic food when we can afford it, but I don't believe that most people understand what the term "organic" really defines. It does not just mean that no insecticides were sprayed on the vegetables. It also means that no chemical herbicides, fungicides, or fertilizers were used in the fields of production for at least a three-year period. The USDA recently amended the rules to prohibit using the term "organic" to label any genetically modified product.

It is obvious to all of us why we don't want chemicals sprayed on our foods. Rachel Carson opened the eyes of many Americans when she wrote her classic book, *Silent Spring*. Partly as a result of her book, the insecticide DDT (sold for decades to farmers as part of the "modern" way of farming) was eventually banned. Since then, many new generations of chemicals have been created and tested. Many of them may be safe if used as directed. I don't accept that they are all safe, or that they are all used as intended. I do know that I can trust my own chemical-free soil to produce vegetables that are tasty—and safe.

Many home gardeners avoid Death Row, the pesticide row, at their local garden center. But many still feel the need to buy chemical fertilizers such as 10-10-10, or the delicious-looking blue Kool-Aid for plants, Miracle-Gro. Organic gardeners believe they can get better results using composts, manure, and natural mineral additives to the soil.

Chemical fertilizers may not be dangerous to you, but they are not good for your soil and plants in the long run. The fertilizer industry has done a good job of making Americans think that soil is only there to give plants something to grab onto, that what plants really need can be produced in a factory and purchased by you. That is not so. The fertilizer industry works on the premise that you need to feed your plant. In contrast, organic farmers feed the soil so that *it* can feed the plant.

Planting a tiny seed in order to get a delicious tomato a few months later is truly miraculous, if you stop to think about it. Millions of chemical reactions or combinations of elements must occur in very specific ways. Over the millennia, Mother Nature worked out systems to accomplish this. Plants use energy from the sun to create their own food from water and carbon dioxide in a process known as photosynthesis. They also get needed elements from the soil. A healthy soil is full of living things that work in concert with your plants to create healthy growth the way nature intended, and the way plants grew before the advent of the fertilizer industry.

A key to successful organic gardening is providing lots of compost, or decayed plant or animal products. Compost does several things that make your plants happy: it provides organic matter, it holds water, it keeps the soil fluffy enough for air to circulate through the root zone, and it feeds the microorganisms that make the soil healthy.

Of course, there are liabilities as well. Beware of fresh cow and horse manure, as both are full of viable weed seeds. You can compost them, or age and turn them to reduce weed problems. I like to stockpile manure and use it after two or three years. Some farmers are now starting to produce composted manure for sale by the truckload to gardeners. It's worth every penny you pay. Composted cow manure is also available in plastic bags, but since more is better when it comes to manure, this can get expensive.

A single teaspoon of healthy soil can contain 5 billion bacteria, 20 million filamentous fungi, and a million protozoa. Some of these are microorganisms that can fix nitrogen from the air; others help roots obtain minerals, or attack disease-causing pathogens. Some of these organisms will be killed, or their effectiveness diminished, when you add chemicals to your garden. Herbicides, fungicides, insecticides, and yes, even fertilizers can affect the health of the microorganisms, and of your soil.

Chemical fertilizers are water soluble, which also means that rain or watering can wash away the elements that you have bought to feed your plants. A soil that is rich in compost and microorganisms makes nutrients available as they are needed by plants. Adding soluble nitrogen suppresses the growth of nitrogen-fixing bacteria. (Fixing nitrogen means taking nitrogen from the air and combining it with oxygen and hydrogen to make it available to plants.) So adding chemical fertilizer can make the soil even more needy of fertilizer over time, and some commercial fields become nearly sterile.

But there *are* good things that come in fifty-pound bags. Limestone is one. It is a source of calcium, and usually magnesium, two minerals needed by your plants. Here in the northeast the rain really is acid, which causes the soil to be acid. If the pH of your soil gets too acidic, certain minerals get bound up and unavailable to plants. Wood ashes can be substituted for limestone. A pound of ashes is equal to two-thirds of a pound of limestone. Kits are readily available for home testing of pH, and these will tell you how much limestone to add to get your soil to a healthy pH.

Rock phosphate is another good mineral to add to your soil. It comes in a bag, and is essentially ground up rock, which slowly dissolves and makes itself available over at least a four-year period. It doesn't migrate through the soil, so it needs to be thoroughly mixed in, not just applied to the soil surface. Phosphorus is needed by plants to develop strong roots, set flowers, and produce fruits.

Greensand is another good product used by organic gardeners. It looks like its name: green sand. Suspiciously enough, it comes from New Jersey. Apparently it comes from an ancient underground sea bed, and is a good source of potassium and, even more important, of trace minerals that are essential for healthy plants and soil. Greensand is useful in breaking up heavy clay soil (as is compost). Potassium promotes development of strong cell walls, which helps plants to survive environmental stresses like cold and drought.

In recent years a number of companies have been formed to produce and sell organic fertilizers. I am partial to one called Pro-Gro, made in Bradford, Vermont. It is made from dried whey, cocoa meal, compost, seaweed, ground oyster shells, and other natural goodies. Although the bag lists the three main ingredients as a 5-3-4 fertilizer, it contains many other nutrients. That is because it contains material produced by plants, and by animals. It is a slow-release fertilizer, and some of its components are effective for years. Similar products are made throughout the country; just look for the term "organic" on the bag.

I feel good about being an organic gardener not just because it's good for the environment and lets me eat healthy foods. I am also an organic flower gardener, and believe that I have healthier, more vigorous plants because of it. Just as a healthy, well-fed child resists illness better than a malnourished one, my plants are healthier because they are organic. Although I can't prove it, I am convinced that my tomatoes taste better because they are organic. And most of all, I like growing things the way my grandfather did. Sometimes I have a feeling he's smiling on my garden.

A Rose by Any Other Name Is Just as Sweet

Mickey Mantle. Chickadee. Monarch butterfly. You know exactly what these names refer to. Gardeners, particularly flower gardeners, encounter dozens of names each growing season. But we don't just get simple names like daisy to learn, we also are faced, often times, with the Latin names. *Rudbekia hirta. Iris siberica.* Many gardeners shy away from learning the Latin names of plants, shaking their heads and waving their arms. "Nope. Not me. No way." I'm going to recommend that you learn a few Latin names.

Why bother learning Latin names? For starters, it's an accomplishment. I remember reading Ann Landers 40 years ago when she advised starting each day by making your bed. Why? Because it only takes a minute, and you feel better knowing that you have already accomplished something. Learning a Latin name is much the same. It is an accomplishment.

And you know what? Latin is easier than English or French or Spanish to sound out. No silent consonants. See it, pronounce it. There was a comedian whose mantra was "I don't get no respect." Learn a half a dozen Latin names, and throw them into a discussion with other gardeners. They will immediately upgrade you from dilettante to devotee. You'll get some respect.

Another reason to learn Latin names is that they are absolutely precise. I visit a lot of gardens in the course of a growing season, and when I talk to gardeners who have just moved here from Georgia or California or Minnesota, they often talk about plants that I don't know. I mean I do know them, I just don't know them by the names they use. What I call lungwort others call striped dog, still others Joseph and Mary plant. But if you say *Pulmonaria longifolia*, there is no question as to what flower you mean. Even if you just say *Pulmonaria* you are ahead in the game.

We name things we see and care about, our dogs and cats, for example. But those names only matter to us. Someone has gone to the trouble to name all the plants known to mankind, and to make them recognizable to everyone. When you learn the Latin names you join that international community of people who care about plants.

Okay, it's cold and snowy out there, and we can't garden. So go to the library, or select one of your own books of flowers. Settle in for your first lesson. Look up your favorite flower by common name. Iris? That's easy, the Latin is *Iris*. But wait a minute, there are several iris.

Each Latin name normally has two parts; the first name, which is capitalized, is the genus. The second word is not capitalized, and is the species, which is the most specific name. Within most genera (plural of genus) there are several related species.

So under iris there is *Iris cristata*, or crested dwarf iris. Then there is *I. ensata*, Japanese iris. Whenever you are talking about species within a genus, you can use just the first letter of the genus, in this case *I.*, instead of writing out *Iris*. You may be familiar with *I. pseudacorus*, or yellow flag Iris, which grows big and tall on the banks of ponds and streams. If you are a gardener, you must know *I. sibirica*, or Siberian iris, that lovely ephemeral (usually) blue flower of early June. Lastly (for this discussion, anyway), there are the bearded iris, the showy ones, which come in many colors. They are just called iris hybrids. The iris hybrids are flowers that breeders have developed by cross-pollinating (breeding) two different species within a genus.

So now you see, perhaps, why it is good to learn the Latin names. If you just say "iris" it doesn't tell the listener which one you mean. And in Japan or Holland, they have different common names than we do for *Iris ensata*. Horticulture is a worldwide activity, but the Latin names stay the same everywhere.

Are you ready to learn a few more Latin names? I'll just give you a few that are interesting in their derivation. *Hemerocallis* is the genus for daylilies, and is Greek for "beautiful for a day"—appropriate since that is how long each individual blossom lasts.

Latin Names of Some Common Flowers

Aquilegia hybrids	Columbine
Aster novae-angliae	New England aster
Cleome hasslerana	Cleome, spider flower
Dicentra spectabilis	Bleeding heart
Digitalis purpurea	Foxglove
Echinacea purpurea	Purple coneflower
Monarda didyma	Beebalm
Paeonia hybrids	Peony
Papaver orientalis	Oriental poppy
Phlox subulata	Creeping phlox

Strawflowers are really *Helichrysum bracteatum*. *Helichrysum* is once again from the Greek: *helios* means sun and *chrysos* means gold. And the species name is related to our word bract, meaning a much-reduced leaf associated with a flower, in this case the stiff "petals" around the blossom. Our common sunflower is *Helianthus annuus*, literally "sun flower." The species name *annuus*, means annual. Simple? You'll get the hang of it with time.

Yarrow is another flower with an interesting Latin name. It is *Achillea millefolium*. The *Achillea* refers to Achilles, the mythical warrior. It is said that he made a salve from it to soothe and heal the wounds of his warriors. Millefolium means, literally, a thousand leaves. *Folium* looks a lot like foliage, doesn't it? And this is a plant with very finely divided foliage. Makes sense to me.

So go ahead and give the Latin a try. Learn a few names on a cold day, and dream of spring when you'll be looking at these wonders of nature as you speak their names. They might just appreciate your learning *their* names as much as you do when a distant acquaintance remembers yours when you see him on the street. And think about being upgraded to the "Serious Gardener" category—a little Latin goes a long way!

March Is a Good Time to Prune Fruit Trees

The maple sap is running, my snowdrops (*Galanthus nivalis*) are blooming, and warm sunny days have turned my thoughts to gardening. Like many gardeners, I am ready to start tilling the soil. Unfortunately, it is still quite a long time until that will be possible. In the meantime I have to do something to keep from going nuts. Pruning my apple trees will help.

March is the month, traditionally, for pruning fruit trees. It is fine to prune fruit trees in April and May, or any time until the flowers buds open. But now is when we need to get outdoors and do something. I have one full-sized apple tree, and I love having a good excuse for climbing it, saw in hand. Adults aren't supposed to climb trees, but I love to do so, and suspect that there are plenty of others who feel the same way. Climbing up into the blue sky on a sunny day is as close as I'll get to flying.

However, most people don't prune, even good gardeners. There is something irrevocable about lopping off a branch, particularly a good-sized one. Perhaps we think of trees in human terms, where an amputation is a serious operation. But pruning helps the tree. For fruit trees the benefits are not only aesthetic, but will give you better yields of fruit. So get outside on a nice day and try your hand at it.

First a few principles of pruning. What you are going to do, by pruning, is to help the tree let light get to all its branches. Trees need sunshine on their leaves in order to create food by the process of photosynthesis. If you have too many branches, particularly those that parallel each other or crisscross the tree, the interior of the tree is shaded out, and it cannot produce as much food.

It is important to know where on the branch to cut. Do not cut off a branch flush to the trunk or larger branch where it originates. There is a a swollen area called the collar where each branch is attached. This collar produces protective barriers against invading disease. A flush cut (tight to the trunk) removes this important area and opens a large area to disease. The collar bulges at the branch's at-

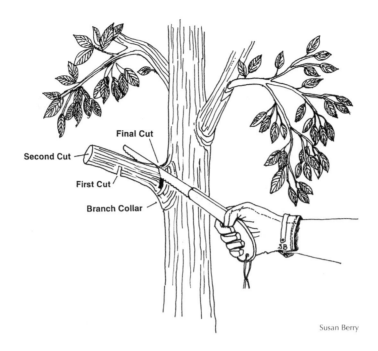

Final Cut

Second Cut

First Cut

Branch Collar

Susan Berry

tachment point and usually has a wrinkled aspect to its bark. You will want to cut just beyond the collar.

Fruit trees often have numerous "water sprouts". These start out as pencil-thin branches popping straight up from larger branches. Unless you prune each year, of course, they will get big and make the interior part of the tree a jungle. They are easy to recognize, and a rookie pruner might begin here, while building up confidence. Last year's water sprouts can easily be snipped with a pair of bypass pruning shears. Bigger ones will need a pruning saw.

A few words about tools: Don't use the anvil type of pruning shears on your fruit trees; they crush the branches, leaving wounds which are open to pests and disease. Bypass pruning shears cut like scissors, and work well on small branches. Don't try to cut branches bigger than the manufacturer's recommendations, or you will spring them, and they will never work well again.

I spoke to a friend of mine whose husband has a chainsaw, and loves to use it. She tries to keep him inside during the pruning season (or on a short leash), and with good reason. Although a chainsaw can be useful for taking off a large branch, rarely is one needed, and they can quickly reduce your favorite apple tree to a skeleton.

For a long time the accepted rule of thumb was that it was all right to prune out a third of a tree in any given year. Arborists now say 20 to 25 percent is a better limit. Removing too many branches means less food produced for your tree. It won't kill the tree, but may stress it out.

If you want to prune well, buy a new pruning saw. The old bow saw that you got when Timmy was a Boy Scout is rusty, dull, and the wrong shape. Ask for a tricut pruning saw, and you will get what you need. Pruning saws generally taper to a sharp point so that they can get into the tight spots that you will encounter.

Some fruit trees are infected with viruses, which can be spread from tree to tree like flu through a preschool. The way to prevent this as you prune is to sterilize your saw and pruners after you finish each tree. A 10% solution of household bleach will do the trick nicely. I put mine in a quart sprayer or old Windex bottle.

Cut out any deadwood you see. You can do this any time of the year. Even without leaves, dead branches will be obvious to you: The bark will be dry and flaky, and there will be no buds for new leaves. Take your fingernail and scrape the bark of a twig. If it doesn't show green, it is dead.

When cutting big branches it is important that you not let the weight of the branch tear it off before you have cut all the way through. This can result in tearing off strips of bark, opening unnecessary wounds, and creating places for disease to enter your tree. Prevent it by cutting off the branch with three cuts. First make an undercut roughly 12 inches out from the trunk on the branch, cutting about one-third of the way through. Then go a little farther out the branch (away from the trunk) and make a top cut, which will sever the branch. Finally, remove the stub just outside the collar, cutting perpendicular to the axis of the branch.

As you work on the tree, take time to stand back and see what you have done. Remember, you are trying to open up the tree to let in light, and to eliminate branches that are shading others. Try to make the tree beautiful. It should be pleasing to your eye, not a mishmash of branches. It might help to observe apple trees in a working orchard before you begin, in order to get a better idea of what one should look like.

Pruning really isn't so tough, and once you get the hang of it you'll wonder why you never did it before. And remember the advice I got from an old orchardist when I was dithering about a branch I

> Increase the water you give your indoor plants beginning in March, especially your rosemary if you have one. With lengthening days your plants will start their spring growth spurt and will suffer (or die) unless you increase the amount of water you give them.

wished I hadn't cut off so impulsively: "Don't worry, others will grow in its place."

Trees are like gardeners, remarkably resilient. So go out on a sunny Saturday, and try your hand at sculpting your tree. It will produce better, look better, and you will feel better for "doing something" while waiting for spring to really arrive. And bring a few branches indoors, put them in water, and they may please you by blooming in a few weeks.

Vermont Ladyslippers

As a boy of twelve, Bill Ballard was walking in the woods near his home in Greenfield, Massachusetts, when he came upon a stand of wild ladyslipper orchids in bloom. He was awed by their beauty. He was thunderstruck. "I fell to my knees and wept," he told me nearly eight decades later. Bill went on to become a well-known fish embryologist, but ladyslippers were his passion. He feared that as land was developed and habitats lost, these scarce and temperamental orchids would go the way of the dinosaur. He decided he had to do something about it.

Professor Ballard did much to save habitats and develop an environmental consciousness in his community of Norwich, Vermont. But even more importantly, he did something no one else had ever done: propagate ladyslippers in the laboratory. Prior to that, scientists had believed that ladyslippers could only grow outdoors in a symbiotic relationship with a specific fungus. It takes nearly 2 years for a ladyslipper in the wild to germinate, develop a root system, and finally produce two small green leaves that will produce its food. Up to that point, it gets nourishment from the fungus.

After retiring in 1971, Bill spent a lot of time sloshing around swamps in red, high-topped sneakers, studying ladyslipper habitats. But he was also growing ladyslippers from seed in a sterile growing medium in his laboratory at Dartmouth College. He raised them to a point where they could survive on their own in the wild without the fungus. He published a paper on this that caught the eye of a young aerospace engineer, Scott Durkee, of New Haven, Vermont.

Scott saw his first ladyslippers in 1988, and he, too, was enchanted by them. Over the next 10 years Scott perfected his own techniques for growing ladyslippers from seed in the lab. He and his wife, Elizabeth, started the Vermont Ladyslipper Company, which they run out of their home, a modest white farmhouse on the edge of a windswept field in dairy country.

Being a Vermonter and an engineer, Scott built his own equipment for working with these orchids, such as the "glove box" he needed for working in a sterile environment. The glove box has long-sleeved rubber gloves going into a Plexiglas box where he can painstakingly transplant the tiny seedlings into a medium free of airborne fungus spores.

Instead of buying a glove box for $3,000, Scott built his own with materials from Aubuchon's Hardware—for under a hundred dollars! He raises plants in sealed containers lovingly placed in plastic shoeboxes. He has improvised and cobbled together an interesting array of devices and techniques to do what few others in the world can do: grow northern orchids in a lab from seed. And it all works just fine: Scott and Elizabeth now have 50,000 ladyslipper orchids in various stages of development, and a business that is taking off.

Almost anyone who is willing to make a little extra effort can grow ladyslipper orchids. Don't try digging up plants in the wild. They are on the endangered species list, it's illegal, and you'll probably kill them anyway. They can be purchased as dormant, bare root plants in April or October from Vermont Ladyslipper Company. Some nurseries now buy them from Vermont Ladyslipper in October and pot them up for sale in other months. Ask how they were propagated, and don't buy them unless they were laboratory grown.

Each type of ladyslipper orchid has very specific requirements for growth. Pink ladyslippers (*Cyripedium acaule*) need a poor, dry, acidic soil. Showy ladyslippers (*Cyripedium reginae*) need wet, neutral or sweet soil. Both types need part sun, but neither is happy in full shade. The Durkees' literature explains what you need to do in order to make your soil suitable. They even explain how to create a wet place to grow the showy ladyslippers by burying a plastic garbage bag, creating a mini-bog.

Bill Ballard passed away in 1998 at the age of ninety-two. But his legacy lives on, and Scott Durkee is doing something Bill only dreamed of: making ladyslipper orchids available to the public. Now you don't have to steal them if you want some on your own land. They are commercially available, so you can buy them.

A Gardener Dreams of Spring

Every year when the snow turns brown and skies turn gray with mud-season rains I am saved from declining into a psychological slump by two things: the increased hours of daylight, and my snowdrops (*Galanthus nivalis*). Every year—or almost every year—on March 4 I go outside and pick my first flowers of the year. I remember it is March 4 because it is the birthday of a loved one. It is always a delight to grace the table with fresh cut flowers, even those so small and unassuming as snowdrops, so early in the year.

Most people don't have spring flowers until April or later, but anyone can. March is the time to go outside, look around, and do some planning for next year. Our snowdrops grow on the south side of the house, about 6 feet from the house. If they were a little closer to the reflective warmth of the house they might  bloom reliably in February. We have daffodils that snuggle right up to the house, and they first poke their noses up in late February, but they won't bloom for a few more weeks. Crocus will bloom in March, too, if they are planted in the right spot. So walk around your property today and note where the snow melts first, and plan to plant some early bulb flowers next September.

For many years when I was busy with other things I didn't bother starting plants indoors. It seemed like too much trouble to nurture little plants on the window sill for months when I knew I could drive five miles in any direction and find a reliable greenhouse that would sell me tomato plants just the right size at just the right time. For many people, buying tomato plants at a local greenhouse is the best choice, but the seed catalogs do offer some things worth considering. Beyond something to dream about, that is.

You might consider ordering seeds if you are a cook who would like to have hot peppers of varying flavors and intensities. In general, greenhouses here have little variety in hot peppers. Peppers are rated in Scoville units, starting at 300 to 700 for Hungarian wax peppers, increasing to 3,500 to 6,000 for cayennes and jalapeños, and peaking at a blistering 200,000 to 350,000 Scoville units for Habaneros. I have been able to determine that the units were named after Wilbur Scoville, an Englishman, who started measuring heat in peppers in the early part of this century. What I have not been able to determine is how he measured the heat. I like to imagine him serving little tea sandwiches to proper English lords and ladies, but with peppers beneath the watercress. Did he measure heat by face color or expletives?

Certain vegetables are not usually purchased as plants in six-packs. Root crops (like carrots and beets) are always planted as seeds. Potatoes are planted as chunks of sprouting potatoes. Lettuces and other greens can sometimes be purchased as six-packs at your local greenhouse, but are direct seeded by most gardeners. Most vine crops, from cute cornichon cukes to the behemoth blue Hubbard squashes are easy to start directly in the ground. Vine vegetables germinate relatively quickly, but some melons need to be started indoors in order to bear fruit before frost. Unlike those tiny carrot seeds, they are large seeds that even your six-year-old can plant.

As much as I like to buy locally and support our local vendors of seeds and plants, I have come to enjoy reading seed catalogs and ordering some seeds by mail. It gives me the opportunity to really read the descriptions and think about what I can realistically expect to grow in my garden. This is the time of year to plan your garden, to draw maps and set priorities. Go outside and measure your garden space so you can decide now how many rows to plant in tomatoes. Get your hands on a catalog and dream about what you would like to grow. There is a wonderful range of plants to choose from.

I have come to enjoy planting heirloom and unusual plants. I recently ordered seeds for a red-cored Chantenay carrot, another heirloom. I dream of biting into perfect orange carrots and seeing a ruby red center. I don't know if they will live up to my expectations, but it gets me through mud season thinking about it. Or maybe I'll plant some Punjabi purple carrots from India, where carrots originated.

If you are new to the area or haven't done much gardening, you can learn much from your neighbors about what grows well here. Most gardeners love to give advice and will be helpful to anyone who wants to get started. So if you don't have any seed catalogs, ask a neighbor to let you borrow one. Probably you will also get advice about what lettuce, spinach, or carrots have worked well in your own neighborhood.

If you are ordering seeds from a catalog you should pay attention to the number of days to harvest. For things like lettuce and carrots, which are planted directly, the number is quite simple. For tomatoes, peppers, or eggplants and others that can be injured by frost, it is *assumed* that you know that the "number of days to harvest" on the package means time from *the day you transplant them*, not when you first planted your seeds indoors in April. I generally pick seeds with quicker growing schedules, all things being equal.

Being a gardener means that I am an optimist. Who else but an optimist would believe that it is possible to grow beautiful and tasty vegetables by burying insignificant specks of matter in dirt? Yes, we could have floods or a drought, but I believe that by early summer I will be harvesting comestibles from the garden that are chemical-free and delicious. I'm already dreaming of that first fresh tomato, that first crisp cuke. And it helps me muddle through mud season.

Growing Vegetables All Winter Long in an Unheated Greenhouse—In Maine

Winters in New England, even in the best of years, can seem too long for many gardeners. We long to eat our own fresh vegetables, to know the joy of food picked and eaten within hours. There are limits to what we can do without a heated greenhouse, but those limits have been redefined in recent years by the work of a Maine organic gardener and writer, Eliot Coleman.

Coleman eats and sells fresh vegetables all winter long without using fossil fuels or expensive technology. He describes all this in his book *Four-Season Harvest*, published by Chelsea Green Publishing (1999, paperback). On a snowy day in late March I drove to Harborside, Maine (on Penobscot Bay), to visit him and to witness his operation.

Eliot and his wife, garden writer Barbara Damrosch, live in a simple house on a rutted dirt road seemingly out in the middle of nowhere. Coleman had gone to Harborside in the late sixties to meet Helen and Scott Nearing, authors of the 1954 classic *The Good Life*. The Nearings liked him, and offered him a piece of their land at $10 an acre, the price they had paid many years earlier. Eliot turned down their offer. He insisted on paying a higher price, compounding the effects of inflation. He has lived there off and on for thirty-two years, farming full-time since 1991.

The Nearings devoted their lives to hard work, self-sufficiency,

and intellectual excellence. They became role models for many people of the "back-to-the-earth" movement. Eliot Coleman followed their example, living softly on the earth, gardening organically, and developing ways to minimize any adverse impact his farming might have on the environment.

Coleman's farm is at 44°N latitude, roughly halfway between the equator and the north pole. It lines up with southern France and northern Italy, but has a very different climate. The warmth of the Gulf Stream and the Mediterranean Ocean keep the climate warmer there, but the length of the day and the strength of the sun are the same. The average January temperature in southern France is 40 to 45°F, although they do get freezing temperatures.

Harborside, Maine, is in USDA Zone 5. During the month of January the average temperature is 21°F. Even so, Coleman believed he could grow cold-weather vegetables without heaters. He was right.

The heart of Coleman's system is a standard single-layer plastic-covered hoop greenhouse. This is the outer shell of the system, the equivalent of a windbreaker you might wear on a windy day.

Next he uses row covers, each a layer of spun agricultural fabric that is kept a foot off the ground by wire wickets. The row covers allow 95% of the sun's light to pass through, hold in heat, and keep up the humidity. This would be the sweater you would wear under the windbreaker. His soil is rich and dark, which absorbs the sun's heat. It releases heat all night long, like a soapstone stove after the fire has gone out.

Next Eliot had to select the right vegetables to grow in the system. He knew that he couldn't grow tomatoes or eggplants without burning lots of fuel oil, but that there are many salad greens that will survive freezing temperatures without complaint. He and Barbara traveled through France and Italy some years ago looking at hardy winter crops and how people grow them there.

Their growing plan involves planting hardy crops in the fall, beginning in August and continuing through October, to provide greens all winter long. The plants do most of their growth during the warmth of the fall, and then coast through the coldest, darkest parts of the winter unharmed. Those still in the ground in March start a growth spurt as the days get longer.

The greens get frozen every night, surviving temperatures in the high teens as long as they warm up during the day, which they do, even on cloudy days. The system of protection rarely lets temperatures dip below 18°F at night, even if it is well below zero outside. Greens picked frozen will go limp and unattractive. Greens picked at midday are not frozen, and they not only are tasty but salable. Eliot and Barbara do brisk business selling salad greens all winter long.

The selection of greens they grow includes many most of us don't know, things like mache or "corn salad" (*Valerianella locusta*), and claytonia or "miner's lettuce" (*Montia perfoliata*). They even grow dandelions from seed! More common crops include carrots, beets, leeks, spinach, chard, and a wide variety of lettuces.

When the days start to lengthen in March the crops begin to grow again. For most plants this is a good thing. Carrots, however, must be harvested by the end of February, as carrots lose their good flavor once they start their second season of growth. They are sweetest during the coldest months, Eliot told me. As I walked around the greenhouses I was amazed at the quantity, variety, and health of everything I saw. It made my mouth water for my own spring salads.

Eliot Coleman is an organic gardener, which means he uses no chemical fertilizers and no pesticides. Most greenhouse operations rely heavily on pesticides. Coleman believes that healthy plants are much more resistant to attack by disease and insects, so he concentrates on providing optimum growing conditions for the plants.

In his book *Four Season Harvest*, Eliot explains that stressed plants change their protein metabolism, building up amino acids in their leaves and stems. These amino acids attract insect predators. This fascinates me. It gives scientific evidence for what so many organic gardeners have observed: Plants grown in a good, rich organic soil are less likely to be attacked by bugs.

Plants can be stressed by heat, incorrect watering, or excessive fertilization, among other causes. Greenhouses that are pushing their plants to grow big and fast stress their plants, making them more susceptible to insect damage, thereby requiring pesticides.

One of the advantages of winter production is that many pests are lethargic, dormant, or dead. The hot-weather bugs aren't interested in a greenhouse where the temperature often dips down into the twenties at night.

The plastic greenhouses Eliot uses are designed to be portable, even the biggest of them. He can pull them forward or back with a tractor, allowing him to capitalize on the cleansing effects of the sun, rain, and cold weather to help eliminate insect pests that might otherwise become chronic problems.

Meadow voles can be a problem, because they love fresh salads as much as Barbara and Eliot do. Eliot uses mouse traps baited with strawberry-flavored Bubble Yum brand chewing gum to keep their numbers down. In case you're wondering, I asked. For best results, don't chew it first.

People have criticized greenhouses for using so much plastic sheeting, which is made from petroleum products, so Coleman did the math on it. He figured out how much petroleum is used to provide plastic for one of his greenhouses, how many lettuces he can grow in it during its useful life span, and how many gallons of diesel it would take to truck the same amount of lettuce from California. He figures his lettuces only use 6% of the energy required by trucked-in lettuce. And they're a lot fresher.

Eliot Coleman uses no plastic or cardboard to package his vegetables for market, selling it in reusable wooden boxes. His lettuce mixes are carefully washed and then dried (in the biggest salad spinner I have ever seen), so that the greens are ready to use, an attractive feature for restaurants.

When I asked Eliot what training he had in agriculture, he explained that he was largely self-taught. His degrees are in English and Spanish literature. While teaching at Franconia College in the

1960s, he took one day a week to study agriculture. He read his way across the shelves of Dartmouth's Baker Library from 630.1 to 634.0, "Agriculture" in the Dewey decimal system. "I read every book I could find," he said. More importantly, Coleman questions what he reads, does his own experiments, and keeps good records.

Eliot Coleman is not only an organic farmer, and one who would make the now deceased Helen and Scott Nearing proud, he is a businessman. He makes his living farming, and has figured out that each crop must return $1.50 for each square foot of greenhouse space that it occupies. If a vegetable can't be sold at a profit, it's off the list. He is constantly looking for more efficient ways to do things.

It is heartening to me, an amateur organic gardener, that there are people like Eliot out there, finding improved ways to grow things organically. He's the kind of guy who is always looking to build a better mouse trap. Or to catch voles with strawberry Bubble Yum, if that's what it takes.

Chapter 2

April

April Is the Time to Start Seedlings Indoors

The deep snows are melting. The spring sun has some real warmth to it, and it brings hope to gardeners. Winter has been defeated. Spring and summer are headed our way, and fast. Snowdrops once again grace our table, daffodils are playing catch-up. This all means that it is time, once again, to start seedlings in the house.

But first, why should you bother starting your own seedlings? Variety. Price. I do it to keep sane. Although some greenhouses are getting very good at offering many different annual plants and vegetables, they can't offer everything. Growing heirloom vegetables can be wonderful if you would like to taste the flavors your grandparents knew. Or you can start one hundred flowers for the cost of a couple of six-packs of plants from the greenhouse. A mass planting can be expensive if you buy plants someone else tended. And of course tending to seedlings helps us to keep busy during the mud season.

Many people have tried starting tomatoes or other plants by seed and been disappointed. Let's look at the common causes for failure, and how to avoid them.

First, people too often start their seedlings too early. This often means that the plants get leggy and weak. By starting in mid April you have already minimized that problem. Yes, if you are just starting now, your tomato plants will be shorter than those you buy at the farm stand at the end of May, but they will catch up quickly once they get their toes in warm earth and bask in the hot June sun.

You can minimize legginess by using supplemental lighting and growing them at the right temperature. Adequate lighting is very important for any plant. Many hardware stores sell inexpensive 4-foot-long, two-bulb fluorescent fixtures that will make your plants purr. Don't waste your money on fancy "Gro-lights," anything will do.

The trick is to have your lights at the correct distance from the seedlings. This can be accomplished by suspending the lights from the ceiling over your plants. Place the lights about 6 inches above the plants, and as they grow, raise the lights as needed. Your local hardware store will sell you the appropriate fasteners to go in the ceiling, and some light-weight jack chain. Plant stands are also available, though pricier.

Warmer is not better when it comes to growing seedlings. Sixty-two degrees works well for me, although there is natural sunlight on them, so they get warmer than that during the day. It's ideal to have them in a room which cools down to the 55 degree range at night.

If you have had a problem with your seeds not germinating in the past, there are three common causes. Most likely it was due to the growing medium drying out. This is easily fixed by either wrapping your flats with Saran wrap, or placing plastic covers over your planting flats.

Clear plastic covers are available that fit over the trays that hold the little six-packs of seedlings. They are the easiest solution, and although they cost more, they are usable year after year, and I recommend them. Lift them off after everything has started growing.

Secondly, some seeds need a specific temperature to germinate. Seed companies are getting better about explaining that, but not all are perfect. Generally 65 to 70 degrees is fine for germinating flowers, and all vegetables that I know of. Some flowers need it a bit warmer, and a few want it to be quite chilly. Larkspur, for example, will not germinate in warm earth; it starts best at 40 to 50°F, so I do it outdoors.

Lastly, some seeds need light directly on them in order to germinate. These plants need to be planted on the surface of the soil and barely covered up. Lettuce, some flowers, and many weeds fall into this category. Seed packets should tell you this, or the catalog you ordered from. Seeds in this category don't even try to grow unless they are near enough the surface to succeed. Many weeds are programed to wait until you bring them to the surface to germinate. Of course they risk drying out, which is also lethal to a tiny seedling.

New seedlings are very tender, and are susceptible to a fungus, commonly found in garden soil, that causes death by "damping off." They literally keel over and die, and there isn't much you can do about it. Although you can sterilize garden dirt by cooking it in your oven at 250°F for forty-five minutes, this is akin to skinning a skunk. You might do it once, but it stinks to high heaven, and nobody wants to eat dinner afterward.

Buy a bag of soilless mix designated for starting seeds. It is a peat moss mix with perlite and a little fertilizer. It doesn't have much nutrition for your plants, but they will be going outside around June 1 anyway, and if you want you can fertilize them with a water-soluble fertilizer. I like Neptune's Harvest, a liquid organic fertilizer, and despite its fishy past, it doesn't smell bad or attract the cats.

To plant your seeds, buy some of those little black plastic six-packs and fill them up with soilless mix. Water well. This stuff usually will not cooperate. Water sits on the top, and does not soak in. Or it will run right through. Since these six-packs are not sturdy, you need to buy the trays they sell with them. Be sure to buy the kind that have no holes in the bottom.

You can put water in the tray and let the mix soak up water from

Other gardening notes: If you buy tulips at the grocery store, be sure to trim their stems under water before placing them in a vase. And add three pennies to the water. It will help keep them from going by too quickly. Another trick is to put them in an unheated space like the entryway when you go to bed at night. Hot temperatures finish them off quickly.

the bottom, but it will happen very slowly. It may take hours to be well moistened. Drain off any excess, and you are ready to plant.

Seeds, in general, should be planted at a depth equal to two to three times their length. For big seeds like squashes or watermelon I create a hole with a grapefruit knife, drop in the seed, then cover with soil. Little seeds I place on the surface, then just sprinkle a little planting mix on top. I use a retired kitchen sieve, and shake it over the seeds for a fine layer of soil.

I always plant two seeds per compartment. If they both germinate I snip off the frailer plant after a week, so that the remaining plant can do better. Plants don't like competition, even from their brothers or sisters. Tough to do, but necessary.

Most people plant lettuce seeds directly in their gardens, but I like to start some in the house now. A couple of six-packs of lettuce started early will cut the grocery bill for salad greens sooner. They transplant well, and I love that light green color of the leaves as they develop under lights in my bathroom. I have some growing outdoors in my cold frame, too.

As much as I love living in New England, I do believe spring should come a little sooner. If you are feeling cranky and out of sorts because of the snow and mud, I recommend planting some seeds in the house. I feel better every time I look at a little tomato plant. It reminds me that soon summer will be treating us to fresh vegetables and gorgeous flowers . . . if we make it through black fly season, which comes first.

Building an Old-Fashioned Hot Box, and Other Tricks for Jump Starting the Gardening Season

Avid gardeners are always looking for ways to extend the growing season, particularly in New England. Recent weeks of cold, raw, gray, rainy and generally unpleasant weather have been making me wonder if summer will ever come, or if perhaps I should move somewhere more hospitable. Don't get me wrong. I love the vagaries of the weather, it's just that sometimes enough is enough. To combat these feelings I decided to try building a hot box so that I could start growing more things outside now.

Gardening books written before World War II often make mention of hot boxes as a way to extend the growing season, but I had never seen one, nor met anyone who had one. My grandfather always had cold frames, and I have built them myself as a way to keep eating lettuce late into the fall. A hot box is similar to a cold frame, but it uses the heat generated by the fermentation of fresh horse manure to create heat, enough heat to keep the plants warm all night, and to keep them content despite day after cloudy day.

In order to build a hot box you will need an old wooden storm window approximately 30 × 60 inches, a sheet of 2-inch-thick blue Styrofoam insulation, some clear 4-mil plastic sheeting, six cement blocks, a couple of scrap two by fours, and two large wheelbarrows of fresh horse manure.

Finding the right horse manure is the hardest part of this project. The first manure pile I visited had too much straw bedding mixed in, so that the pile wasn't "working." There was no heat being generated. The next farm had a pile that was just right. The manure pile was 76 degrees on a day when it was 40 degrees and drizzling, and it was literally steaming. There was some straw and some sawdust mixed in, but it was a nice juicy manure pile whereas the first one was dry. I have a soil thermometer, but you don't need one—just check that it is warm to the touch. Or look for steam on a cold day if you prefer.

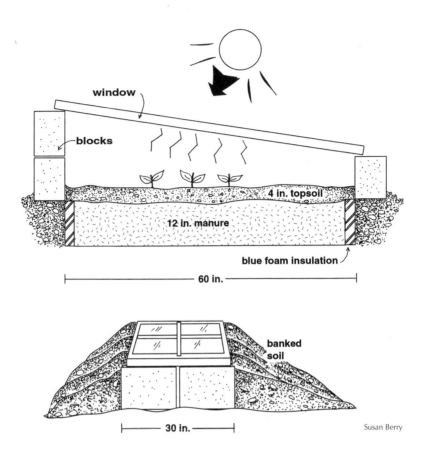

window

blocks

4 in. topsoil

12 in. manure

blue foam insulation

60 in.

banked soil

30 in.

Susan Berry

I selected a site on the south side of my barn that gets lots of good sunshine. I dug up the sod, and set it aside for use later. Then I dug a pit the size of my storm window and a full 12 inches deep. Next I insulated the side walls of the pit with the Styrofoam insulation. I used a hand saw to cut the 24-inch-wide piece of blue board up the middle. I cut two pieces that fit into the hole as sides, and had enough left over to do the two ends. The ground right now is 40 degrees, and much heat would be lost laterally if I hadn't used the insulation. I suppose in the old days they did without it, so you could too. I happened to have the insulation, and it seemed like a good idea at the time.

I shoveled horse manure into the pit until it came up to ground level; then I added 4 inches of good compost/topsoil mix on top. At each end of the hot box I placed cement blocks as supports for my storm window. I wanted the window to slope to the south, so I made the head end higher by using two layers of cement blocks there, and one layer at the foot end.

For the sides of the hot box I used the chunks of sod, then mounded the rest of the excavated dirt up against it. If you had bricks or boards or extra cement blocks around, they would do just fine for sides. To make a more airtight fit for the window I lay two pieces of lumber on top of the dirt and sod.

Since the old storm window was peeling its white paint, and I didn't know if it contained lead, I wrapped the window in clear plastic sheeting. I am growing vegetables in the hot box, and don't want to get any dumber by ingesting lead. The plastic also helps hold heat in for those extra cold nights.

The results have been impressive. The day after I built it, we had suffered the indignity of 2 inches of wet snow during the night, but it was 60 degrees inside! The heat from the fermenting manure warms the soil, and keeps the air warm enough for tender plants even without sunshine. I planted seedlings I had started in the house, including a tomato and a pepper, and they are doing nicely. Mostly I planted cold-weather crops like lettuce and broccoli, but I did risk one of my precious artichoke seedlings, and it seems pleased to be outdoors. I also planted lettuces by seed, and they germinated in two days! Bottom heat is good for germination.

Each morning after it warms up outside, I prop open the lid of my hot box 2 inches all the way around. This allows air to circulate and it keeps it from getting too hot inside if the sun comes out. One very hot, sunny day I removed the storm window and put it aside.

If you want to warm up the soil in your garden to give a quick start to lettuces outside, there are a number of other things you can do. The simplest is to hoe up a small raised bed and cover it with clear plastic. When you make a raised bed, the wet spring soil will dry out more quickly. The clear plastic will trap the sun's heat (if you are lucky enough to see the sun) and warm the soil. You can leave the plastic on after planting seeds, but remove it as soon as they germinate, or you will kill them. It is easy to achieve 100 degrees under the plastic.

I built three miniature green houses to experiment with. Gardener's Supply Co. (1-800-863-1700 or www.gardeners.com) sells wire hoops that can be placed in the soil to create mini-greenhouses 3 feet wide and 16 inches tall. Three hoops are adequate for a 4-foot-long hoop house. The company also sells "garden fabric" to drape over the hoops, and I got some of that. It provides a windbreak but lets 85% of the light pass through. I covered one hoop house with the fabric, one with clear plastic sheeting, and one with used bubble wrap I got from a furniture store. I sealed up the edges of the hoop house with dirt, and I closed the front with a scrap of lumber placed over the plastic. The plastic and bubble wrap houses quickly heated up to 100 degrees on a sunny day, which was great for warming the soil, but not so good for growing plants. The garden fabric was great—it is a spun fiber that breathes, so it never got hotter than 85°F inside.

Unlike my hot box, the hoop houses cool off quickly at night. If you start things in a mini-greenhouse with garden fabric, be aware that it won't keep your plants protected on a very cold night. You will have to cover it with a bedspread or blanket if the temperature is going to descend into the lower twenties, or you will risk killing non-hardy plants like tomatoes. Gardener's Supply claims that it will provide frost protection down to 28 degrees, and at least where I live and garden, we will see several more nights colder than that. But I'm willing to try almost anything (short of a deal with the devil) to get my tomatoes ready to eat a little earlier this year.

Spring Lawn Care: Organic or Chemical?

Americans love lawns. We have over 15 million acres of lawn. Huge sums of money are spent each year by people—mainly guys—on growing and maintaining lawns. There is quite a spectrum when it comes to interest in lawns. At one end of the spectrum are the teenagers who have to push the mower around the yard before they get the car. At the other are those people who keep their lawns perfectly free of weeds and never let it get longer than 2.25 inches, who fertilize regularly, and who apply fungicide, herbicide, and insecticide whenever there is a hint of a problem.

I am closer in approach to the teenagers than to the latter group. I admit I love dandelions, and don't worry about crabgrass. I cut my lawn regularly, and that's about all I do for it. In order to write this article I talked to two lawn specialists: one organic and one purely chemical in approach. The organic approach made the most sense to me, but I'll tell you about both.

First, a few basics of lawn care. Don't think of lawns as green carpets, think of lawns as lots of individual plants that are forced to live in very close proximity. This means that each plant is competing with its neighbors for nutrients, and unless you have a naturally rich, deep loam topsoil, you will have to supplement the soil with fertilizer if you want a "Better Homes and Gardens" type lawn.

Bagged fertilizer comes in many strengths, and is labeled with three numbers (such as 10-20-10), which indicate the ingredients as percentages. In this case the fertilizer is by weight 10% nitrogen, 20% phosphorus, and 10% potassium. The rest (60%) is inert filler. Nitrogen helps a plant grow robust green tops, the phosphorus promotes root growth, and potassium helps the grass build strong cell walls to resist stresses like cold, drought, or heavy traffic. Grasses need thirteen other minerals for growth, but they do not come in your bag of chemical fertilizer.

Even if all the needed minerals are present in your soil in adequate amounts, they may be bound up, and not available to your grass if the soil is too acid or too alkaline. It is a good idea to test the acidity of your soil, especially if you are about to seed it. Simple kits are readily available at garden centers. A neutral or slightly acid soil (pH 5.5 to 7) is best for the lawn. You can make your soil less acid by adding limestone. Limestone is not fast acting, and fall is really the best time to apply it if you want to top dress your lawn, but a little now won't hurt. Use limestone, not powdered lime, and you will not burn the grass.

I went to Fenway Park, the home of the Boston Red Sox, and talked to Joe Mooney, who has been head groundskeeper there for the past thirty years. Joe uses a totally chemical approach. First he explained that a lawn will not green up until the soil temperature reaches 50 degrees. He begins the season with a 14-3-3 fertilizer with a built in fungicide. Most other experts recommend a spring fertilizer with more phosphorus than nitrogen in order to help the roots before pushing green growth. The fertilizer Mr. Mooney uses gives the grass a quick burst of green growth, and the fungicide is important because he grows Kentucky bluegrass, which is susceptible to fungus when it is fed a lot of nitrogen. The general rule for growing bluegrass is that you need to feed it five pounds of nitrogen per 1,000 square feet per season, but the turf at Fenway gets much more than that. Joe Mooney knows intuitively what to do, and when. Bluegrass needs full sun to do its best, which translates to at least six hours per day.

Home and garden centers sell complete lawn "systems." If you want to go the chemical route, read the bags carefully before you buy them. Also read the warnings and hazards that are listed on the bags containing insecticides, herbicides, and fungicides. And remember, they tell you this information and still hope you will buy their product. I won't use anything that requires me to wear protective masks or clothing. I often see signs posted on lawns by lawn care companies warning you to stay off the lawn for a set period of time after application. Those toxic chemicals don't just disappear, and if my lawn is "safe" after three days, where have the chemicals gone? Downhill? Downstream? To my neighbor's yard? No thank you, that's not for me. Even if it breaks down, I don't trust the by-products.

I also spoke to Lindsay Strode of Cape Organics in Harwich, Massachusetts. He has been installing and maintaining organic lawns for about 10 years, and is a wealth of knowledge. Lindsay started by saying that good soil is the key to a good lawn, and that good soil is full of living organisms. Bacteria, beneficial fungi, worms, and insects work in concert with the plants in a healthy soil to create a healthy lawn. Chemicals that kill or damage the living organisms create imbalance, and more opportunity for a pest to become a problem.

The turf at Fenway is pure bluegrass, a monoculture that could be wiped out by a disease quite quickly if not for the chemicals. Lindsay recommends lawns be seeded with a mixture of grasses to create a diverse population that is more likely to stay healthy. His favorite mix for sunny locations is 19% Veranda tall fescue, 19% Kittyhawk tall fescue, 19% Barlennium perennial rye grass, 10% Chewings fescue, 9% Aaron Kentucky bluegrass, and 10% white clover. The main thing is to buy a good mix, and one that is appropriate for your site. The amount of sun you get is very important, so buy some shady lawn seed to use in areas where you don't have full sun. It may look a little different from the grass you plant in full sun, but will be healthier.

North Country Organics, our Vermont-based organic fertilizer manufacturer, makes a bagged fertilizer called Pro-Start, which Lindsay Strode uses on lawns in the spring. It is a 2-3-3 fertilizer, a little lighter on the nitrogen than Pro-Gro, my old standby for use everywhere. But the best thing you can do, he says, is to spread a thin layer of compost or composted manure on your lawn. He scatters it with a shovel and then smooths it out with a rake, a layer one-quarter to one-half inch thick. If your lawn has been a chemical lawn, the compost will help to reinoculate the soil with useful bacteria and fungi.

Thatch is a problem on some chemically treated lawns. Thatch is a layer of grass clippings that have not decomposed because the chemicals have killed the microorganisms that break down the grass. Instead of using a dethatcher to remove the thatch, you might consider renting an aerator. This is a motorized machine with tines that dig out plugs of lawn perhaps ⅜ inch in diameter and about 2¼ inches deep. If you use this first, then spread compost, you will not only allow water and air to get to the roots, but you will also get microorganisms into the lawn most effectively. Don't bother to rake up the plugs. In a healthy lawn they will decompose quickly.

Milky spore is a treatment that helps to reduce the Japanese beetle grubs that moles and skunks love. It is a bacterial treatment, and Lindsay tells me that it can be quite effective over a long period of time. Like any organic solution to a problem, it is not a "quick fix." Read the directions carefully before you buy it, as it is not an inexpensive treatment. I have heard lots of anecdotes from people who have used it and liked the results, especially those whose roses and other plants had been decimated by Japanese beetles in the past. Once established, the milky spore should continue to live in your lawn for years.

Spring is a good time to clean up the lawn and give it a little of the fertilizer of your choice. You can scatter some seed over the dead spots, and cover with a very thin layer of good topsoil. Grass seed generally needs light to germinate, so don't cover it deeply. Keep the seed from drying out by covering with a little straw. Fall is really the best time to do major lawn improvements.

An organic lawn will have insects and grubs, both good and bad. It will have dandelions and the occasional weed. I can live with that. And I might just live longer with that. I don't need to have a Fenway Park environment around my house, I'd rather have a healthy environment around it.

Starting a Garden from Scratch

If you have thought it would be too much work to have a vegetable garden, think again. There are some tricks to saving labor and getting good results, right from the first year. Think about juicy, red tomatoes, corn picked while the water boils, cucumbers with skins you can eat. I think it's worth the effort. Here are my tips for the beginning gardener.

First you need to select a good site. Full sun is what you want, but you can do it with as little as six hours of sun per day. The more sun, the happier your plants will be. More sun means bigger, earlier tomatoes, and more of them.

Then you need to learn about your soil. Each state has an extension service with a laboratory that can test your soil. It makes sense to get your soil tested and learn as much from them as you can. Get a pH test done to find out if your soil is too acid or too alkaline, so that you can make adjustments as needed.

Pay a little extra and find out how much organic matter is in your soil, as this is a key ingredient to a healthy soil. You will need to add organic matter each year anyhow, but this number will help you see what you are starting with. Good soil has 8% organic matter. In a suburban subdivision you might be lucky to have 2%. There is a test that can also tell you whether you have a heavy clay soil or a nice loam, so if you're not sure what you have, get a "soil texture" test done.

Moisture is important to plants, but avoid a site that holds water and is soggy all summer if you can. I have a wet site for my garden, but as with most obstacles, there are ways around the problem. It does mean I can't get started as early in the spring as I'd like. Creating raised beds helps a wet site to drain better, helping to solve the problem.

If you are going to start your garden in what is now a lawn or field, you must not let someone come in with a big rototiller and chew up the the grasses. This is very important!! The grasses and weeds will not die, and will plague you all summer, and for years to come. Each scrap of root can regenerate a new plant.

Many rental centers have something called a sodlifter available. It is a motorized machine that will cut strips of sod and slide a blade underneath it, so that you can roll up your sod and take it away. It is a heavy machine, does not do well on steep banks, and isn't great about turning corners. But it is an amazing labor saver. In a couple of hours time you can do what would take the best of gardeners a full weekend—if you didn't get discouraged first! If you are starting from a field, mow the grass short before starting.

My suggestion for the size of a first vegetable garden would depend on how much time and energy you have, but if you are renting a sodlifter, I'd advise doing the biggest plot you think is practical. You can always cover up part of the sod-free zone with mulch or black plastic if you don't want to use it all this year. Once you taste those tomatoes, you'll want more space next year, or you can rotate your garden back and forth between two plots.

For a family of two, a plot 20 by 20 feet should be adequate. You will need more than that if you plan to plant pumpkins, squashes, and cucumbers, as they can take up a lot of space. But for a first year, don't bite off more than you can chew.

If you only want a little garden (say 8 feet by 10 feet) for a few tomatoes and a little lettuce, you can do the job by hand. Cut the sod into one foot squares with an edging tool or a shovel, loosen the sod with a garden fork, and shake the excess dirt back into the garden. Compost the sod in either case.

In most suburban lots the soil near the house is pretty awful. It is often the subsoil that was removed when the contractor dug the basement, then spread out over the lot. Loam, or topsoil, is worth its weight in gold, and most of us have to figure out how to improve what we inherit to turn our soil into a good loam.

The key to good soil is adding organic matter in large quantities. Most households can never generate enough compost, so you are going to have to find another source. Many dairy operations now sell aged or "hot composted" manure. Fresh manure is usually full of weed seeds, but turning it to aerate it will heat it up enough to kill the seeds. Manure also comes in plastic bags at garden centers, but that gets expensive if you are planning a large garden. Old leaves are great if you have them.

Double digging is a technique for preparing the soil for a new garden. It is particularly important in an area with heavy clay soil. It's a lot of work, but worth it. Good soil will result in a good garden. Heavy, unimproved soil is almost guaranteed to disappoint you.

Start by removing all sod or grass, as already described. Then dig a trench by removing the soil in a strip a foot wide and deep. Save the soil in a wheelbarrow or on a tarp. Then take a garden fork to loosen up the soil in the bottom of the trench. Do this by stepping on it, then pulling back on it to loosen the soil. Do that all the way down the trench.

Add compost or manure to the bottom of the trench, as much as you can afford, preferably 2 to 4 inches. Then dig a second trench, but put this soil into the first trench, mixing in some more compost as you go along. Loosen up the subsoil in the second trench, and repeat. And repeat until your back hurts and you have blisters on your fingers. Actually, if you wear gloves for this activity, you will avoid the blisters.

After the first year, you won't have to double dig anymore. But each year you should add compost, and some bagged organic fertilizer. The organic fertilizer is made from things like seaweed, dehydrated whey, and compost, and has many different minerals that your plants need. A bag of chemical fertilizer such as a 10-10-10 only provides the three basic elements, nitrogen-phosphorus-potassium, but plants need a total of thirteen different elements from the soil to grow well and stay healthy. Think of 10-10-10 as Wonder Bread, and organic fertilizers as gourmet meals.

But actually, you shouldn't think of what you do as feeding your plants. What you need to do is feed your soil and the microorganisms in it. You are providing a good growing environment for the bacteria and fungi and insects and earthworms that work with your plants to provide the minerals needed to your plants, and which give your soil its ability to hold moisture and allow air to reach the roots. You are trying to nurture a light, fluffy soil that is rich and dark with organic matter.

Most gardens can also benefit from some rock phosphate and greensand added to the soil. Do this as you double dig, as the rock phosphate does not migrate through the soil easily. One application of rock phosphate will provide phosphorus for several years.

Greensand is a naturally occurring substance (deposited by the sea eons ago) that provides potassium and trace minerals. It is very good for helping to break up heavy clay soils. Follow the directions on the bags, and rest assured you will not burn even the tenderest of roots with these additives, nor with organic fertilizers properly applied.

I started using raised beds years ago because my soil stays wet in the spring, but have decided that wide raised beds make sense for everyone. Making wide beds allows your plants to send roots out in a wider and deeper pattern than they would in more traditional beds with narrow rows surrounded by hard-packed walkways.

After you double dig and add compost, your garden plot will be higher (and fluffier) than the surrounding land. Take a garden rake and mound up beds that are 24 to 30 inches wide. Leave the walk-ways just 12 to 15 inches wide, raking the soil from the walkways into your beds to help increase their height. Doing this will give your plants maximum space to extend their roots. And by creating wide beds, you end up with less square feet of walkway than you would if using narrow beds. Root crops like carrots and beets will perform much better in a raised bed.

After your plants are in the ground you can save yourself lots of work by mulching them well. This will keep weeds from taking over, and will help to hold in moisture. There are lots of ways of mulching. I favor a system that starts by spreading out four to six layers of newspaper, then covering that with 6 inches of straw or mulch hay. Wet the newspapers before you start, or your newspapers may end up in the neighbor's yard

The newspapers keep early weeds from coming up, keep out seeds from the mulch, and will disintegrate by the end of the season. Earthworms love them. Most newspapers use vegetable dyes, so don't worry about the inks introducing heavy metals to the soil. If the print doesn't come off on your hands like it used to in "the old days," you are safe to use them.

Every new gardener needs a gardening friend with experience. Talk to your gardening neighbors who seem to be doing well, and learn from them. Retired gardeners are often your best resource, as they have the time and the experience to help you. But beware of those who still use chemicals to solve all problems!

If I had just one bit of advice for the new gardener, it would be this: Don't stretch yourself too thin. Start small, improve the soil well, and enjoy the fruits of your labor. But be advised, once the gardening bug grabs you, you will always want to do some more. And what could be better?

Tulips

It's spring, and the gardeners among us are coming out of their winter funks after a particularly long and snowy winter. Snowdrops, crocuses, and daffodils, the early harbingers of spring, are blooming. But it is only when the tulips start to blossom that we know that spring really has arrived.

Tulips have fascinated gardeners for centuries. They are not native to the United States, or even to Holland, where raising tulips is a major industry. Tulips in the wild are not much like those most of us grow. The "species" tulips, those that originally grew wild, are low-growing little guys who sport simple flowers in primary colors. They come from Asia, often growing in mountainous, remote places. Some were carried away by invading Turks when they traveled to the mountains bordering Tibet, China, Russia, and Afghanistan centuries ago. They were being cultivated in Persia and Turkey a thousand years ago.

According to Persian folklore, the first red tulips sprang from the earth where a grief-stricken man, on hearing (incorrectly) of his lover's death, hacked himself to bits with an ax. Tragic. Poetic. Fit for an opera, or perhaps a Country and Western song.

Tulips first came to Europe from Istanbul around 1559, bulbs that were collected by an Austrian ambassador to the Ottoman Empire as representative of the Holy Roman Empire. In the early years, bulbs were given and traded by botonists and collectors around Europe who were fascinated by their beauty. By this time the tulips had been hybridized and cultivated for hundreds of years, and were like our modern tulips in many ways.

Tulips can be propagated either by seed, or by harvesting "offsets," which are little side growths that become flowering bulbs in their own right in a couple of years. The offsets are identical in genetic makeup to the bulb they have come from. Seeds can produce different progeny, depending on the parents, and take six to seven years to flower.

Tulips took Europe by storm. By 1630 breeders had developed thirteen distinct groups of tulips, and many hundreds of named cultivars. Holland was the center of the tulip trade, as the poor sandy soil there worked well for producing them. Prices began to climb sharply, and "tulip mania" was born.

Holland in the early 1600s was benefiting from the spice trade, which often allowed merchants to reap a 400% profit on their investments. The merchants then invested in country homes, art, tapestries, and other signs of their wealth. Thus artisans were fully employed and, though not even comfortable by our standards, were doing better than craftsmen and laborers elsewhere in Europe. The Dutch also believed that if you were successful in what you did, you could rise in social standing, just as we do here in America today. Hard work and industry were valued highly.

At this time, a hard-working craftsman might earn 300 guilders in a year. Fancy tulips were highly prized, and by 1630 some individual bulbs were selling for a hundred guilders and more. There was huge demand, and very limited supply. By January 1637 the top-selling bulbs went for more than 10,000 guilders each, the cost of a fine country estate.

The most valuable bulbs were infected by a virus that caused them to bloom with wonderful streaks and stripes of color. The virus was not understood, but it was understood that certain tulips would produce these amazing beauties, and that most would not.

The offsets of an infected tulip would produce the same amazing blooms. The disease weakened the plants, however, so that a bulb might only produce two offsets a year, and expire after just two or three years. Tulips bred from seed might be completely different, so the real beauties could not be easily mass produced. It might take ten years to produce 1,000 bulbs.

The Dutch at the time were reputed to have been serious gamblers. As it became obvious that the tulip prices were continuing to climb, doubling in a year or less, everybody wanted a piece of the action. Craftsmen were willing to mortage the tools of their trade in order to have money to buy into the tulip trade. It seemed like a sure bet.

The tulip trade got out of control when the rules changed. Instead of selling real bulbs that were on the shelves of bulb dealers during the summer months, people started buying what we would call "bulb futures." A 10% deposit would constitute a sale. The idea was that the price would double before it was time to actually turn over the bulb. At the height of the frenzy, some bulbs were sold up to ten times in a day.

Another factor in the bulb mania was that common, uneducated craftsmen were buying and selling bulbs, and they were earning in a few months (on paper) much more than they previously might have made in a lifetime. Thus more and more people got involved, driving prices up further. Most of the dealings were done in bars, with huge quantities of beer and wine being consumed.

Eventuallly the market got so strong that people were buying and selling common tulips that no one really wanted, and at vastly inflated prices. There were no checks or controls. Fraud was easy to perpetuate. Doom was just around the corner.

The bottom fell out one day when no one bid at an auction in Haarlem. Bulbs were offered, but no takers bid. Panic broke out. Everyone tried to unload their bulbs at once, and they became virtually worthless almost overnight. Within three weeks the country was in turmoil. Prices fell to 1% to 5% of their previous level within a matter of weeks. Courts and lawyers spent years trying to sort out who owed what to whom, but the result was financial ruin for many.

If there is a lesson to be learned from this story I will let you figure it out. But I will leave you with this anecdote. In the Muslim tradition, all flowers belong to heaven. Thus, when a famous Turkish holy man was asked who would go to heaven, he pointed to a gardener. He said that the Hadiths (or oral pronouncements of Prophet Muhammad) declared that people who go to heaven will do there what they most enjoyed in life. So surely gardeners are needed in Heaven! I do not play the stock market and will never be rich, but perhaps I have something to look forward to. In the meantime, I'm enjoying my tulips.

The Wizard of Turf at Fenway Park, Joe Mooney

Today, April 11, 2000, the Red Sox play their first game of the new season at Fenway Park, that wonderful aging ballpark that has been home to so many great players, and a few championship teams. Very few. Like all Red Sox fans, I'm convinced that this could be the year for the Sox. One thing is certain, however: The turf at Fenway Park, one of the few parks that has held out against Astro-Turf and the use of green dye, will look great. This is due largely to the stewardship of Joe Mooney, head groundskeeper at Fenway for the last thirty years. I went to see Joe Mooney recently to find out how he makes the grass so beautiful, despite the early spring weather of New England, which is often cold, and always unpredictable.

Like many of the ballplayers, Joe Mooney started his career working in the minors. He grew up near Scranton, Pennsylvania, where his grandfather worked in the coal mines. As a boy he watched the men coming out of the mines, faces blackened by coal dust, bone weary. He knew that this was not for him. The Red Sox had a farm team in Scranton, and at age seventeen Joe got a job working on the field. Now at 69 years, Joe knows turf as well as anybody in the business. He knows it intuitively. He has no rules for applying fertilizer or fungicide. "It all depends on the weather," he repeats time after time as I quiz him about what he does, when, and why. His

other favorite phrase is, "You just know!" Joe is a big man with a handsome, craggy Irish face that is weathered from decades outdoors.

I asked Joe how he protected the turf from winter cold and the harsh winds off Boston harbor. He explained that they covered the field each December with a layer of white felt. It allows air and moisture to pass through, and some light to penetrate. They rolled up the felt this year on March 5, and the grass in left field was already long enough to cut. Last year they rolled it up March 8, the year before on March 10. How does he decide? "You just know!" Since March 5 he has had the grass cut twelve times.

The art (or perhaps the alchemy) of field maintenance is in the application and timing of the fertilizers, fungicides, and insecticides if necessary. The first application of chemicals to the field went on right after the felt was rolled up. This year he used a Scott product called FF II. It is a fertilizer and fungicide that provides nutrition at a ratio of 14-3-3 (14% nitrogen, 3% phosphorus, 3% potassium).

Joe Mooney took me to the chemical room deep in the bowels of Fenway Park. He explained that he doesn't use just one product, he varies the menu according to the weather and what the turf needs. "You just know." He had bags of Turf Formula (34-3-7), Tee Time (22-0-16), 5% Daconil Fungicide, and Pro-Turf (17-3-17). Joe doesn't believe in liquid fertilizer, nor in plain nitrogen, which can promote fungus. "Too much nitrogen is murder!" he exclaims. Joe does not mince words. Joe knows. He knows when to apply at one-half the rate on the bag, when to use a quarter rate. He would like to occasionally be able to use Milorganite, an organic fertilizer made from the sewage sludge of Milwaukee. "But it stinks! The players complain! Can't use it!" he says.

I think Joe would be perfectly happy if no one ever walked on the field, let alone made a diving, sliding catch in deep right field. When I first arrived at Fenway and was looking for Joe Mooney I asked how to find him. "Put one foot on his infield," someone warned. "He'll find you." Which wasn't quite true. Joe let me walk on the infield, and for a lifelong Red Sox fan, it was a thrill to stand on the infield as if I were playing third base, and to look up at the stands. I'd imagined doing this a thousand times as a youth, and there I was. Joe may be gruff, but he has a big heart.

The grass at Fenway Park is Kentucky bluegrass. It is replaced from time to time, most recently two years ago, and then thirteen years before that. It is installed as sod, pieces 64 feet long and 4 feet wide, which are rolled out onto the field on a base of 3 to 4 inches of sandy soil. When repairs need to be made, Joe sends someone out to the bullpen with a fierce harpoon-like tool to cut up what is needed for the patch.

There are 67 drain holes, which are hidden in the outfield, grass-covered plugs that can be opened if need be. From them, excess rain water can be diverted to Boston's storm drains. The infield pitches gently away from the pitcher's mound, and is covered with a tarp 175 feet square when heavy rains fall. It takes 16 men to roll up the tarp when wet.

During the winter the track around the field is kept free of snow. In April 1998 Boston experienced a major snow storm just before opening day. Joe Mooney's crew was ready. They couldn't plow the field, obviously, so they used snowblowers to get the snow to the sandy track at the edge of the field, and then hauled it off with a front-end loader.

When it comes to turf, Joe Mooney believes that you shouldn't overreact. "The more you try to do certain things, the more you monkey it up," he explained. "Grass is like a human being. If you're hungry, you go to the refrigerator. That's when you fertilize. You're sick? You go to the doctor. That's when you put on the chemicals." He makes it sound simple, and for him it is. "There are no experts, no rules," he says, and again, "You just know."

Joe Mooney rules Fenway Park with a voice that allowed him to give instructions to someone working in right field as we talked behind third base. Everyone showed him respect, from John Harrington, the owner (who checked in with Joe while we talked), to the groundskeepers who carry out his directions. Everyone knows that the season will start off with two acres of gorgeous green grass precisely three-quarters of an inch high because Joe will make it so. I almost wish Joe Mooney had made his career managing teams instead of turf. Maybe by force of personality he would get the Red Sox to win the World Series. It wouldn't surprise me.

Chapter 8

May

The Glory of Flowering Trees and Shrubs

Life in New England has its elements of hardship. There is the sub-zero weather of January, with frozen pipes and misbehaving cars. There is mud season, with days of rain and deteriorating back roads. And there is black fly season, making life outdoors a battle with biting bugs. But oh my goodness, there is also spring, and it is all worth it.

Spring comes in fits and starts, beginning with the early-blooming snowdrops and crocuses, lurching forward (and sometimes seemingly backward on cold days) toward the leafing out of trees and the blooming of our shrubs and trees.

The shadblow serviceberry (*Amelanchier canadensis*), an under-stated, white-blossomed native understory tree, is one of the first to bloom. It never gets very big, growing at the edges of woods and in wet places. Its bloom is fleeting, but for me it is a sure sign of spring.

It is rarely planted, but its close cousin the downy serviceberry (*Amelanchier arborea*) is used more often. It can have a nice shape, pleasant white flowers, and edible berries birds love. I'm told they taste like blueberries, but the birds always get to them before we can.

Another early bloomer, but sometimes an unreliable one in my neighborhood, is forsythia. This brilliant yellow shrub, though often unkempt, cheers the heart with the daffodil colors of sunshine. After harsh winters some forsythia only bloom on their lower branches where the buds were protected by a layer of snow. Horticulturists have worked hard in recent years at propagating hardier strains including New Hampshire Gold, Meadowlark, Northern Gold, and Vermont Sun, all of which do well in my zone 4 climate.

The rhododendrons and azaleas that are commonly planted in front of homes are closely related, and a recent poll of gardeners listed them as the most popular shrubs in America. There are some 900 species and uncountable named cultivars. They interbreed promiscuously, so new hybrids are continually being created.

The P. J. M. rhododendron is one of the most common, an early bloomer with lavender-pink blossoms and dark evergreen leaves. Its rounded form stays 3 to 6 feet tall, but can spread out over a wider zone. I have to admit I don't like the color, but obviously many people do. White "rhodies" are more to my liking, especially as they show up nicely in dark corners. Rhododendrons and azaleas don't require much sunshine, nor very good soil. They prefer acid soil, and an acid organic fertilizer such as North Country Organics' "Holly-Gro" helps them to perform well. Scratch some in underneath them each spring to help them perform.

Azaleas tend to be smaller and to have smaller leaves. Those in the Northern Lights series of azaleas are very hardy and have some of the most garish colors available. Orange. Pink. You get it. Not for me, thanks, but enjoy.

Magnolias are available that perform quite well in New England, even though many gardeners think they only bloom in parts south. They are small to medium-sized trees that have dramatic white or pink blossoms 3 to 6 inches in diameter. In harsh winters they may loose their flower buds, so plant them in protected places, out of the wind.

The star magnolia (*Magnolia stellata*) is hardy to USDA Zone 4, gets to be 15 to 20 feet tall with a spread of 10 to 15 feet, and has lovely white flowers. The Loebner magnolias (*Magnolia × loebneri*) can get to be 25 to 30 feet tall. Dr. Merrill is a very nice white one. For some nice color (lines of purple-pink along the center and fuschia on the back of the petals), try the Leonard Mussel hybrids of the same species.

Apples and crabapples are wonderful trees both for their blooms and for their fruit. Even organic gardeners can grow eating apples, especially if you choose one of the newer disease-resistant varieties like Liberty or Freedom. Talk to your local nursery about what might work best for you.

The fruit on many crabapples is enjoyed in the winter by birds, though totally ignored on a few varieties. I have been told that Snowdrift, a white one, is a favorite of our local birds. Indian Magic is a nice pink-purple crabapple, and Prairie Red is a good red one. If you don't intend to eat apples, then select a crabapple, as they give a fine floral display, and don't leave such a mess of apples on the ground in the fall. There are hundreds of varieties, some of which are very resistant to diseases. My favorite is Donald Wyman, a very resistant strain that is red in bud but opens to a white. Most crabapples reach 15 to 25 feet in height at maturity, and are often nearly as broad. Weeping crabapples are also available and can be quite lovely.

Common lilacs (*Syringa vulgaris*) are among my favorite plants. They usually are very fragrant, and have colors that speak to me. I love the form of an old lilac, and they are very hardy. Skiing through the woods in winter I sometimes find them near abandoned cellar holes, signs of thriving farms decades ago. They like an alkaline soil, so tradition has it that one should put some wood ashes around the base of each lilac in March. You can do it any time, and can use agricultural lime if you don't have a woodstove.

Some lilacs send up "suckers" from their roots, shoots that will develop into full-sized plants in a few years, creating hedges where you might not have intended them. Some lilacs have been bred to stay put, thus saving you the trouble of pruning back the suckers. Miss Kim, bred at the University of New Hampshire, is a hybrid that does not sucker and is daintier in leaf and flower than most. Lilacs come in a variety of colors from white to pink, magenta, violet, blue, and deep purple. A few get a nonlethal white mold on their leaves in August, but a breezy location helps to prevent it. Raking up their leaves in fall will help to prevent reoccurrence.

Viburnums are hardy flowering shrubs or small trees, though many have very coarse leaves and may look best at the edge of a woods. The American cranberry bush viburnum (Viburnum trilobum) is tough and produces lots of reddish berries for birds in the winter. The Onondaga variety of *Viburnum sargentii* has quite a striking blossom in June.

If you are thinking about planting a tree or shrub, consider its ultimate size carefully before you plant it. Do not plant it where snow or ice falling off a roof will injure it. Try to see a mature specimen before buying it. Some municipalities have lists or maps of trees planted, others do not. Some neighbors will know the name of the particular variety they planted, and most are flattered if you knock on their door to ask.

Your best resource is usually a good tree nursery that has a knowledgeable staff. Think about parts of your property that need the color of a flowering tree or shrub, and remember that there are things that will bloom now, and others in mid to late summer, even one (witchhazel, *Hamamelis virginiana*) that will bloom in October. Of course, if you buy a tree in bloom you will know its exact color, which is important to me. Don't be in a hurry to buy the first thing you see, and remember to water deeply twice a week all summer and into the fall unless the ground is soaked.

Many of us have lived in other parts of America and remember plants from our youth that are not common here. I say, take a chance. Thirty years ago I dug up a small Japanese maple (*Acer palmatum*), a wonderful maroon-leafed one from my parents' home in Connecticut, and brought it to Cornish Flat, New Hampshire. Theirs was 40 feet tall, and as broad. Thirty years later mine is a chubby, thick-stemmed tree only 5 feet tall, but it pleases me. I believe that being a good gardener means taking some risks, pushing the limits. If you want to try something at the edge of its hardiness zone, plant it out of the wind, and mulch its roots in the fall. Who knows, the tree spirits may bless you.

Mrs. Marguerite Tewksbury, Organic Gardener

Mrs. Marguerite Tewksbury has been a market gardener for nearly sixty years, raising vegetables for sale from her home in Windsor,

Vermont. She still drives her 1950 Ford Ferguson tractor, and despite her small stature she weeds the rows of her 6,000-square-foot vegetable patch with a full-sized rototiller. There may be other eighty-five-year-old women who do that. But one of the things that makes Mrs. Tewksbury special is the fact that she has been an organic gardener for nearly fifty years.

When Mrs. Tewksbury and her late husband, Olin, bought their home in 1941, it was blessed with good soil, river bottom from the bordering Connecticut River. As most people did in that era, they had a large garden and kept a few animals to keep the grocery bills low. They used the manure from their cows, pigs, and hens to improve the soil, and before long they had so much garden produce that they began to sell some.

Many of their customers came from across the river in Cornish, New Hampshire, and one wealthy customer kept asking Marguerite if she knew anything about "organic" gardening. Mrs. Tewksbury had grown up on a farm in Barnard, Vermont, and had two years of college after high school, but she didn't know anything about organic gardening. But she was interested. Then one day, without any explanation, *Organic Gardening and Farming Magazine* started to arrive in the mail. She read it, she thought about what it had to say, and it made sense to her.

In the 1950s most farmers and gardeners wanted to be modern.

The American chemical industry had done a good job of convincing the public that a better world could be had through the use of chemicals. Got an insect problem? DDT will get rid of them. Mildew on your roses? We have a fungicide for you. Weeds a problem? We can take care of them, pronto. And most gardeners believed what they were told, and bought chemicals to bring in bigger, better looking crops. Most people at that time believed that the chemicals, if applied as directed, were harmless to you. Rachel Carson, J. I. Rodale (of *Organic Gardening* magazine), and Mrs. Marguerite Tewksbury believed otherwise. I think they were right.

What *Organic Gardening* magazine promoted, starting back in 1942 and continuing to this day, was the idea that chemicals, whether used as herbicides or fertilizers, are detrimental to a healthy soil. It does not say that spreading a bag of 10-10-10 fertilizer will poison your food, but it does say that it may inhibit the natural processes of a living soil. That fertilizers made from minerals and products made by living things are better. The magazine's philosophy is that the soil should be full of living things: bacteria, fungi, worms, and insects, which work together to supply your plants with what they need in the ways that naturally evolved over time. That organic matter in the soil helps it to have a good tilth, or structure, which lets air and water pass though it and get to the roots of your plants as they need it. And that chemical fertilizers only provide some of what plants need, and ignore many micronutrients that are important to plant health and taste.

Manure, preferably aged manure, is a central part of Marguerite Tewksbury's soil improvement program as an organic gardener. She hasn't had animals for quite some years, but gets some manure to use in her garden each year, particularly for her tomatoes. She warned against using fresh horse manure, which she said was "just like planting weeds," as the weed seeds pass through horses unharmed. She recounted the story of using "hedgehog" manure, which she said was very good. She said that a friend of theirs had a shed which had been occupied by porcupines. Her husband, Olin, made a deal with the fellow—he went and cleaned out the shed, so he could try it out in their garden. It was excellent. It is pelletized like rabbit manure, which is also excellent.

Leaves are another important part of Mrs. Tewksbury's gardening system. "I gather all the maple leaves I can in the fall," she said. "I've got bags and bags of them down in the second barn. I like them dry when I put them out, they're so easy to put down. But you've got to put them on thick, or the weeds will come right through. They're awfully good mulch, because you don't have to worry about them afterward. They just turn into soil."

I liked an analogy Mrs. Tewksbury made. She said that plants are like children. Some children just catch everything that's going around, and others don't, or can easily throw off a cold. Plants grown organically just do better, they are the healthy ones. And Mrs. Tewksbury knows not only plants, but children. She raised three of her own, and when they got big, she started teaching fourth grade. She started taking courses so that she received her bachelor's degree in 1964, 30 years after she left the Normal School at Castelton State.

Marguerite Tewksbury is still a teacher in many ways. Whenever we talk, she shares her wisdom with me. She taught me never to fertilize peppers. When her plants bloom, she scratches in some wood ashes, usually doing this twice, which enhances pepper production without a lot of unnecessary green growth. "That way, peppers don't turn into trees, which they're so apt to, if you fertilize them—you get trees and no peppers," she said.

The lesson I liked best was to freeze sweet peppers for use in salads. She said that she washes and slices green peppers, and freezes them without blanching. When she makes a salad, she takes out slices of pepper from the freezer, and tosses them with the salad. By the time she eats the salad they are thawed, and have the taste and consistency of fresh peppers. An hour later they would be limp, but for immediate consumption they are fine. I'm growing an extra six pepper plants this year.

In addition to her market gardens, Marguerite rents out garden plots. She does not insist that all the gardeners follow strict organic practices, but she told me that most of them end up as organic gardeners when they see how well she does. She sells Pro-Gro, a 5-3-4 organic fertilizer, at a price that brings in gardeners from outside as well.

Mrs. Tewksbury has patience, which is important for organic gardeners. If she has a pest problem, she will try different organic approaches. She understands that there will be garden pests that bother her plants, and that there is no miracle cure for the organic gardener. Last year Mexican bean beetles were a problem, but she froze quite a few beans before the beetles became too much of a problem. For a few years Japanese beetles devastated her red raspberries, and she couldn't beat them. So she switched to fall raspberries, a variety called Heritage, and last year she got in a great crop, picking berries right into October. So she continues to experiment, to observe, to learn. She is willing to lose a portion of the crop rather than use chemicals.

I asked Mrs. Tewksbury if she had any advice for beginning gardeners. "I always say you've got be willing to work hard," she said. "You can't give up because you weren't successful the first time, because nobody is. And I think you've got to be willing to pull weeds. People don't like to pull weeds. Until the plants get themselves established in good shape, you've got to pull weeds. I have quite a lot of weeds by fall, but you shouldn't let them get ahead of you."

Mrs. Tewksbury spoke lovingly of her late husband, Olin, and how hard a worker he was. Marguerite struck me as being an incredibly hard worker herself. Not only does she grow vegetables for sale, she fills two large freezers full of vegetables each year for her own consumption, cans tomatoes, makes vegetable juice, and still finds time to volunteer at the local library and drive "the elderly" to doctors appointments. She admits that old age is not a fun thing ... this whole thing of getting aches and pains, well, she just doesn't "cotton to it." She doesn't say that keeping active and eating organically keeps her healthy and vigorous, but I have a feeling that it does.

On Gardening with Children

As a child and as a young man I spent a lot of time with a wonderful grandfather who loved to garden. Grampy didn't "teach" me about gardening, we just spent time in the garden while doing things that needed to be done, and talking. We made manure tea to feed the tomatoes. We turned the compost pile to aerate it, and if the worms were particularly juicy, we quit work and went fishing. We pulled weeds, but never got too compulsive about it. One of my earliest memories of the garden is riding back to the barn in his old wooden wheelbarrow, trying to outrun a thunderstorm.

So I learned a lot from Grampy, pretty much by osmosis. Those were some wonderful times, and I feel grateful that I learned to love the garden at a young age. Many parents spoil gardening for kids by making it either (a) a chore required before fun can be had, or (b) an opportunity to teach their kids about plants or the proper work ethic. My philosophy is that gardening should be just plain fun. I recently went to visit Emily Cromwell, a friend whom I consider a "Supermom," to talk to her about gardening with her children, Carlos and Moe, ages four and six.

Emily agreed that gardening with kids should be fun for both parent and child, and added that kids need to see results, both short and long term. At Carlos and Moe's preschool last fall the children went to a gardening center and selected some hyacinth bulbs to plant. They selected the colors they liked, and then went back and planted them. I have suggested radishes to parents as first planting adventures, as they germinate in three days or less, and young children like to see rapid results. But the hyacinths were great. The results were months away, but the flowers were dramatic in color and smell when they finally bloomed. And the bulbs are big enough that four-year-old children can handle them easily. It's a nice introduction to gardening.

The real reason I went to talk to Emily was to learn about the sunflower fort that she and her husband, Mark Woodcock, built for and with their children last summer. They were given a kit by a neighbor, but it is easy enough that you can do it yourself with seeds available anywhere. The sunflower fort is a space for kids that gives them some privacy and a place to play near the garden while the adults are in the carrot patch weeding or doing other chores that might not interest kids. And despite the living walls, parents can still see through the stems and stalks to be sure that the shrieks heard are of glee, not agony. Private spaces are important to children, and this is much quicker than creating the forsythia fort I had as a youth.

Here is how to build a fort. First, you have to be willing to tear up some lawn in a sunny place. Get string and stakes, and mark out the inner perimeter of a fort, perhaps 8 by 10 feet. Perhaps smaller for small children, or smaller yards. Then repeat for an outer edge, 24 inches from the inner one. Mark out a doorway, and don't disturb the grass there, or inside the fort.

Using an edging tool or shovel, slice through the grass in nice straight lines. Then comes the hard work, pulling the sod. I would use a potato fork, a great old-fashioned tool that resembles a garden rake but has only four or five tines, each 8 inches long. It would allow me to peel back the sod quickly. Lacking one of those, you can do it with a hand weeder, or by using a standard garden fork. Cutting 1-foot strips with the edger will make the sod removal easier.

Once the sod is removed, you need to loosen the soil, which can be done with a rototiller or by hand. Ideally you have some compost on hand to mix in, particularly if you have heavy, compacted clay beneath the layer of sod. Most new houses only get 4 inches of "topsoil" spread on the ground after the bulldozers have tidied up the lot. Generally the subsoil was excavated from the cellar hole, and is pretty worthless for growing things. So buy some bagged compost or manure to add to the soil if you don't have any, and mix it in. Sprinkle in some Pro-Gro or other organic bagged fertilizer to help the soil. I wouldn't use any chemicals, particularly herbicides, in an area for children.

Let your children smooth the soil with a rake, and it is time to plant. Planting is fun. Help your children space out the sunflower seeds, but don't worry if they plant them too closely, you can thin them later. I would suggest creating a furrow with a stick, and having them place the sunflower seeds in it about 6 inches apart. Sprinkle a layer of dirt over the seeds. The general rule for planting seeds is to cover them with two to three times as much dirt as the length of the seed.

Carlos, age six, recalls that the fort used two rows of sunflowers. I like the idea of a tall row on the inside, then another, shorter variety outside that. The inner row should be about 6 inches from the grassy edge. Space the two rows about 8 inches apart, or follow the directions on the package. After planting the sunflowers, add some cosmos, or any other bright, robust annual as the outside edge of the fort. You can plant seeds, or get six-packs of seedlings from a farm stand if you want quicker results.

Waiting for seeds to germinate is always tough for kids, even this one. I still race down to the garden each day in the spring to see what has come up during the night, and they will too. One thing they can do each day, and should if it doesn't rain, is water their seeds. A watering can is better than a hose, as they are less likely to blast the seeds out of place. Watering makes them feel useful, and it will ensure a much higher germination rate. Seeds that dry out will not succeed.

Children need child-sized tools, and fortunately they are now readily available. I'm a firm believer in buying good-quality tools, even for kids, but your budget may not allow that. It is important, I think, for children to feel ownership of their garden and their gardening tools. So take your kids along and let them select a tool or two that feels good to them.

In your vegetable garden be sure to plant some things that will taste good to your kids raw. Edible-pod peas and cherry tomatoes are good for grazing, and most kids will eat carrots right out of the ground, dirt and all! Encourage your kids to go in the garden and grab a snack any time they want.

Kids love flowers, and you may want to plant some around your vegetable garden that they can pick. Flowers are also useful in the organic garden, as they attract beneficial insects and give them a place to rest. Some, like marigolds, are said to repel bad bugs. Larkspur is said to hold a fatal attraction to Japanese beetles. White sweet alyssum is said to deter deer, who allegedly find the odor repulsive. (I do wonder who interviewed the deer on that question.) Children like to cut flowers and create bouquets to present to Mom, Grammy, or a loved friend. Get them safe scissors and encourage the practice. Plastic scissors might even live in their fort. It's true that they might occasionally snip something you don't want cut, but so what? They are learning to appreciate the beauty of nature and the joy of growing things. It may be one of the best gifts you can ever give your children.

Growing Flowers in Containers

Mother's Day is traditionally a time for giving plants. I remember that as a small boy I always went to the local nursery to get my mother a box of field-grown pansies for that occasion, and she and I would plant them outside the kitchen window. As I got older I spent more and got more sophisticated in my purchases, but I always got flowers of some sort. It's a nice tradition, and one that can involve the children of the family in planting a nice big container for Mom or Grammy to put by the door or on the porch for the summer.

Containers are nice gifts. They can provide flowers or greenery in places outside where you might not otherwise have something: on the deck, or where the soil is rock hard and full of stones, for example. Weeds are not usually a problem. Once planted, the only work required of your container garden is to water it regularly, and to snip off the spent flower heads.

If you are not an experienced gardener, my first bit of advice is to go to a local nursery that has helpful people who know their plants. If you go to a chain store, chances are that you will not be able to find people who can really answer your questions.

Before you go you will need to know where the container will be located, and how much sun it will get every day. Shade plants in sunny spots cook before the summer is half past. Sun-loving plants on a north-facing deck might survive, but they won't be happy, and consequently they won't bloom well. Check the clock to see when the sun shines on your porch, and when it disappears. Afternoon sun is more potent than morning sun, especially in August.

Next, you need to decide what sort of container you want to buy, as this also will affect what plants do well for you. Unglazed clay pots are traditionally popular, but they have the disadvantage of drying out much more quickly than plastic containers. If your loved one is good about watering house plants, she probably will do well with plants in clay pots. If, on the other hand, she has three preteens to chauffeur around to various athletic events, two preschoolers, and full-time paid employment, you might do well to select a planter made of plastic or one of the decorative fiberglass or composite pots. They are much more forgiving if a watering is forgotten. Garden centers are even selling larger containers that are plastic and have a reservoir that will "self-water" the plants.

Wooden containers such as half whisky barrels or homemade window boxes are also excellent. They have much better insulating value than clay or plastic, which is particularly important for containers left in the hot afternoon sun. Remember, the roots are usually right up to the edge of the container, and for some plants these roots easily bake.

The hardest part of container gardening is selecting the plants themselves. Look around the nursery, and read the descriptions on the printed tags. Ask for help, but be patient, especially just before Mother's Day. Most nurseries put shade plants and sun lovers in separate places, which is very helpful.

For a large container I would select three different types of plants. First, select something that will get tall to go in the middle of the container. This should be something that you particularly like, as it will be the most noticeable. Next, select some plants that will "trail," or cascade over the sides. Lastly, select plants to intersperse with the viny things, but that will stay fairly low.

Oh yes, then there is the issue of colors. Mothers rarely complain, and undoubtedly whatever you and the kids do will be much appreciated. If your children are helping to select the plants, suggest they think about their mother's favorite colors in clothing. She probably doesn't wear orange and purple together, for example. If you have teenagers, they are probably sneaky enough to find out what flowers Mom likes best without giving away your plans.

A few basic rules of color composition might be in order. In general, related colors look good together, such as blues and purples or pinks and reds. Yellows with oranges. Sometimes contrasting colors make a grouping come alive, though there should be a predominance of one color, with just a dash of the contrast. White flowers and silver foliage look wonderful at dusk, and bright yellows are great in the morning. But as Casey Stengel might have said, "There ain't no 'countin' for taste." Just get stuff that looks good to your eye.

To prepare a container for planting, begin by scrubbing it out if it has been used before. Then provide for drainage. Old-time gardeners will tell you to put "crockage" in the bottom of your pot, broken pieces of clay pots. Lacking crockage, put an inch or two of small stones in the bottom. Be sure your container has a way for the water to get out, and make holes if it doesn't. Window screen placed at the very bottom will help keep soil from leaking out onto the deck, and keep slugs and bugs from crawling inside to hide.

A 24-inch pot filled with dirt is way too heavy for most people to move around the deck, but you don't need to fill it all with dirt. Been looking for a use for those awful styrofoam peanuts that come via UPS? Put a thick layer of them on top of the crockage, as much as 6 inches deep (depending on the size of the pot).

The soil mix is very important. Most hanging planters or store-bought containers of flowers are filled with a lightweight mix that is

Recipe for Container Soil

I use the following recipe for potting with good results: In a large wheelbarrow mix together 2 heaping shovels of garden dirt, 1 small shovel of sand, 2 heaping shovels of compost, and 2–3 shovels of fluffy material (peat moss, soilless planting mix). Vermiculite and perlite are also fluffy, inert ingredients available in small bags at garden centers. The first absorbs water, the second doesn't, though water will adhere nicely to its exterior. Lastly, I mix in a cup of Pro-Gro or similar organic fertilizer. This stuff is slow-release fertilizer, so frequent watering won't wash it away (unlike most chemical fertilizers).

largely peat moss and vermiculite. It has little nutritional value, so you have to fertilize all summer long with a liquid fertilizer to supply nutrients. I recommend making your own mix.

Most people do not plant perennial flowers in containers. This makes sense for a number of reasons. First, annuals will bloom all summer if you pinch off the dead flower heads, but most perennials only bloom for a few weeks at best. Perennials will probably not survive a New England winter in a pot as pots lack the tempering effect of the surrounding soil. If you plant shrubs in containers you will have to protect them when winter comes. Perennials also cost more, so you can have more annuals for the same cost.

A few final words of warning: Ask at the greenhouse when you buy your plants if they have been "hardened off." If not, you need to introduce your plants, which have been coddled and protected in a greenhouse, to the harsh sun and drying winds of the outdoors. Find a protected spot that gets only morning sun and is sheltered from the wind, and place your plants there for four or five days. If you can move them inside at night, they will be most appreciative. Failure to harden off the plants probably won't kill them, but it will delay their growth in the weeks ahead. It's worth the effort.

Most container annuals are frost sensitive, so be sure to protect your plants on cold, clear nights. In my part of New Hampshire May 30 is generally accepted as the first frost-free day, but you can check with neighbors or the greenhouse where you bought your plants.

Cover your planter at night with an old sheet or towel if you are not sure what the weather will do.

I have two last bits of advice. Snip off spent flower heads daily to keep the blooms coming all summer. And don't overwater. Providing too much water is one of the most common causes for failure with container plants. Waterlogged soil doesn't let the roots get the oxygen they need, and may also cause root rot. There is no simple formula for watering. Be observant; visit your plants daily. Plants grow best if the soil is allowed to dry out before watering, as this encourages the roots to grow out in search of water. If you see your plants wilt, don't worry, give them a drink and they will usually bounce back. Most plants are as tough and resilient as their gardeners.

The Art of Weeding

May is black fly season where I live, and those pesky critters are out to sabotage my garden. Not literally, of course, because it's my blood they want, not my plants. The weather recently has been good for working in the garden, and I've been out there, but not without a little grumbling about the biting flies. I find that some bug repellent applied to a baseball cap helps to keep them at bay, though one gardening friend uses a beekeeper's hat, long-sleeved shirts, and gloves for absolute protection.

This is an important time to be out in the garden. There is something that you can do now to greatly reduce work for yourself later on. In a word, it's weeding. If you can eliminate most of the weeds in your flower beds (and in your vegetable garden) early in the season, you will be rewarded later on. And I don't mean in heaven. Your work now will save you twice the effort later on, or more. The ground is softer in the spring, and weeds are not as well established as they will be later on. Weeds pull more easily now, and they are less brittle. So now is the time to get them.

Virtually every plant has but one goal in life: to reproduce itself. Generally plants do this by creating flowers, which produce seeds. Weeds and grasses often spread by sending roots laterally, then sending up new plants. A few plants such as brambles can move by dropping branches to the ground and then rooting themselves. There are even a few oddballs like the seedless orange that depend on humans for propagation.

At this time of year the dandelions are hard at work making flowers to propagate themselves, but most other weeds are just getting started. Grasses are busy creeping from your lawn to your flower beds unless you have created a nicely dug moat around your flower beds, or installed plastic or metal edging to foil their plans.

There is an art to weeding. Some people give up because they don't do it correctly, and the weeds come right back in just a few weeks, which is very discouraging. Many weeds can regenerate themselves from just a scrap of root, so it is very important to get the whole durn thing. Weeds are not cooperative about being uprooted, as clearly it is not in their best interest.

If your soil is hard packed, I recommend loosening it with a garden fork before attempting to pull a large, well-established weed. Push the fork in as far as you can, pull back until the soil starts to lift, then do the same from another side. Then gently ease the weed out. Wiggling it sometimes seems to help. Weeds with a long, deep taproot are the toughest, things like dandelions and thistles. Steady pressure is better than a quick yank. Shake off the top soil before discarding the weed.

I like to use a hand tool to grab the underside of a big weed before I try to pull it out of the ground. For years I used a little three-pronged scratcher, and it worked just fine. Its tines can get underneath the body of the weed, giving you a handle to pull with instead of a weed body. Many weeds seem designed to separate from the roots in case a grazing animal like a cow gives it a yank. Or a Yankee gardener. But now I use a "Cape Cod Weeder," and I like it better.

The Cape Cod Weeder has become an extension of my hand. I use it to loosen soil, pull weeds, dig out rocks, cut through sod, and a dozen other tasks. It is a simple tool about 14 inches long with a wooden handle, a shaft about 4 inches long, and an eye-shaped blade at a right angle to the shaft. It is easier to get under a weed with this tool than with the traditional three pronged weeder, and the long wooden handle lets me pull with both hands if I need to. Left-handed friends tell me it is a right-handed tool.

Recently I spent a lot of time trying to resurrect a weed-infested flower bed. Grass had invaded, along with chickweed, bedstraw, dandelions, bugleweed, and others too numerous and noxious to mention. I like to attack a patch of grass by digging out the big clumps with a garden fork first, and then kneeling down to work with the Cape Cod Weeder. This allows me to be close to what I am working on, and to rake through the loose soil with my weeder to gather up small weeds and broken bits of root. The single blade of the weeder allows me to extract weeds invading clumps of perennials without damaging them.

Good gardeners are observant. While weeding, look carefully at the weed roots. Notice their color and texture. The Bermuda grass that has invaded my flower beds has a white root that runs sideways for long distances, and is quite different from the roots of most flowers. If I see that it has invaded a clump of flowers, sometimes I will dig the entire clump up with a shovel, turn it upside down, and carefully extract those white roots. Then I replant it immediately and no harm is done to the plant.

After a thorough weeding of a flower bed I like to add some nutrition for the soil. I "top dress" the soil by adding a 1- to 2-inch layer of compost, or composted manure, and scratching it in. This is also a good time to add some bagged organic fertilizer. Organic fertilizers enrich the soil, feeding the microorganisms that reside there. The bacteria, fungi, earthworms, and other living things present in a healthy, chemical-free soil help to make nutrients available to your plants.

If you want to mulch your flower beds to keep the weeds down, mulches are readily available in a variety of types, colors, and textures. More than 4 inches of mulch is not needed, and may actually serve to keep rain from reaching the roots of your plants if the shower is brief. Because some nitrogen is required to feed the microorganisms that break down bark mulch, some fear that using it will hurt the soil. This should not be a problem if you rejuvenate your soil with compost and fertilizer every year or two. Bark mulch is not recommended for vegetable gardens except for things like asparagus and berries. Mulches keep the soil cool, so you may want to wait till summer to add it.

This year I was given a pair of gardening gloves that I like a lot. Never in my life have I gardened with gloves. But these are wonderful, and they seem to be available in many stores and catalogs. They are a knit glove impregnated with a latex palm, and come in different sizes. They are not hot, they have great gripping power, and they are sensitive enough to feel the thin throat of an emerging weed.

I've always heard that you could keep your fingernails clean while weeding by clawing a bar of soap before you head to the garden, but at fifty-something I rarely remember.

I am often asked what to do for a "maintenance-free" flower garden. Although I am tempted to tell people about Astro-Turf or blacktop paving, the answer is simply that there is no such thing. Flower gardens take work on a regular basis all summer long. Weeds are a great excuse to be outside, and to get away from the worries of other work. But you can minimize the weeding later if you get outside and work on the gardens now, in May. I just wish somebody would develop a better way to keep the black flies away.

Planting Your Garden

Marauding deer, hungry woodchucks, bum backs, bad knees. Black flies, slugs, bugs, and blisters—it's a wonder that there are so many gardeners in North America. But, as I battle the bugs, visions of sugar peas dance in my head. As I take a bite of a freshly picked asparagus spear, I know why I garden. And if there is a heaven, I know it has organic, home-grown tomatoes all year round.

If you are selecting a new garden site, chose a place that receives a minimum of 6 hours of sun per day. More is better, and afternoon sun is better than morning sun. Avoid sites on a steep hillside if you can, as they are prone to erosion and to drying out too quickly. Try to keep 50 feet from maple trees, as they extract much nutrition from the soil.

Traditionally, gardeners in my part of the world plant their tomatoes and other frost-sensitive plants (peppers, eggplants, cukes and squashes, annual flowers) on Memorial Day weekend. The old-timers warn us that the last frost usually coincides with a full moon, and this year the full moon is on Sunday May 30. I will be listening carefully to the weather man, and, as I live in a cold spot, I might not plant until early June. Some risk takers have probably already planted their tomatoes, but as I raise mine from seed, I tend to be more cautious.

Vegetables started indoors or in a green-house need to be hardened off prior to being planted in the garden. New plants are very tender and are susceptible to being dried out by the wind or burned by the sun if taken from their sheltered life in the greenhouse and put di-rectly into the garden. So you should put them outside in a place where they will just get morning sun, and where they are sheltered from the wind. They need three or four days to toughen up, so be sure to buy your plants well in advance. This goes even for tougher plants like broccoli or lettuce. Bring your plants in at night, and they will do better than if left out on a cold night.

Rototillers have become widely used, and there are few who do all their garden preparation by hand. Whether you are preparing a new bed or using last year's, I do not recommend just rototilling in all the grass and weeds that have appeared seemingly overnight. It's extra work now, but weeding the garden before rototilling, or pulling up the sod for a new garden, will save you work later.

If you buy plants in six-packs you may notice when you remove the plants that their roots have formed a thick mat against the edges of the container. It's good to tease the roots out away from this mat, even if it means you break a few. This will encourage the roots to grow out into the soil more quickly.

Preparing the soil for planting is the most important part of the cycle of growing vegetables. A good soil for growing vegetables is rich in organic matter, and is neither too sandy, nor too heavy with clay. Plants get their oxygen and water from the soil, so it needs to be fluffy enough for both to pass through it. The root hairs, which are the point of exchange between the soil and the plant, are finer than your hairs, so your soil should not be so compacted that they can't extend outward in search of nutrients or moisture.

Each year organic matter (anything produced by plants or animals) is broken down by the process of oxidation and used up by microorganisms in the soil, and nutrients are absorbed by plants. But this also means that in order to have the best soil possible, you need to add organic matter each year, particularly if you grow "heavy feeders" like corn. Compost, or composted manure, is great for your soil.

You can make your own compost from kitchen scraps, grass clippings, weeds (but avoid weeds with seeds forming), and leaves. Some people work hard on their compost piles, layering things green and brown, adding soil, and aerating it with special tools or by turning it over. These people make good compost in a year or less. It also works to just accumulate a lot of compost and let it sit for two or three years, and then use it, which is what I do. The lazy (or busy) person's compost. Incidentally, you should never use cat or dog droppings in the compost pile.

Garden centers sell bagged composted cow manure, which is a good (but expensive) way to add organic matter to your soil. Most dairy farmers sell manure by the truckload, and some even age it so that it is not so likely to enrich your garden with weed seeds. Horse manure usually is very weedy, but sheep manure is not. Fresh chicken manure is very concentrated, and can hurt your tender roots, so age it or use it sparingly. I like to put a 3- or 4-inch layer of composted manure on the garden every year or two, and add manure every year right where I plant my tomatoes. Potatoes should not be planted with added manure, although they do well where manure was added the year before.

Prepare the soil for each plant carefully and it will repay you later. I loosen the soil and stir in some compost and bagged organic fertilizer before setting the plant in the hole. Firm the soil around the plant, and give it a good drink of water. Never put in tender young plants in the heat of the day. I prefer planting in late afternoon, and a cloudy or rainy day is ideal.

Water is vital for new plants. Immerse your six-packs in a bucket of water until the bubbles stop prior to planting. Add water to the hole you create for the plant before you plant if the soil is very dry.

Let the water soak in before you install the plant. After planting, make sure your soil stays moist until the plant is well established. Buy a rain gauge or put out a glass to catch rain. Most plants need at least 1 inch of rain per week.

The core of the vegetable garden for most people is the tomato crop. There are numerous ways to plant your tomatoes, but most gardeners agree that it is good to plant much of the stalk as well as the root ball. I pinch off the lowest leaves, then lay the roots and most of the stalk in a shallow trench. I bend the top part of the tomato plant so that it sits up straight. The buried part of the stalk becomes roots and helps to nourish the plant. This also turns tall, leggy tomato plants into nice stocky ones that won't blow over.

Let's face it: Planting seeds is a bore. Lettuce, carrots, beets, peas, beans, and lots of others are generally planted by seed. For carrots and lettuce, which have tiny seeds, it's nearly impossible to plant just one at a time. I like to take a little extra time to space them out well, however, because then I don't have to spend so much time thinning them later. There are numerous mechanical devices for planting small seeds, but I've never found one that I like.

After the seeds are on the soil, cover them with two to three times as much soil as the length of the seed. That's not much, for most. I use an old kitchen sieve to help me. I put in some good loam, and shake it over the seeds until the right amount has fallen. Firm this down, and water gently so as not to disturb the soil.

Gardening does take a certain amount of effort. But remember what the old folk tune tells us: "There are only two things money can't buy . . . true love and home-grown tomatoes." It *is* worth the effort.

Chapter 4

June

Peonies, Like Diamonds, Are Forever

June days often come to us like gifts from the gods. Warm, sunny days and fluffy white clouds in skies of azure blue contrast with the rain and chill we've experienced throughout much of the spring. Most of us want to be outside, even if that means playing hooky from "the real world" to work in the garden.

I like to ask my gardening friends a rhetorical question: If you could grow only one flower, what would it be? Most object, saying that it is impossible to choose just one, no more than they could choose to keep just one of their children. But I know what I would choose. I would grow peonies, especially one called Festiva Maxima. It is an old-fashioned double peony, one my grandparents grew, one I grew up with. It has lush, full white blossoms with a little splash of red in the center, which I have always assumed was a drop of blood from a princess of long ago. And it has a scent that will sweeten a room, a smell so fine that it makes me smile.

Growing peonies (*Paeonia* spp.) is not an art, but they are fussier than many other plants. However, a properly planted and nourished peony will live and bloom for the rest of your life. With a little care, it will outlive your grandchildren. If you do not own a peony, now is the time to buy one. Buy one in bloom so that you can see the color, smell its scent. Peonies come in a wide range of colors and types of blossoms, and not all peonies are fragrant. Pick one that you love. Or two or three. But remember, peonies are forever.

Peonies have roots that develop into tubers, like long, narrow sweet potatoes, but that can extend down two feet into the earth. And since peonies are heavy feeders and hard work to move, it essential that you prepare a good nutritious place for it to live and grow.

Pick a site in full sun, or one that has at least six hours of sun per day. Peonies need rich soil, but you can create that. They like a moist soil, but not a soggy one. Avoid a site full of tree roots, because they will compete for nutrients with your plant.

I prepare a site for a peony by digging a hole 18 to 24 inches deep and wide. In the bottom, I put a good 6 inches of compost or aged manure and stir it around. In a wheelbarrow I make a mix of good garden dirt and composted manure, in roughly equal quantities.

With the dirt I mix in 2 cups of Pro-Gro (a bagged 5-3-4 organic fertilizer), 1 cup of rock phosphate, and 1 cup of greensand. Rock phosphate is a ground rock that, as it dissolves over a multiyear period, releases phosphorus to the soil, encouraging good root development. The greensand was formed as an undersea deposit and is an excellent source of trace minerals and potassium. Potassium helps build strong cell walls, giving plants the ability to survive stresses like drought or cold. Garden centers sell green sand, especially recommending it for people trying to break up heavy clay soils.

I fill the hole with my mix of soil and nutrients, and pack down the soil well so that there won't be much settling of soil later on. The stems of the plant originate at buds or "eyes", which should be only an inch or two beneath the surface of the soil in your pot, and after it is planted. A peony planted too deeply will not bloom after the first year. Use your fingers to scratch away the dirt to assure that the peony has not been planted too deeply in its pot at the greenhouse. If the roots were pushing against the edges of the pot, you should tickle them a little to free them up once you remove the peony from its pot. Then place it in the hole, and fill in around it. Press the new soil down firmly with your hands, and water it well. A small peony plant might not bloom for a year or two after planting, even if it was in bloom when you bought it. I've read that it takes five to seven years for a peony started from seed to bloom, though I've never met anyone who has done so.

Once your peony is well established it will produce magnificent blooms, and often these blooms are so heavy that they fall to the ground when it rains. The solution is to provide some support. Peony cages made of heavy galvanized wire are the easiest way to provide the support, and these are readily available at garden centers. You need to put them in place before your peonies are in bloom, as it is nearly impossible to do later, even with two people trying. If you forgot to do it, you can build something using stakes and string.

Another type of peony is the tree peony (*Paeonia suffruticosa*). These are like shrubs, as they get woody and do not die back to the ground each winter. They can achieve a size of 4 feet tall and wide, with blossoms 6 to 8 inches wide. I have read that mature tree peonies can produce 75 to 100 blossoms over a two-month period! They are not fast growing plants—I have one that is blooming now after a wait of four years. Plants from seed are often not true to type, so grafting is commonly used to propagate them. No wonder they are so expensive to buy. They have been cultivated in China for 1,600 years, and were widely used in the Imperial Palace gardens. There are some 300 varieties of tree peonies. Mulch them well in the fall to protect the roots.

I am often asked about the ants that seem ever present on peonies. Are they harmful? No. A number of gardeners I know were told by their grandmothers (forty or fifty years ago) that the ants were there to open the buds. I was taught, however, that the ants are gathering a sweet substance excreted by the buds, or milking aphids attracted to it. When I went to my books on flowers to confirm this, there was no mention of the ants, no scientific explanation. So maybe the grannies were right. I think I'll try to find my hand lens so that I can see for myself what those ants are doing.

Furry Friends—and Foes

According to the Chinese calender, this is the year of the hare. According to my gardening friends, this is the year of the chipmunk, woodchuck, the mole, the vole, and the deer. Some gardeners are ready to do battle with the threat to their garden; others shrug and hope there will be enough food for all. There are lots of folk remedies for garden pests. Some of them work some of the time, but none work all of the time, I suppose. Many gardeners are ready to try almost anything to rid themselves of pests. In order to determine which animal is attacking your gardens, it is necessary to learn a little about their habits.

Woodchucks are voracious garden predators. They are strict vegetarians, fond of clover, grasses, weeds, twigs of trees and shrubs, and garden vegetables. They like beans, peas, melons, and corn, and will nibble on many other plants. They are easy to catch in a Hav-a-Hart type trap using watermelon or Red Delicious apples. The correct size of trap is important. Use one that has openings that are 12 inches square, and is 36 inches long. Place it in one of their runways if you can figure that out. Setting the trigger on a Hav-a-Heart is tricky, so consult a knowledgeable friend if you can't make it snap shut with a very light touch to the bait. Their burrows are usually easy to spot, as they leave quite a bit of dirt outside the front door with a 5-inch opening, usually on a hill.

The most bizarre woodchuck cure I have ever heard was told to me by a woman who swears it works, but it sounds wacky to me. She claimed that you can keep woodchucks out of the garden by surrounding the garden with one-gallon milk jugs spaced 6 feet apart. Fill them with water so they won't blow away. Does a milk jug look like a space alien to woodchucks? It does sit up in a perky fashion, ever so slightly like a portly woodchuck, but still . . .

Fortunately, my losses to rodents are minimized by Emily the Wonder Dog, the ever-vigilant Defender of the Garden. Or by her reputation and smells, since at twelve years old, she is no longer as

fast as she used to be.
The one time a wood-
chuck did appear, she
chased it into a stone
wall and sat there till
(her) dinner time. The
woodchuck escaped
during the night and
never returned.

Moles, also rodents,
are commonly blamed
for all kinds of garden
atrocities that they most surely did not commit. They are carnivores
who eat earthworms and grubs. They tunnel under the surface of
your lawn looking for the larval form of Japanese beetles and other
delicacies, so although their tunnels may be an aggravation, moles
do some good, too. And they don't eat your bulbs or plant roots.

I've had very good luck chasing moles away with a castor oil
emulsion that I read about in *Organic Gardening* magazine. Here's
what you do: Mix 1 tablespoon of castor oil (available at local pharmacies) with 2 tablespoons of liquid soap in a blender until it gets
stiff like shaving cream. Then mix in 6 tablespoons of water. Use 2
ounces of this mixture in 2 gallons of water in a watering can, and
sprinkle on the lawn. When you buy your castor oil make sure it is
the old-fashioned type, not the new, improved descented type. Obviously, you will need to make up quite a bit of the stuff to sprinkle
if you have extensive lawns, but I have been told that you can just
do the perimeters. There are commercial mole mixes that are also
based on castor oil. They are probably the same basic recipe, but
more expensive.

Chipmunks appear to have experienced a large upsurge in numbers in my area this year. Although they will take a bite out of a ripe
tomato or squash, they feed primarily on seeds, nuts, and fruits. They
will also eat beetles, slugs, cutworms, wireworms, frogs, salaman-
ders, and bird's eggs. They do occasionally steal bulbs, and are fond
of lilies, but never daffodils, which are poisonous. Chipmunks live
in burrows underground that are accessed from a hole about 2 inches
in diameter, though often this entrance is not obvious.

Voles are very common here, but are not well known by most-people. The meadow vole looks a lot like a mouse, but has reddish or blackish brown fur. It is 3½ to 5 inches long, with a tail that adds another 2 inches or so. My books show me that mice have longer tails and more prominent ears, and voles weigh a little more. Voles make tunnels in grass, and generally live above ground. When they burrow in the soil, their holes are just an inch and a half wide. They are the culprits who eat the bark off fruit trees in the winter, and they will munch on root vegetables, leafy vegetables, hay, and grain crops. In the wild they eat leaves, stems, roots, fruits, seeds, flowers, bugs, mushrooms, and carrion. They are prolific breeders, with females breeding just after they are weaned at age three weeks. Since owls and hawks depend on them for up to 85% of their diets, it's a good thing they breed early and often. Gardeners may disagree.

Deterring small rodents, whether chipmunks, mice, or voles, is never easy. Cats and dogs help in keeping numbers down, but you may not want a pet, or perhaps yours is too well fed to bother. I have read that a mixture of four parts cayenne pepper to one part garlic powder is good at deterring rodents, and that it can be put down openings to their dens, or sprinkled around plants that are being bothered. I know someone who put mothballs (not a good idea for organic gardeners) down the tunnel made by chipmunks or red squirrels. The rodents threw them right back out!

Last fall I planted more than a thousand tulip bulbs for my customers, and used cayenne pepper in each hole. There was no noticeable loss to rodents last winter, but that doesn't establish cause and effect. Also, I doubt that hot pepper lasts for more than one season, and in the garden a good rain or a watering will wash it away. Cayenne is also expensive. Blood meal is available as an organic fertilizer, and is thought to repel rodents. Bone meal is also used by some for the same purposes, but may attract dogs. A Labrador retriever digging in your garden can do more inadvertent damage than a busload of hungry voles. You can't win!

Trapping woodchucks and other rodents with a Hav-a-Hart is easy enough, and I have deported my share of red squirrels over the years. I talked to local naturalist Ted Levin about these traps, and he explained that they are not as kind as I had thought they were. He said that few rodents are going to survive relocation as they will be easy picking for predators. I know some people who live-trap garden pests, then submerge the cage, rodent and all, in water. They figure it is a quick sure death, but I, for one, couldn't do that. Ride 'em out of town, give 'em a chance, and leave 'em a snack. That has been my policy.

Raccoons love corn, and are as wily as can be. Mrs. Muriel Cole of West Canaan, New Hampshire, wrote me to say that she grows squashes around her corn to keep raccoons away. She said she has done it for thirty years and it really works! When I spoke to her recently she said that she believes the coons don't like the feel of crossing the prickly vines as they have sensitive paws. She suggested training the vines right up the corn where you can.

Electric fencing placed low has worked for some people, but you really have to love your corn to do that. Another trick that I've heard (but not tried) is to set two radios in the garden at night, each set on a different talk radio station. One station apparently doesn't work for long. So Rush Limbaugh, you have a job to do! You can be the gardener's friend!

Constructing a Bentwood Arbor

I've always felt that a vegetable garden should be a thing of beauty as well as a source of healthy, tasty, low-cost food and an excuse for not doing housework. My gardening grandfather always grew flowers in and around the vegetable garden, and I have maintained the tradition.

A few years ago I built a bentwood arbor, or archway, as an entrance to the vegetable garden. It was a late, wet spring, and I was dying to get started growing things, but the ground was soggy, so I couldn't. One Sunday afternoon I went out to the woods and cut some saplings, and built an arbor. When things dried out we grew scarlet runner beans up it, and by midsummer it was covered with lush green leaves and bright orange flowers.

From a design point of view, an arch or arbor draws attention, and encourages people to pass through. Arbors are wonderful all year, even in winter when their graceful forms stand out sharply against the snow.

Making a bentwood trellis or arbor is relatively easy to do. If you want to build one, you will need a good sharp hand saw, preferably a tricut pruning saw, and a pair of pruners or loping shears. The arbor described here used about 100 feet of copper wire, which is available at your local hardware store. Copper is preferred over iron wire as it doesn't rust, and can turn a handsome verdigris color with weathering. I like #14 copper to work with, but the thinner #16 is also good, and is more flexible. A pair of pliers, preferably needle-nosed pliers, is also needed.

Begin by finding a free source of saplings. I prefer using maple saplings, but ash is also good. Black birch and poplar are a little too brittle. For this article I tried also oak and elm, both of which are okay, but less flexible than maple. Look for tall, thin saplings which are 1 to 1.5 inches in diameter near their base. The thinner the sapling, the more flexible it will be, but also the less structurally solid. Build your arbor the same day you cut the trees if possible, so that they don't have a chance to dry out.

You will need a total of a dozen saplings to build this arbor, including six good, strong, straight saplings 10 to 12 feet long for the uprights. Mine has an opening 54 inches wide, large enough for me to pass through with a fully loaded wheelbarrow. It is 42 inches from front to back, and stands about 9 feet tall.

Determine the size and location of your arch, and use a measuring tape to lay it out and make it symmetrical. My garden soil is soft enough that I could push the uprights into the ground, but in dry, hard soil you will need to make holes in the ground with an iron bar or pipe.

Prepare six saplings for the uprights by snipping off all the side branches. I put three uprights in on each side about 20 inches apart. These uprights are bent in pairs until they meet, then overlap, creating a rounded top to the arbor.

Bending the green wood to form the top of the arch required me to stand on a step ladder. I slowly bent each piece, flexing it a little at a time, starting from the thin end. If I heard fibers starting to crack, I let go of it so that it wouldn't break. I had a piece of copper wire about 18 inches long draped around my neck, ready to tie the bent pieces together. I overlapped the uprights and brought them together, then wrapped them with wire so they wouldn't go *sprong* and fly apart, as they wanted to. This job would definitely be easier with two people and two stepladders.

It is important to try to make each of the three arches the same height. Don't worry if the uprights are not perfectly parallel at this time. You will fix that in the next phase, which is adding some crosspieces, that tie the three uprights together.

Prepare some sticks for use as crosspieces, which are 48 to 52 inches long and ½ to ¾ inch in diameter. Weave the first crosspiece through the three uprights about 4 feet off the ground. Attach one end with wire, wrapping it around the joint, then twist it tight with your pliers. Measure the distances between the uprights to be sure they are parallel. Then tie the other end. Be sure to tuck any loose ends of wire in so that they can't catch clothing and such. Repeat the process on the other side of the arch, and then again at the top of the arch.

The basic framework is now done. You should continue to add crosspieces every 2 feet or so, and diagonals and whimsy as you like. I put a big heart on each side of mine, using two very thin branches. Each half of the heart required a piece nearly 7 feet long, thin and flexible. Because I will grow scarlet runner beans up the trellis I added some extra vertical pieces at the bottom to give them something to grab onto when they first start growing. I pushed short sticks into the ground so that the young beans could easily reach the first crosspiece. I didn't even bother attaching these uprights, and will have to replace them in a year or two as these thin sticks will rot out sooner than the thicker uprights.

Because this arbor will last less than five years, I don't plant perennial vines here. Scarlet runner beans will cover the arbor in a few weeks. Hops are incredibly fast growing, and a handsome variegated form is available in some places. Morning glories are another option, or even mixing them with scarlet runner beans to have different colors. Purple hyacinth beans (*Lablab purpureus*) and annual sweet peas (*Lathyrus odoratus*) are other very handsome options.

Most families have but one serious gardener. There are exceptions, of course, but even in those with two gardeners, teenage children are not usually excited about gardening. Building a trellis or an arbor might be an activity in which even a nongardener would enjoy participating. It's done in a day, looks nice, and allows one to use (latent) artistic talents. And if your kids whine about working on it, tell them to send their complaints to me!

Creating Outdoor Play Spaces for Children

When I was about eight years old my father built me a tree fort. It was not an amazing technical feat, but it was amazing to me that he would create something for me to play on that was so high in the sky. It seemed pretty scary when I first climbed up into it, though in reality it was only 8 to 10 feet off the ground and built with appropriate side rails. But it seemed to me that I could fall off and be killed or, at a minimum, maimed.

In retrospect, I realize he built it for several reasons. We had moved into a new house, and he wanted us to like our new home, and feel that we were there for keeps. We had moved many times before, but this time we weren't renting, and the tree fort was proof of it. It was also his way of saying he trusted me to be careful, that he knew I wouldn't do something stupid up there. And lastly, my father liked to build things, and I bet he had fun building it, too.

I believe that it is important for children to have their own outdoor play spaces, and that those created by their parents are much more special for children than those which are purchased. Some play spaces can be created by artful placement of shrubs, others can be created using rocks, trees, and branches harvested from the land, and still others built with salvaged or purchased lumber. In each case, however, it is important to think carefully about the placement of the space in relation to your home, the land, and your existing trees and shrubs. The age and maturity of your children are also very important factors.

Urban—and most suburban—house lots are generally pretty unremarkable. Green grass, maybe some evergreen muffin-shaped shrubs in front of the house, and a maple tree if you are lucky. There is not much to lure an eight-year-old away from a television or an interactive video. I think kids need places to play that are comfortable to be in, which includes shade. They need places to hide. They need plants, which will also attract bugs, snakes, toads, and other animals you don't want in the house. Native trees and shrubs can help provide all of that.

Kids need and like privacy. That is part of the allure of forts. Generally, forts are too small for adults to enter. And they can be defended from intruders, both real and imaginary. Growing up in suburban Connecticut, I loved my tree fort partly because all those wolves and bears couldn't get me. Well, maybe the bears could climb up, but I could hold them off with a sharp stick if need be. And other kids? Had to know the password.

Young children may not be ready for a tree fort, but a nice grouping of shrubs will create a space that will give them the sense of privacy. New shrubs are generally spare enough that parents can see through the branches to keep an eye on their young ones. And as the kids get older, the shrubs will grow, giving more privacy. My grandfather planted forsythia bushes in a long oval arrangement, and we liked to play in the middle. These bushes were thick enough that we were sure no one could see us, though that may not have been the case. Azaleas, rhododendrons, arborvitae, and some viburnums would also work well. Highbush blueberries would be great, and provide snacks in season!

Obviously, most people will not want to plant shrubs for their children in the middle of their lawn. Pick a site that is off to one side, preferably one that nestles up against a natural feature like a wooded area, a barn, or a hillside. If you spend time in a vegetable or flower garden, you might want your children's play space within sight or at least earshot of your garden.

Think about using two or three different types of shrubs to create the space. You might want to flank the entry to it with one type of shrub, the "walls" with another. You could install a trellis or build a bentwood arbor as an entry and grow scarlet runner beans or other vines over it. You might be able to create the feel of a castle by planting something at the four corners that will grow tall and narrow, like certain arborvitae. You are only limited by your space, your budget—and your imagination. Get your kids to talk to you about what they might like, as they generally have lots of (grandiose) ideas.

Shrubs are probably better to use than trees. Trees keep getting taller, and one day—hard to imagine though it may be—your kids will abandon the fort. Shrubs are easier to reign in and keep under control. Flowering shrubs are nice, particularly ones that have a pleasant smell. It is all part of helping your children to enjoy the out of doors and the world of growing things. And there is no television in their fort, or any need for one.

After you have planted your shrubs, crawl around on your hands and knees to see if there are any potential "owies." Find any sharp roots and stones poking up before your two-year-old does. Grass is a wonderful carpet for kids, but as your shrubs or trees get bigger they will shade out the grass. You may want to add a 4- to 6-inch layer of finely ground bark mulch over the surface.

I recently visited two gardens that had nice play spaces for children. First I visited the home of garden designer (and grandmother) Judith Reeves, in Hanover, New Hampshire. Toward the back of her town lot she has a few trees, and has created a very nice little children's nook. There is a path that beckons to any youngster.

Once you enter the secret space, there is a simple wooden structure for her grandchildren made from two wooden packing crates and a ladder. Simple, inexpensive, and fun. If I'd been small enough, I would have climbed up onto it myself. Because of its location it is quite private, and has the added element of climbing up onto something, which children love. Perhaps it's a ship on the tall seas today, and Tarzan's home tomorrow.

I also toured the children's garden at the Brooklyn Botanical Garden in New York City recently. The feature I liked best there was a simple kid-powered water pump. It was a pitcher pump such as is still available at hardware stores for about sixty dollars. You pump the handle up and down, and water comes out. They had it placed in such a way that the child pumping could watch the water progress down hill through a series of plastic pipes that had been sliced in half and painted to look like bamboo troughs.

Actually, I was fascinated by the water pump. And it reminded me that children's gardens need interactive elements, and that water is one of the best. Assuming you don't have a well that you can incorporate into your garden, use your imagination to see what you can come up with. There are shallow plastic pools for fish or water gardens readily available—perhaps one could be incorporated into your design. Or an old sink or bathtub left over from renovations—

yours or a neighbors—might be used with a hose or buckets and a bilge pump. A galvanized watering trough for livestock has great potential. Your kids may end up getting soaked, but hey! It's good clean fun.

Slugs, Bugs, and Feathered Garden Pests

The garden salad bar is now open! Slugs to the right, beetles to the left. And here comes a squadron of Japanese beetles in fighter formation! Sigh. Sometimes it seems like we gardeners are in constant battle with critters of one type or another.

Crows love tender young corn plants, hence our efforts with scarecrows. But scarecrows won't fool a smart crow for long. Lore has it that shooting a crow and suspending it from a curved sapling by string will work, but that requires killing one, which I won't do, and putting up with the unpleasantness of it. But a friend of mine, a commercial farmer, fooled me—and the crows—by hanging a piece of black plastic instead of a crow. As I drove by I saw the "crow", and figured Harold had shot one and put it to use. But no, he said it was a piece of black plastic, perhaps 30 inches long and 8 inches wide, bunched in the middle and tied with string. He hung it in the field, and the crows stayed away. It doesn't have to fool them for very long, just until the corn seedlings are too big to carry away.

Tender young plants, particularly squash family plants, are quite susceptible to bugs such as the striped cucumber beetle, particularly when they have just a couple of small, tasty leaves. Commercial growers, particularly organic growers, have been using row covers for years as a way to keep insects off their crops and to keep early crops a little warmer. Row covers are made from a spun synthetic material that is lightweight, air and rain permeable, and allows 85% of the light (or more) to pass through. Wire hoops are sold to keep the garden cloth (also sold under the trade name Remay) up above the plants. As it is so lightweight, you can just spread it out over the plants. Check your garden center, or look in one of the many gardening catalogs. I know Gardener's Supply (1-800-863-1700) sells it. The garden fabric also will protect your plants against a light frost. Be sure to remove it by the time your squashes start to bloom, so that the good bugs can come and pollinate them.

Japanese beetles are perhaps the most dreaded of six-legged garden pests. They can devour your roses or raspberries in a jiffy. Japanese beetles are just one of many foreign pests. They first appeared in New Jersey in 1916, and gradually moved north. They do have some natural predators, but the lawn care industry insists on applying broad-spectrum insecticides to lawns, which kill the good, the bad (and the ugly). Japanese beetles are prolific and mushroom in population when there are no predators. This accounts for their high numbers in areas such as new housing developments, where fresh soil (not containing predators) is brought in.

Many people hand pick them, dropping them into a jar of soapy water. If this is your preferred method, do it early in the morning while they are still lethargic—even if you are, too. That way not so many will get away. In the heat of the day, many will fly off when you try to grab their friends.

Milky spore is a long-term approach to reducing Japanese beetle populations. It is a bacterial disease that affects the grubs, but not beneficial insects, plants, or warm-blooded animals. It can be applied any time when the ground is not frozen. I've never experimented with it, as I never have had a serious Japanese beetle problem. According to friends of mine it works well, but is most effective when an entire neighborhood does it together, as the beetles can fly in for lunch at your house, even if they were born next door. It may take two or three years to be fully effective, but should last for ten years or more.

Beneficial nematodes are another approach to control. Nematodes are tiny worms that can be introduced to the soil to prey on Japanese beetle grubs as well as (allegedly) Colorado potato beetle grubs, cutworms, root weevils, and flea larvae. They do not affect earthworms, plants, pets, or people. Gardener's Supply sells them by mail order, but does mention that they keep working "as long as the soil stays moist." That could be a problem in many summers, and it's hard to know exactly what is going on beneath the turf.

One approach *not* to take is buying the sex-scented Japanese beetle traps. Yes, they do catch a lot of beetles. But a lot more beetles come to check out the scene than are caught, and it seems many eat lunch before looking for sex! If you want to try them, give some to your neighbors, and maybe they will lure your beetles away.

Being an organic gardener means trying different approaches to pest problems. Each gardener will find that different solutions are required for his or her particular environment. People reach for the poisons because they bring quick death. Spray it on, and watch the bugs gasp and die. Next time you are tempted to do that, remember those Japanese beetles that are so troublesome. They are not a problem in Japan, where natural predators keep them in check. When you spray toxins on, you kill the good insects along with the bad. The toxins wash off your roses in the rain, killing things you don't even know about.

Slugs are not a problem for me in most years, though they will occasionally lunch on the hostas. It may well be that the beneficial insects—parasitic wasps and others—that like living in this toxin-free zone keep them under control.

Saucers of beer are well known to attract slugs, leading them down the road to cirrhosis and death. Well, death anyway. There are also a variety of commercial slug baits, some of them acceptable to organic farmers.

Diatomaceous earth is a very fine, very sharp white powder that, if sprinkled around your plants, works like razor wire for slugs. It is sold at most garden centers. I have used coarse mason's sand as a cheaper alternative, and it seems to work in the vegetable garden.

I lose some things from insect damage from time to time, but I'd rather do that than poison my lawn, or my flowers, or my vegetables. Or Emily the Wonder Dog. Proving cause and effect is very tough for the backyard gardener—did I have less bugs because I'm organic? Hard to say. But I have never met an organic gardener who tried it for three years and didn't see an improvement. That's good enough for me.

An Afternoon in the Garden with Jamaica Kincaid

As a garden designer and an ardent gardener, I never turn down the opportunity to see the gardens of another gardener, especially a passionate one. There is always something to learn. Thus I felt very lucky when I met Jamaica Kincaid at a workshop, and she agreed to let me visit her home near Bennington, Vermont, to see her gardens and to talk about plants.

Although Jamaica Kincaid is best known as a writer of fiction, she wrote a book, *My Garden [Book]* (Farrar, Straus, Giroux, 1999, cloth), that is both highly personal and full of information about specific plants, including many plants I had never seen or read about. I leapt at the opportunity to spend a Saturday afternoon with Ms. Kincaid learning about plants, and came away with a list of plants that I simply must have.

Jamaica Kincaid was born and raised in Antigua, in the West Indies. She remembers reading Wordsworth when she was young, and trying to imagine the daffodils he described, their smells, texture, beauty. When she moved to New York as a young woman (working as a nanny, like the Lucy in her early *New Yorker* stories), her employer took her to Central Park to see the daffodils in bloom. Although she loved the daffodils, it made her angry to realize that her colonial education had forced her to memorize a poem that, but for coming to New York, would have meant nothing to her. Plants and flowers continue to affect Jamaica strongly.

Some fifteen years ago, Jamaica Kincaid moved to the Bennington, Vermont, area. And although she still qualifies as a "flatlander," she has learned to cope—grudgingly—with our winters. She told me that if she were designing our climate she would have ten months of spring, and only one week of winter.

Jamaica, her husband, and two teenage children live in a large, brown-shingled house on a hill overlooking a meadow. It is surrounded on three sides by large evergreens. As we gardeners know, shade plants are often subtle, and it is more difficult to get the long-

lasting, brilliant colors of sun-loving or tropical plants. But Jamaica is undaunted by challenges. She will not cut down these trees, as she loves the way "the wind sings in the pines."

In her shady gardens she grows all sorts of plants, including things like the umbrella plant, *Darmera peltata*, which seem tropical because of their huge leaves. She has a *Crambe cordifolia* (colewort), which displayed huge, exquisite, crinkled leaves. By now it must be sending up 4-foot spikes of delicate white flowers reminiscent of baby's breath. Most crambes have coarse leaves like rhubarb, and need to hide behind something like the roses, but her specimen was so much nicer than any I'd seen elsewhere, it motivated me to try to find one.

She speaks in very personal tones about plants she loves, and sometimes feels they are teasing her, or misbehaving in order to get her attention. Throughout her book she shares her feelings about the frustrations of getting the garden just right, and I don't think it will ever be exactly right for her. Jamaica gets great joy from plants, but the garden is also full of trials and tribulations for her.

Like many[1] serious gardeners, Jamaica uses Latin names for everything, as common names are not consistent, though she admits that common names usually sound better. Some I had her spell out for me, like the *Peltoboykinia tellimoides*, but even so I can't find all of them in my standard plant texts.

Jamaica loves nursery catalogs, and drools over them much of the winter. They help her survive the melancholy of months without time in the garden. She has developed friendships with many of the people she buys from. She traveled to China on a plant-collecting trip with Dan Hinkley of Heronswood Nursery, in Kingston, Washington. I came back with notes like "*Lathyris vernus*. Purple. Must have. Heronswood." By now I can't remember the plant, but this winter I'll study a Heronswood catalog and find it. Clearly from its name it is a perennial sweet pea, but it must be an early one that grows in (partial) shade. Jamaica tells me that Heronswood is probably the best supplier of rare and unusual plants, though I admit that I've never bought from them. I was put off by them years ago when I realized I would have to pay five dollars just to get the catalog! (You may reach them by phone, 360-297-4172, or see their web site, heronswood@silverlink.com.)

Most of us know the common cyclamen, which is sold in grocery stores in the winter for its profuse, lovely and colorful flowers. Jamaica introduced me to *Cyclamen neapolitanum*, a relative of the houseplant, which will grow in the shade and is hardy to Zone 4 (it can usually withstand winter temperatures of minus 20 or 25 degrees Fahrenheit). I ordered some bulbs from Dutch Gardens (1-800-818-3861), and each week I check on them, but so far there are no signs of life. I am beginning to get discouraged. Perhaps it is a conspiracy. Or maybe I'm just worrying the way Jamaica might.

Jamaica Kincaid is very generous with her time and with her plants. I had brought her a clump of plants that I love, descendants of some I grew up with (snowdrops, *Galanthus nivalis*). I went home with six plants from her garden, including a wonderful blue anenome (*Anemone nemerosa*) that I had never seen before. It's always a good idea to visit a serious gardener's home bearing a gift, of course, because you are most likely to go home with something new and nice. We gardeners are like that.

This is the time of year when garden clubs offer tours of gardens, and I recommend going to as many as you can if you want to be a better gardener. You may learn some new plants, or see some great combinations. Bring a notebook, and be sure to seek out the garden's owners with your questions. Like Jamaica Kincaid, they will be pleased to tell you about their special plants.

Jamaica's garden is a wonderful, personal reflection of a bright woman with a feisty and creative approach to life that she brings to her garden. And it is a thing of beauty, which is really what each of us tries to create in our own way.

Chapter 5

July

The Deer Dilemma

Deer are a problem for many American gardeners. Historically, deer populations were kept in control by cougars and wolves, but these have been exterminated in the eastern parts of the United States. Dogs and coyotes are not much of a threat to deer except when snow is deep and crusted. Hunters try to keep nature in balance, but in many areas the deer populations are growing rapidly. As woods become house lots, deer lose browsing territory and turn to the suburban garden for food.

I have read that the deer population in all of North America was about 500,000 in 1900, but that it now has reached 15 million and is rising. These hungry critters have got to find something to eat, and will. For many discouraged gardeners this means that they feel they have to give up growing some of their favorite plants, things like tulips that deer consider delicacies. There are ways to protect your plants, and alternatively, there are plants that deer don't particularly like.

I have had very good luck keeping deer out of gardens with deer repellent, but I live in a part of the world with adequate supplies of wild fodder for the deer. I have gardened for people who have had deer problems. Whenever a problem arises, I go to my local grain and feed store to buy coyote urine, and the little air-wick bottles they sell with it. Predator urine has been shown to work in the past, but the problem was that it washed away with rain. Now you can buy little plastic containers with cotton in the bottom, holes in the sides, and a rain-cap lid with hanger. It exudes vile smells that make deer lose their appetites.

Deer appear to have regular lunch routes. Hostas at the Smiths for breakfast, tulips at two next door. To break their cycle you have to place these stinky things within 6 to 8 feet of each deer treat. You are supposed to refuel the containers every thirty days, but I haven't found that to be necessary. Once they have crossed you off the list, you are home free. Oh, and by the way, humans can't notice the smell, except when filling up the containers. I won't comment on the ethical questions of keeping coyotes caged up in order to collect their urine, but I know it's not a job that I would want! I have heard of people who regularly urinate outside to keep the deer away, and who claim it works. Try it if you like, but don't blame me if you get arrested!

Sprays are available to discourage deer from eating favored plants, but these can't be used in the vegetable garden. Some contain hot pepper, others rotten eggs, and a few have both. Try them on shrubs that suffer during the winter, and look for one that contains waxes, as it will last longer.

We have a dog, Emily, and no deer problem. I credit her dog smells with keeping deer away. In the winter they come by looking for apples that fall on the snow, and once on Christmas eve they finished off our Brussels sprouts that we were counting on for a Christmas treat. But who knows, maybe that was reindeer. I'd like to think so.

Deer netting is available to keep deer out, but this requires setting up 8-foot poles around around the perimeter of your garden. While that may be acceptable around a vegetable garden, even a badge of determination, it doesn't make sense for most flowers and shrubs around your house. Deer have even been known to crawl under net fences, so burying-the fence is sometimes needed.

Selecting decorative plants that deer don't like is perhaps the best long-term solution. Start by taking a walk in the woods to see what is growing there. If deer aren't eating paper birch (*Betula papyrifera*) or black locust (*Robinia pseudoacia*) in the woods (they usually don't), then they probably won't eat them in your yard. Ask your neighbors, they may have already sacrificed several nice shrubs to the Deer Lunch Program.

There are several criteria that you can use when selecting perennials. First, deer don't like things with furry leaves, I'm told. Lamb's ears (*Stachys byzantina*), for example. They don't like things with thorns or spikes, though they may carefully gather rosebuds for breakfast. And they don't generally like plants with aromatic foliage such as yarrow (*Achillea millefolium*). Lastly, they are not stupid, so they keep away from poisonous plants, things like monkshood (*Aconitum carmichaelii*). Daffodil foliage is ever so slightly toxic, so they generally keep away from it. There are exceptions to every rule, and a hungry (or vengeful) deer will eat anything but the bird bath.

Companion planting helps protect plants if the deer problem is not too severe. White sweet alyssum is said by some to repel deer, and garlic or onion family plants help. You can surround your appealing plants with disgusting—to deer—plants, and maybe they will be spared. Fritillaria (*Fritillaria imperialis*) is a bulb plant that is so strong smelling that I can smell it from a couple of paces away. I plant it with tulips in hopes of keeping not only deer but rodents away, and believe it helps.

There are books available that list plants that deer tend to avoid, and you should probably buy one if you live in an area with a deer problem. *Gardening in Deer Country*, by Vincent Drzewucki, Jr. (Brick Tower Press, paperback, 1998), is the one I have, and it is fine.

I recently saw an ad for a sprinkler with a battery-operated motion sensor. When a deer or other pest comes by, the sprinkler sends out a stream of water. Sounds like it should work, though not in the winter, obviously, when deer are most aggressive toward shrubbery. This might be interesting if your teenager decides to slip out the window for a midnight rendezvous!

I am a believer in doing what needs to be done. If you really want tulips, figure out a way to do it. A chicken-wire cage over a bed of tulips could be set out each fall, and removed once the tulips have bloomed. It sounds drastic, and clearly is not the solution for everybody. In fact, I've never seen it done . . . yet.

Gardening without Rain

Sunday at 2 P.M. Temperature in the shade is 90 degrees, a brisk breeze is blowing. Lawns are looking parched, flowers are limp, vegetable gardens everywhere are in desperate need of water. This is a drought. People with wells are already rationing water, and many lawns will not get sprinkled tonight. The weather may be nice for golfers, boaters, and tennis players, but this is a tough time for gardeners.

So what can the gardener do in a drought? There is much that you can do to help your lawn and plants in the short term, and much to think about in the long term. In this book I have been espousing organic gardening, and I would like to use a real-life example of what organic gardening can do in these dry times.

Last fall I prepared a flower bed in Hanover, New Hampshire, for planting this summer. I had worked in a 4 to 6-inch layer of composted manure. I had added Pro-Gro bagged organic fertilizer and added greensand and rock phosphate. To keep down the weeds I had put on a 4-inch layer of bark mulch. When I started planting late last week I was delighted to see that the earth was moist, despite the drought. Each time I dug a hole for a plant, there were several earthworms. The soil was light and easily worked.

At the same house I went to another flower bed and dug up a flower for transplanting. That bed had not been improved last fall, nor mulched. The difference was radical: The earth was bone dry, there were no earthworms, and the plant was half the size I would have expected.

That example confirms for me what I already believe: Organic gardening is not something politically correct, but a system that helps the soil to be a vital, living resource that nourishes and protects our plants. A healthy, organically nourished soil gives plants resistance to environmental stresses like heat, drought, and extreme cold.

But let us assume that you haven't been an organic gardener, you have relied on 10-10-10 fertilizer, or Miracle-Gro. Or that perhaps

you have added a little compost to your vegetable gardens, but not to your flower gardens. What can a person do to keep a lawn and gardens alive and happy without rain?

The first problem area for many is the lawn. If you can't water your lawn, leave the grass long. It might be a little unsightly, but it will be worse if it turns totally brown. So don't cut it during the drought. Taller grass shades the soil and helps keep it from drying out. Three and a half inches is a good height for the blade. Your lawn will be healthier if you don't use a bagger to catch the cut grass, as this will act as an organic mulch, albeit a thin layer.

If you planted trees or shrubs this year *or* last year you will need to water them regularly. You may have thought that last year's trees were well established and could be left alone, but watering them now is worth the effort. If you can reach your new shrub with a hose, give it a good soaking and then leave the hose on it at a trickle for a while to really let the water soak in. Build a ring of dirt around the tree to contain the water if you haven't already. Although cheap hoses are nothing but aggravation, it might be worth buying a couple of 50-footers if you have new shrubs that are out of hose reach.

If you water with a bucket or watering can, you have the advantage of knowing how much water you are giving your plant. Too many times people squirt some water on a lawn or tree, but really don't get much to the roots. Five to ten gallons per tree or shrub is needed two or three times a week. Exactly how much is needed depends on the soil type, size of the plant, exposure, wind, and temperature. If you see leaves curling up or browning along the edges, your plant is stressed out and in dire need of water. A 4-inch layer of bark mulch around the tree will help keep the soil moist, but keep the mulch away from the trunk.

My vegetable garden is an important source of organic produce for me. I mulch my vegetables with newspaper covered with straw, or with grass clippings, which keeps down the weeds and retains moisture. If you don't use mulch and we have no rain for a long time, you may notice that your soil is not very receptive to watering, that water tends to run off rather than soaking in. Mulch will help with this.

I don't like to use a sprinkler that waters the entire vegetable garden. I prefer using a watering wand, which allows me to water individual plants and doesn't waste water on walkways and between plants. I like to give each plant some water, go on to the next, then return to it. The first dose softens the surface, and the second drink lets water really penetrate to the roots. This is particularly important for plants like squashes, which I grow in hills, as it helps reduce runoff.

If you have planted perennial flowers this year you will need to water them even if they are well settled in. If you are still planting flowers, mix in lots of compost or well-rotted manure with each plant. Fill the planting holes with water and let it soak in before planting.

When planting in dry times, be sure to immerse your plant in a bucket of water for a few moments (or until the air bubbles stop) before you remove it from its pot. It is much easier to soak your plant in a bucket than to get the water down to the bottom of its roots from above. Check your new plants every day, and water at least every other day for the first week, longer if necessary. If you notice that it wilts during the heat of the day, water more and add mulch.

People often have strong feelings about whether to use bark mulch or not. I feel that it is not really needed in a well-established perennial bed that is full and lush. The plants are big enough to shade out the weeds. I top-dress the soil with an inch or two of composted manure, which serves as a sort of mulch until the earthworms carry it down into the soil. Although I tend to find time to do it in my own garden in the early spring or late fall, you can do it at any time.

Too Much Rain?

Too much rain can be a problem for some plants, and some gardens. Plants like phlox and lilacs are often subject to mildew, an unsightly but nonlethal white coating to the leaves. In rainy times, the problem can become severe. Spraying toxic chemicals won't help: By the time the mildew is visible, it is already too late. Improved cultivars are available that are mildew resistant. You may want to replace some plants if you have a problem every year, and if it bothers you. Or if you can move your plant to a sunnier, breezier location that will help next year.

If your garden is in a low spot that holds water after a rain, there are several things you can do. The most drastic is to bring in a backhoe and have someone install drainage pipes and gravel. You can improve the soil by adding lots—and I mean lots—of compost. Truckloads. Lastly, create raised beds so that your plants are 6 to 12 inches higher than they were. This along with the compost will solve the problem for most gardens.

In new flower beds, or where plantings are sparse, bark mulch does help conserve water and keep weeds down. While it is true that bark mulch uses up some nitrogen from the soil as it breaks down, I believe that a good soil full of compost and organic fertilizer does not suffer from the use of the mulch. In times of drought, a layer of mulch will help any planting.

I reread the opening pages of Steinbeck's *The Grapes of Wrath*, which describes the beginning of the drought of the great Dust Bowl era. The picture he paints is much bleaker than what we have experienced this summer, but we do need days of rain to refill our wells and raise the water table. So welcome this week's rain, even if it spoils your parade.

Some of Summer's Best Bloomers

I love flowers. I love looking at them, smelling them, growing them, arranging them in a vase. I love reading about them. In fact, I have even been accused of suffering from plant lust. But unlike Jimmy Carter, I do not admit to harboring feelings of lust, especially not in print.

It is true, however, that I have a very hard time going to a greenhouse or nursery and not buying something. A good-looking plant, especially if it is in flower, is a temptation for me. Like many gardeners, I want to try growing just about everything. What I have found out is that although there are hundreds of interesting plants to try, not all of them are worth garden space. This is about some of the plants that I love, have grown, and feel are garden-worthy.

One of my favorite plants is the delphinium. It is a tall plant, growing to 3 to 6 feet. Although there are lots of different colors available, the most common colors are shades of blue and purple.

Delphiniums have a flaw, and because of it some gardeners avoid them. They grow tall, so often they flop over and break in a rainstorm. Stakes can prevent this, but if you have lots of delphinium, it is a lot of work to stake them all up, and the stakes are not usually handsome. They are excellent cut flowers, so after a rain I usually end up picking some that have been damaged, which is okay by me. If you pick a delphinium and leave the lower part of the stalk, often it will present you with side shoots that bloom a bit later.

Last fall I redid a bed that had some lovely delphiniums, and as a result I learned something about them. I had removed many of the other flowers in the bed, added lots of composted manure, Pro-Gro organic fertilizer, rock phosphate, and greensand. These are the standard additives I use, and I've described their benefits in previous articles. My delphiniums stayed in place, but the soil around them was improved for the first time in a few years. I noticed that they were taller and more lush this year. The best thing was that most of them were not damaged at all by last week's heavy rain and wind.

So do some organic soil improvement this fall, and it will help your delphiniums.

My technique for tying up individual delphiniums or other tall flowers is to get a bamboo stake and push it firmly in the ground behind the plant, so that it is largely hidden. I prefer stakes that are a little shorter than the flower. Next I attach the tie wrap or string firmly to the stake so that it won't slide down the stake. Then I tie a loose loop around the part of the plant I want to support. I try to avoid tying it tightly so that the plant can grow, and so that it moves gently and naturally in the wind. You can also try encircling a group of delphiniums with some of the 4-foot-tall green enameled wire fencing that is available at nurseries and home centers.

Another plant I love is foxglove, *Digitalis purpurea*. It is a biennial, not a perennial, which means that it takes two years from seed to flower, and after the second year it does not return. It is a tall plant, commonly 2 to 3 feet, with lots of pink or purple flowers along the stem. Its Latin name, *Digitalis*, means finger of a glove, referring to the shape of the flower. Its common name really means fairy gloves, as fox is just an old name for folk, or fairies.

Often gardeners buy foxgloves in bloom and then are disappointed when they do not reappear the next spring. They produce lots of tiny seeds, and usually will self-sow if left to drop their seeds. Observe the shape, color, and texture of the leaves this year so that you will remember them next year and not pull out the young plants. Foxgloves in the first year produce no tall stalk, just a basal rosette. One named cultivar, Foxy, will bloom the first year if started early enough in the spring.

Although foxgloves make great cut flowers, be sure to leave a few in the garden. Once the flowers have turned brown and dry I cut the stalk and shake seeds out over areas where I would like some foxgloves in two years. They like full sun, but will grow in part shade, so I often shake seeds out at the edge of a woods where they will grow up among the weeds and understory plants. I don't prepare the soil, I just trust in nature, and am usually rewarded with plenty of plants. At other times I shake out seeds in loosely worked soil in the vegetable garden, and raise the first-year plants there, transplanting them to places in the flower beds in the spring of their second year.

Another great plant is the Shasta daisy, or *Leucanthemum* × *su-*

perbum. It is a white daisy, and there are many different named varieties. My favorite is Thomas Killen, which has very strong stems and large handsome flowers excellent for cutting and bringing in the house. It keeps well in flower arrangements.

Although some reference books list the Shasta daisy as a Zone 5 plant, my personal experience is that most times it is hardy here even though we are in Zone 4. (The zones are useful in selecting plants based on their survival in different climates. The colder the winters, the lower is the number.)

Shasta daisies are not long-lived plants. To keep them growing in your garden forever you need to dig them up every other spring, divide them, improve the soil, and replant. That will help keep them vigorous. Even so, you will lose some plants from time to time, but they are worth the effort.

There are lots of plants whose virtues I could extol, but for sheer ability to survive and look good year after year, the daylily (*Hemerocallis*) takes the cake. The common orange daylily is one of the most common flowers in bloom in New England because you can't kill it. I once dug some up on a Sunday afternoon, left them in a pile at the edge of the lawn, and forgot about them. They survived the summer dry spells, the cold winter winds, and are a handsome blooming patch of daylilies to this day, years later.

Daylilies get their common name from the fact that each flower usually just blooms for a day. But because each stem has many buds, they bloom over a longer period of time, even in a vase, where they will open sequentially if provided with sunshine.

There are thousands of named varieties of daylilies to choose from. It is relatively easy to crossbreed daylilies, and consequently there are many different colors, heights, and bloom times.

Most daylilies bloom for three weeks or a month, and then they are done. There are, however, "recurrent" daylilies. The recurrent daylilies bloom for much of the summer, taking a little time out, perhaps, in the heat of August.

The most common recurrent daylily is Stella d'Oro. It is a rich gold color, very vigorous, and a little shorter than standard daylilies. Another nice variety is Happy Returns, which is a lemon yellow. For variety you might try a Pardon Me, which has more of a burgundy petal color, with some yellow inside the throat. All are very nice daylilies that will give you years of pleasure.

It's easy to develop a mentality that eschews the ordinary, the known. Some gardeners strive to have unusual flowers, things none of their friends have. Perhaps they will be the first on their block to have what will become the newest rage. That's all right; I like to try the new and unusual, too. There is something to be said for the classics, however. The perkiness of a daisy, the stateliness of a delphinium, the cheerfulness of a daylily will always give me pleasure. To me these plants are like a good violin quartet—I will enjoy them this year, and every year.

Scary Plants to Watch Out For: The Invasives Are Coming

Weeds. *Webster's New Collegiate Dictionary* defines a weed as "a plant of no value and usually of rank growth; especially one that tends to overgrow or choke out more desirable plants." This is a very subjective definition, as some people may love what you consider a weed. You may arrange great bouquets of wild asters or daisies or black-eyed-Susans on the table, but to others they are just a nuisance in the garden. There are some plants to watch out for, however. Nice-looking plants that will take over.

I recently was at a farm stand that sells fruits, vegetables and plants. I was shocked to see bishop's weed (*Aegopodium podagraria*) for sale, and thought about making a citizen's arrest. There was a small sign that said, "Should be planted where it can be contained." Huh. As if anyone could contain bishop's weed, or its all-green brother, goutweed. Most serious gardeners agree with the assessment that the only cure for goutweed is to sell the house—to a nongardener.

July is the time that bishop's weed and goutweed bloom, so you need to know how to identify them so that they will not spread their seeds. These two spread most often by roots, as their roots invade other plants, and even a small scrap of root can start a new colony. But I wouldn't take a chance with the seeds, either.

Bishop's weed is a green and white plant sold as a ground cover. The leaves are edged in white, have saw toothed edges, and the terminal leaves are in a group of three. They have a delicate white flower that looks like a diminutive Queen Anne's lace. The plant will grow anywhere: sun, shade, wet or dry. It will choke out most any other plant. Goutweed is usually the name applied to the all green form, but they are both the same species. Once well established it is virtually impossible to eradicate goutweed, though (knock on wood) I think I have done so in my iris bed. The green form is much more aggressive and tenacious than the variegated form.

Goutweed is often spread from house to house when neighbors trade plants. So be careful! In my experience, goutweed seems particularly common growing with bearded iris, and I've decided not to risk accepting any from friends, and certainly not if they have goutweed anywhere on their property.

Like most invasive plants, goutweed grows fast, chokes out the competition, and has tenacious roots. I tried eliminating it two years ago by weeding, and getting all the roots out. No luck. A scrap of root is all it takes. Last year I lifted all the iris in the bed, and really combed through the dirt for even the finest scraps. No luck. This year I dug down a foot, and wheelbarrowed away the dirt, roots and all. I dumped it onto a huge sheet of heavy plastic, and after it was all removed, I closed up the plastic and dumped fill on top. Then I put down a layer of landscape fabric in my iris bed, and brought in new dirt. So far, so good. It was a lot of work, but felt good to reclaim a section of flower bed that I had lost.

If you don't have the will to beat this weed, there are still things you can do to contain it. First, don't let it go to seed. Cut off any flowers as soon as they show up, and DO NOT PUT ANY PART OF THIS PLANT IN YOUR COMPOST PILE!!! Put it in your household trash, or incinerate it. Second, try to contain the weed. Cut it back, or mow it down every time it rears its ugly head. Buy some plastic edging and encircle it, though it may go under it unless you buy stuff that is 9 or 12 inches deep. Lastly, cut it back to the ground as often as you can.

Another invasive plant is Japanese knotweed (*Polygonum cuspidatum*), commonly referred to as "bamboo" because of its resemblance to it. It will grow to 8 feet in height on hollow stems, and was imported from Japan over a hundred years ago as an attractive landscape plant. It spreads rapidly by rhizomes (underground stems) that reportedly will travel up to 65 feet from the mother plant. Small pieces of the plant can regenerate a new one, so stream beds are particularly vulnerable as ice and water can spread pieces that then start new colonies. I've heard that even the usual chemical weed killers won't get it. One person I know dug down 8 feet and still found roots present. Very discouraging. I've read that it has pushed its way up through two inches of asphalt. This is the making of a science fiction movie like *The Eggplant that Ate Chicago*.

Again, if you can't beat it, try to contain it. Cut it down every chance you get. Before breakfast, lunch, and dinner, perhaps. Actually, Chris Mattrick of the New England Wildflower Society (and an expert on invasive plants) told me that cutting it back three times a year for three years will do much to wear it down. Plants depend on green foliage to fuel their existence by photosynthesis, so if you really want to wear them down, keep cutting them down and they may ultimately get tired and give up. I doubt it, but at least you will keep it from spreading.

Remember that small pieces can start a whole new colony, so dispose of the stems where they can't start up a new one. It blooms in the fall, and I recommend cutting off the flower heads, even though seeds are not necessarily viable. Rake up your cuttings and incinerate them or put in sealed plastic bags. Leave the bags in the sun till the contents turn to mush (about a month). Never let scraps get into a stream, since they will infect other places.

Purple loosestrife (*Lythrum salicaria*) is another gorgeous plant commonly sold by nurseries and greenhouses. Large colonies of this tall purple flower grow in wet places everywhere, blooming in the late summer. Resist the urge to buy some or dig some out to bring home. Because purple loosestrife is so beautiful, some nurseries sell variations of the wild plant. Even though the greenhouse people may assure you that the cultivars they are selling are "tame" or even sterile, don't buy them. Each plant in the wild produces about 2,000,000 seeds, and some of the "sterile" hybrids can fertilize wild plants, creating new varieties. Purple loosestrife is very tough to dig out once established. Hybrid plants sometimes crossbreed and revert back to the parent stock. In some places purple loosestrife has choked out nearly all other wild species of plants. If you have it growing on your property, please cut all the flowers off it on a regular basis so that it won't spread. And try to dig it out if you can.

Another "problem plant" I am often asked about is poison ivy

(*Rhus radicans*). As an organic gardener I have not found a quick fix. Pulling it out is dangerous for those with allergies. Do so in winter if you dare, though I wouldn't. All parts of the plant are poisonous. I have tried eliminating it with a number of organic approaches including a strong solution of borax and water, and by spraying on white vinegar. Both approaches damaged the poison ivy, but did not eliminate it. Be consoled, if you have it, to know this: Its berries in the fall are highly prized by migrating birds.

My final bits of advice: Speak up at greenhouses selling invasive plants. Go for the citizen's arrest. Threaten never to buy another plant unless they stop selling invasives like bishop's weed and purple loosestrife. Be prepared to back up your threat. And be VERY careful when trading plants. If your friends have goutweed, it might be best not to accept any plants. Organic gardeners do better overall, but we are a bit handicapped when it comes to an arsenal for destroying invasive plants. I can live with that. And will live healthier because of it.

Edging and Mulching

We garden for many reasons. We grow tomatoes for an early taste of heaven. We grow flowers for their beauty and their scents. We keep a lawn to have a bit of order in our chaotic lives. Most of us aspire to do more, but run short of time or energy or money. Or all three. Some of us continue to expand our gardens even when we know, rationally, that we shouldn't. But even for the compulsive gardener there are ways to keep things looking nice with a little less work. Which means, of course, that we can take on new projects. I'll never completely catch up, I'm sure.

Just about every house has some lawn around it. And even for the lawn minimalist there is the problem of the ambitious lawn, lawn that wants to extend its domain into the flower beds or the vegetable garden. The hostile takeover. Lawn rarely spreads by seed. Even if you go on vacation, it hasn't enough time, normally, to produce seed and spread it into the gardens. Lawn spreads underground by extending it roots, then sending up new blades. Again and again.

There are a number of ways to confine your lawn to its proper place. Plastic "pound-in" edging is readily available, and works quite well. It is particularly useful where the ground is soft and there are no rocks or roots—at the beach, for example. It comes in 6-inch sections that interlock. I have used it, but rarely does it pound in. If you use a shovel or an edging tool to slice through the turf first, it pounds in quite well. I find it most useful for containing aggressive plants like bee balm (*Monarda spp.*) or mint (*Mentha spp.*) in an existing flower bed that already has had the roots and rocks removed. One can make a circle or a square with it. Plastic edging also comes in rolls, but it is flimsier and more difficult to work with than the stuff that comes in 6-inch sections. There is also steel edging, which is seen most commonly in public spaces as it is quite expensive. It comes in 20-foot lengths, which means it's hard to transport. It bends, but does not turn sharp corners.

For most of us, the best way to confine your lawn is to dig an empty "moat" around it. If you want straight edges, mark the edges of your garden bed with mason's twine, a thin braided nylon twine. Wrap the twine around nails or pegs, or an old screwdriver, and stretch it tight. Then begin cutting through the sod.

It is worth buying an edging tool for the job (unless you can borrow one from a sympathetic neighbor). The tool has a crescent-shaped steel cutting blade on a long wooden handle, and you use it by stepping on it to slice through the grass. Angle the blade away from yourself at a 45-degree angle before you step on it. Then you need to remove the sod and dirt to create a ditch that separates the lawn from the garden bed. You can use a hoe or a three-prong scratcher or a soil scoop to clean out the ditch. When the grass roots want to move laterally, they find air, and give up.

Mulching is a great way to reduce your labor in the garden. Mulch helps to keep weed seeds out of the soil, and smothers weeds trying to get established. You still must get weed roots out, but mulch helps keep the soil soft and moist, so pulling weeds is easier. It keeps the soil cooler in the summer and warmer in the winter. Earthworms do much good for your soil, but disappear deep into the soil if it is too hot and dry. A good layer of mulch will also reduce erosion on banks, or the sides of raised beds. Depending on what type of mulch you use, it can add organic matter to the soil as it breaks down, improving soil consistency. And it usually keeps things looking tidier.

Mulch comes in many forms, colors, prices. Mother (or Father) Nature keeps the woods nicely mulched with leaves or pine needles, which accounts for the good soil in old forests. I know that some people worry that nitrogen is used up from the soil as bark mulch breaks down in flower beds. I've never seen signs of it, and it seems like the most natural process in the world. Unless you see yellowing of your plants that are mulched, I wouldn't worry about it. Or if you wish, sprinkle some slow-release fertilizer on the surface before you mulch.

We hardly ever weed our vegetable garden. Not from sloth, but due to a good layer of mulch. First we weed the garden well in the spring. If there are a lot of tiny weeds, sometimes I use a special propane torch to burn them. It is a 3-foot wand with a burner on one end and a bottle of propane (the same one that fires up the outdoor grill) on the other. It is a quick way for an organic gardener to nuke some small weeds. It is available through gardening catalogs such as Gardener's Supply in Burlington, Vermont.

Anyhow, the next step is to cover the walkways and around plants with four or five sheets of newspaper. Then we pile on 4 to 6 inches of hay or straw. We use at least a dozen bales each year, so we get cheap mulch hay from a farmer even though it has seeds. We have found that the newspaper helps keep the seeds out of the soil, and it hasn't been a serious problem. Straw has no (or few) seeds, but costs five times as much. We don't mulch until the soil has warmed up in the early summer. The newspaper breaks down over the course of the summer, and earthworms love to chomp on it.

I have friends who use sheets of black plastic for mulch, stretching it tight across the garden and only cutting holes where plants are located. I tried it years ago, and it works, but I don't like it. Water tends to accumulate in depressions, creating places for mosquitoes to breed. It doesn't please me to look at it, and the sun's ultraviolet rays break it down eventually, so you end up with a lot of bits of plastic in the soil. You can cover the plastic with straw, but it seems to slide off with time, or as you walk around. As an organic gardener I try to create a soil that is full of living things: bacteria, worms, fungi. I've never read that black plastic destroys any of these things, but I have no proof that it doesn't, and I tend to be conservative about such things.

Flower beds are most often mulched with bark mulch. If you have a pickup truck, the cheapest way to buy this stuff is to go to a sawmill. Generally that mulch is quite coarse, however. Most garden centers sell different qualities and colors of mulch, including "double ground" mulch, which is finer and nicer to work with. It is also is sold in plastic bags, but that gets expensive if you have much to mulch. Select your mulch on a sunny day if the color is important, as the wet mulch is much darker looking than the dry. Some bagged mulch is made from grinding up scrap lumber and staining it. Read the label, and avoid that kind if you can.

Landscape fabric is also sold as an underlayer for your bark mulch. This is a woven synthetic fabric that allows moisture to pass through, but not weeds. It comes in 4-foot-wide rolls, and is pinned to the ground with special staples. Then it is covered with mulch. To plant, one must cut a hole in it. As plants like hostas get larger and spread out, you will need to go back and open the hole bigger every few years. I've used it, but don't really like it. When used on hills the mulch will eventually slide off. It is a pain to put down, and it is a nuisance to cut, but it does help with pernicious weeds.

Cocoa shell mulch is sold in bags, and smells quite yummy for the first week or two, though it makes me hungry for chocolate chip cookies. It is a very fine mulch, but with rain and time it develops a crust so that it doesn't blow around. Buckwheat hulls are even lighter in weight, and are more likely to move around. It isn't for use on steep banks. Weeds can come through this stuff even more easily than bark mulch.

As we all know, there is no such things as a weed-free or labor-free garden. My sister likes to say, "The plants always win." Which is almost true, turn your back on the weeds for a few days and they pop up. But that is okay with me, it gives me a good excuse to avoid vacuuming the house when I want to be outside!

Avoiding Death Row: A Talk with Paul Sachs

It's been a long time since I walked down Death Row, but I recently decided that it was time for a visit. Death Row is what I call the aisle at the garden centers and hardware stores where the chemical poisons are on sale. I thought that I should know what is for sale, since I preach organic gardening to whomever will listen.

Usually there is some spillage on the shelves, and the smell of toxins in the air makes me nervous. I want to go outside, I want to escape the nose-tickling smell of chemicals that affect the nervous systems of insects. I want to avoid fungicides and the "Three Step System for a Perfect Lawn." I cringe at the thought of clueless homeowners spreading powdered death. I shudder at the thought of children and dogs playing on chemically treated lawns. I don't want to touch products that claim that "a single application provides protection against grubs all season long."

Before visiting Death Row I took a drive to meet Paul Sachs, the owner of North Country Organics in Bradford, Vermont. His company produces and markets Pro-Gro, an organic fertilizer I use, and various other products that assist gardeners in growing healthy plants without using chemical pesticides or fertilizers. The company does not sell retail, but its products are widely available.

For the past eighteen years Paul Sachs has not only been selling organic products, but he has made the study of soils, plants, and insects his passion. He has studied them so that he can understand and explain how natural systems work. He has written two books that deal with the causes and solutions to plant problems. He believes that if people understand what makes a lawn healthy, or a plant resistant to disease or insect pests, they can avoid ending up on Death Row.

Lawn care has become a big industry in America. If the chemical companies have their say, not only will we buy fertilizer and apply it four times a year, we will buy insecticides to kill grubs and cinchbugs, fungicides to control mildew, and herbicides to prevent and kill those "ugly weeds." But as Paul Sachs explains in his book *Handbook of $uccessful Ecological Lawn Care* (Edaphic Press, 1996, paperback), much of this is unnecessary. His book details the research that has been done on lawn problems, and the ecological and low-cost solutions.

According to Sachs, many lawn problems will disappear if homeowners raise the height of their lawn mowers to 3½ inches, and allow the clippings to fall and decompose on the lawn. Keeping the grass longer gives more surface area for photosynthesis, producing better root systems. Taller grass shades out emerging crabgrass and other annual weeds. A healthy, chemical-free soil is full of microorganisms that will breakdown and recycle the grass clippings. And this from a man who sells bagged fertilizers, even some for lawns.

I asked Paul Sachs how to keep people off Death Row. People with apple trees, for example. He explained that the first step to a healthy plant is to grow it in a healthy soil. I couldn't agree more. Next, he said, don't kill off the predatory insects, things that will eat insect pests. Chemical insecticides kill all the bugs, good and bad. Allow the orchard floor to grow wildflowers that will provide safe haven for a variety of predators. This has been shown to make a significant, positive impact.

He went on to explain that compost teas are being used by some orchardists as a spray to transmit disease resistance to apple trees. They create a biofilm that is alive and protects the fruit. This isn't as simple as it sounds, as the "tea" has to be made from well-made, well-aged compost and kept aerated with an aquarium bubbler to keep it alive. Stirring with a stick is not enough. And the chunks surely will clog most sprayers. So far, it is a system used mainly by commercial organic orchardists.

A commercial kaolin clay product, Surround, can be used to create a breathable film on fruit. Insects select their targets in many ways, one of which involves the resonance given off by a plant. Coating the fruit with a microscopic layer of clay apparently changes the resonance, and insects don't perceive it as fruit. Smoke and mirrors for bugs. You need to know when to apply it for it to be effective.

Another organic product, Garlic Barrier, works in much the same way, changing the cues given off by plants and picked up by insects. This product can be used effectively on apple trees, but only after pollination, as it can confuse the bees, too. In order to be effective, a twenty-four-hour dry period is needed before and after spaying. This is a product that is simple enough for the average homeowner to use.

I asked Paul Sachs if Garlic Barrier would be effective on roses as a repellent for Japanese beetles. He said it works, but you need to use it early and often. Start in early June, he said, before the beetles have hatched and found your roses, then use it every two weeks all summer. If the beetles get a taste of your roses, it probably won't work. Kind of like blood in the water for sharks, I gather. Once they've had a taste, it's too late.

Paul wrote a book, *Edaphos, Dynamics of a Natural Soil System*

(Edaphic Press, 2nd edition, 1996, paperback), which addresses many issues important for gardeners and farmers. The word *edaphos* comes from the Greek, and means soil or ground. In this book he looks at the variables that affect plant success, starting from the soil.

His position is that whatever we do to the soil, to the environment, has an impact on all the organisms living in it. We do not know all the ramifications, for example, of spreading chemicals on our lawns, or using Round Up to kill those pernicious weeds in the brick walkway. Once we use chemicals to cause an imbalance in a natural system it frequently results in further imbalances, and further "need" for chemical correction.

In his book *Edaphos*, Paul Sachs details some of the results of excess fertilization. He explains that research has shown that "excess nitrogen accumulates [in plant tissues] as soluble amino acids and nitrates, needed components for the formation of protein by insects" (p. 71). This attracts bugs. There is a fine line between too much nitrogen and too little, which can also affect protein mechanisms, again signaling insects to come for lunch.

He points out that "compost is also credited with systemically increasing resistance to disease throughout the plant. It is not known exactly how this occurs" (p. 69). I have always believed that when it comes to compost, "more is better." Sachs preaches moderation in all things, at least as far as the plants are concerned. It makes sense, I suppose.

I try to garden sensibly, and to remember that there are often no "quick fixes" for organic gardeners. It takes time and patience to see what really works. Prevention is better than a chemical cure. I try to remember that Mother Nature developed a system that works fine if we don't mess around with it too much. That it is often when we try to grow things in ways that are contrary to nature and the needs of our plants that problems arise.

I never did make it to Death Row. I went onto the World Wide Web and read the promotional materials from one of the biggest manufacturers of lawn products. I read statements like, "After application, the moss shrivels up and disappears" and "Store in a cool dry place, out of the reach of children." And lots more. I decided that a trip to Death Row wasn't for me, even a quick visit.

The U.S. Environmental Protection Agency recently banned the use of Diazinon, a chemical commonly used to "control" insects, saying "symptoms from overexposure can include nausea, headaches, vomiting, diarrhea and general weakness. Diazinon's use on turf poses a risk to birds, and it is one of the most commonly found pesticides in air, rain and drinking and surface water." But the good news, for all of you who want to buy some, is that it will be available for sale though August 2003. So stock up now. It's available on Death Row.

Chapter 6

August

Shade Gardens

Why is it that most gardeners ignore the shady spots on their property, and focus on growing flowers in full sun? Probably because most of the big, showy flowers are sun lovers. There are many wonderful shade plants, but they are less well known. People tend to plant what they know, what their neighbors have, what they grew up with. I'll bet you've had someone offer you some free daylilies, but when was the last time somebody offered you a bag of hairy toad lilies (*Tricyrtis hirta*) or a nice clump of *Kirengeshoma palmata* (which has no common name), both good shade plants? Generally, shade plants are more slow-growing than sun plants, so neighbors have fewer to give away.

And quite frankly, it's more work planting things in shade when it is created by trees. Trees have roots to contend with. If you are going to plant flowers in the shade of trees, you will need a good sharp spade, a pruning saw you don't care about (for cutting roots, which will dull it up in no time), and a mattock or pick ax. You will have to sever roots, but don't worry, you won't do damage to your trees if the roots are an inch or less in diameter. Cutting bigger roots should be avoided if possible. Create a wider hole than you think necessary so that your plant will have time to establish itself before tree roots invade.

Most spring flowers that are started from bulbs (like daffodils and tulips) will grow just fine under deciduous trees in dappled shade. Planting time for bulbs is in the fall, from mid-September until mid-November. To save on labor and to create a dramatic splash of color, I always plant at least 25 bulbs in one location. I dig a hole 2 to 3 feet across, cut off and pull out the roots, and plant a clump of bulbs. It is much quicker than digging individual holes for bulbs. Plan on planting some in shady areas this autumn.

Not all shade is created equal. There is dry shade, which is the toughest location for many plants, and moist shade, which is quite a different ecosystem. It is important to know what plants do well in your particular shady site before selecting them. Find a nursery or greenhouse that has salespeople interested in shade plants, and start asking questions. Or go to your local library and look for a book on shade plants. And be sure to talk to other gardeners; many are a wealth of knowledge.

Hostas are some of the best known shade plants. There are many varieties available. Although hostas do bloom, they are best known for their foliage, which can be green, blue-gray, yellow-green, or variegated with white or blue or gold edges or stripes. Some hostas make huge mounds of leaves that will shade out weeds; others are delicate and tiny. Many varieties will do just fine in dry shade, but most benefit from added organic matter and some slow-release organic fertilizer each spring and at planting time. It takes at least three years from the time of planting a seed to maturity, so most people buy plants or divide clumps for new plants.

Astilbes are another group of well know shade plants. These plants have frilly foliage and delicate midsummer flowers. Their seedheads linger on all winter if you don't cut them down. Most astilbes will do well in dry shade, but a few require moist shade. I think that in order to have a good-looking planting of astilbes, you need to group several plants. If they like where they are growing they will multiply, but this is a slow process.

Groundcovers are widely used in the shade, particularly pachysandra. It will grow well in dry shade, as will Virginia creeper (*Parthenocissus quinquefolia*), though this can be invasive. For a more delicate ground cover, you can use sweet woodruff (*Galium odoratum*), which has lovely, delicate white flowers in early summer. Lily of the valley (*Convallaria majalis*) is another lovely groundcover that has lovely smelling flowers in the spring. It forms a thick root mat that is impenetrable to anything—including your spade!

It is impossible in this space to describe all the wonderful shade flowers that are available, so I will write about just a few of my favorites. I am fascinated with large plants. I like big. So I grow something called *Heracleum mantegazzianum*, or giant hogweed. This plant takes two to three years to reach blooming size, blooms, then dies that year. (It is called a monocarpic plant because it only blooms once.) In bloom the flower head is on a stalk 6 to 10 feet tall, and the cluster of tiny white flowers arranged in umbels (like Queen Anne's lace) can be 3 to 4 feet wide! It needs lots of moisture, and will grow in either sun or shade in moist locations. The leaves are shaped a bit like maple leaves, but are 2 to 3 feet across! This is a very dramatic plant. I know of two greenhouses that sell it, and suspect it will become more widely available as people learn about it. And the good news is that it reseeds itself, so you only have to buy it once, and you will have plants to give away later. It is hardy to USDA Zone 3 (surviving temperatures to −40°F), and I wonder if it has the potential to become a pest. Maybe we shouldn't grow it near streams, for fear that the seeds will travel far and wide and become a nuisance.

Another great plant for moist shade are the primroses (*Primula* spp.). There are many types, some blooming in early spring, others in summer, depending on the species. They come in various colors, including some very bright ones. In general, they like a moist location, and some will do well in very wet locations.

I love woodland phlox (*Phlox divaricata*), which grows in partial to full shade. The books indicate that it likes a moist soil, but I have it growing in dry shade and it does fine. Perhaps a more moist site would make it spread more quickly. It has low-growing foliage with upright flower stems 12 to 15 inches tall, and lovely pale blue flowers in early summer. *Phlox stolinifera* is another native woodland phlox, a creeping one that prefers moist, rich soil in partial shade.

Ferns can be very dramatic in the shade. They tend to be ignored by many gardeners, perhaps because they produce no flowers, or perhaps because they show up uninvited sometimes, and are thus considered weeds. The Japanese painted fern (*Athyrium niponicum*) can be colorful in its foliage, silvery with purple tones. Maidenhair fern (*Adiantum pedatum*) has delicate-looking fronds that seem to float above the ground on stiff, almost wirelike stems. I love the ostrich fern (*Mattueccia struthiopteris*), which resembles a giant badminton birdie, with fronds reaching up 6 feet or more. All three of these prefer moist, rich woodland soil, but will adapt to drier or sunnier soil if need be. The ostrich fern tends to brown up and die back in late summer in a sunny or dry location, and becomes quite unsightly until you cut it back, which is okay to do as soon as it looks scruffy. The springtime sprouts, or fiddleheads, of the ostrich fern are considered a delicacy by many if cooked properly. All three are readily available from local greenhouses, and are hardy to at least Zone 4.

One last terrific shade plant: fringed or wild bleeding heart (*Dicentra eximia*). Although my books tell me it prefers moist shade, I've grown it many times in dry shade. Besides having wispy, delicate foliage, it blooms reliably all summer long! The flowers range from white to deep purple-red, though I prefer the pinky one.

I've found that growing shade plants is a bit like eating raw oysters or listening to the opera: It's an acquired taste. Many gardeners don't bother, and relegate dark spots to viny ground covers or expanses of bark mulch. But if you take the time to really look at the nuances of leaf colors and textures, if you slow down to enjoy the subtle beauty, you will learn to love shade plants. I have, even though it took me a while to really appreciate them.

Using and Preserving Herbs

I was admiring a friend's herb patch recently, a nice plot of basil and parsley, when she admitted to me that although she uses and loves the herbs when they are fresh, she didn't really know what to do with them in the fall. "Oh," I said. "That's easy, you can dry them, you can make pesto." Thinking about it later, I realized that I do waste an awful lot of herbs each year. Yes, we use our basil to make pesto, which we use all year. And we hang big bunches of herbs from the ceiling in the kitchen. But many years we leave the herbs hanging there all winter, gathering dust and looking unkept. Then in the spring I take them down, and they go on the compost pile. So this year I decided to make an effort to really use all our herbs, and to try some new ways of using them.

I began my research by calling Happy Griffiths, the herbalist at the Shaker Museum in Enfield, New Hampshire. Happy taught me much in the course of the conversation, including some tricks that you will love. She said, for example, that if you are going to harvest and save your herbs, you can rinse them off the day before you harvest while they are still on the stalk. A gentle stream from a garden hose will wash off any dust and dirt, and then Mother West Wind can dry them for you. This is much easier than bringing them in the house to wash them off because you don't have to pat them all dry.

The best time to harvest herbs is just before they produce flowers. This is when the essential oils in the leaves are their strongest. Once they have flowered, the leaves tend to turn a little bitter. But if your basil blooms, for example, don't despair. Just pinch back the plants, and they will produce more edible leaves. Try to use leafy herbs before they get tough and leathery. New growth is always better. Handle your herbs very gently as you harvest them, as bruising them lets essential oils to escape. And process the herbs as soon as you pick them for best results.

The time of day for harvesting is also important. Happy told me to pick in the morning after the dew has dried, but before the sun has gotten too hot. She also said that it is best to pick herbs after a two- or three-day period of sunny weather—not always an easy assignment.

Herbs can be dried in several ways: You can simply air-dry them, you can use a dehydrator or your microwave, or you can dry them in the oven. Herbs that dry well are sage, thyme, tarragon, rosemary, and oregano. Although you can dry tender aromatic herbs like basil, marjoram, parsley, dill, and chives, they tend not to preserve their flavor as well, nor for as long a time. But I dry them anyway, and use them in soups and sauces.

If you air dry herbs, you can hang them by their stems in small bunches in a hot, dry place such as the attic, or remove them from their stems and place them in single layers on newspaper. Sunshine is not the friend of your herbs once you have picked them, so avoid sunlight. And although I admit to hanging my herbs all winter in the kitchen, that is absolutely the wrong way to do it, and I *won't* do it again. Promise. I will check the herbs to see when they are, as Happy Griffiths instructed me, "corn flake chip dry." Then I will pack them in glass jars, and store them in a cool, dark place. Or place them in freezer grade plastic bags, and freeze them. Air-drying herbs can take from 1 to 4 weeks, depending on humidity, air circulation, and temperature. Herbs can mildew in the hot humid air of August, so air circulation is a big help.

You can dry herbs in the oven, but this is difficult to do unless you have a gas oven with a pilot light. The ideal drying temperature is in the range of 77 to 95°F. Most electric ovens won't turn down that low. Place herbs in single layers on cookie sheets, and remove as soon as dry. If you want to try drying herbs in an electric oven, try the lowest temperature setting, and leave the door ajar.

The microwave can also be used to dry herbs in small quantities. Place a single layer of herbs between two paper towels. Microwaves, I'm told, vary in strength, so you will have to experiment a bit. Try 30 to 60 seconds at full strength, then flip them over, reduce the time, and give it another blast. Check it again, and zap again if needed. Store as above.

I've had very good luck drying all kinds of things from cherry tomatoes to parsley in our Mr. Coffee dehydrator. It is a great invention. During tomato season we run it constantly to "sun-dry" cherry tomatoes. I like the fact that drying herbs this way is quick, and the colors stay more natural than by hanging them.

Parsley and chives freeze well. Chop them up and place on a cookie sheet in the freezer so that they will freeze quickly. Once frozen, put them in freezer bags for storage. Happy Griffiths grows the perennial herb lovage, which tastes a bit like celery. She stores it by blending with a little water, then freezing in ice cube trays. She uses it in soups all winter. Experiment with other herbs if you like.

A friend gave me some basil leaves that she had packed in olive oil and keeps in the refrigerator. She packs the leaves in a jar, then covers them with cold extra virgin olive oil. She tries to eliminate any air pockets with a spatula, and by gently tapping the jar on a flat surface in order to get out any bubbles. Oxygen causes the aromatic oils to change—and not for the better. Kept like this in the fridge, basil will stay tasty for a year. But *do* keep it refrigerated to eliminate any chance of botulism.

For a taste of summer in winter you can also make herb butter.

I took a stick of butter and four ounces of cream cheese, and softened them in the microwave. Then I placed them in a food processor with a cup of clean dry parsley, and blended it all together. After it was an even consistency I packed it into an ice cube tray, and froze it. The next day I emptied the tray, and transferred the contents into a freezer bag. It is great on baked potatoes. I tried another batch using basil and garlic, which I liked on bread, or to use for sautéing vegetables.

Another easy way to enjoy herbs is to make herb vinegars. Pour out a little liquid, then put two large sprigs of herb in a 17.5-ounce bottle of vinegar, top it up, and reseal. Leave it on a sunny window sill for two weeks, then change the herbs for new ones and it is ready to use. A crochet hook will help get the herbs out of the bottle. An herb vinegar will last up to two years in a sealed bottle. The most commonly used herbs for this are basil, dill, tarragon, thyme, and rosemary. White or red wine vinegar is recommended, not cider vinegar. Rice wine vinegar is also good, though more expensive. Adding a few chive blossoms will give the vinegar a nice rosy glow, and some chive taste. Hot peppers can also be used in vinegars for a spicy kick.

Summer is a busy time. I regularly remind myself that there is life outside the garden, and try to find time for seeing friends, boating, and just plain goofing off. I've always been good about preserving my vegetables, and this year I'm going to try harder with my herbs.

Growing Blueberries

I love blueberries. I love them warm, off the bush. I love them on my breakfast cereal. I love them with vanilla ice cream in Karen's ten cup blueberry pies (see recipe). I love rereading Robert McCloskey's 1948 classic *Blueberries for Sal*, that wonderful book about a young girl, a bear cub, and picking blueberries.

Blueberries are ripening up now, and the birds are ready to see if they can help with the harvest. This year, I think I have the perfect

system to defeat the birds. Of course, I know that birds are pretty insistent that we share, and may beat me yet.

A mature blueberry bush will produce between five and fifteen pounds of blueberries per year. It will take several years to reach that level of production, and in fact you might never get there unless you follow some basic guidelines to make your bushes happy.

In selecting a site for your blueberry patch you should choose a spot that gets sun all day long. They will tolerate some shade, but the more shade, the fewer and the smaller the berries. Six hours of sun a day is the minimum I would recommend. But they make great shrubs for landscaping even if you don't have the ideal site. They have attractive white flowers in the spring, berries for the birds, and lovely red leaf color in autumn. They won't take over the landscape, nor get so big they hide your windows. And you will get at least a few berries even in more shady locations.

Blueberries do not compete well with weeds. They have a shallow, fibrous root system, and this means that weeds growing under your bushes are competing for food and water. They need lots of moisture but they can't tap into water deep in the soil the way a tree might, so they get thirsty during dry spells. The solution is a good thick layer of bark mulch. It will keep the roots moist and keep the weeds down at the same time. Four to six inches of bark mulch will do the trick. Some people use sawdust, but sometimes it can develop a crust which keeps the rain from penetrating well.

Another key factor for success with blueberries is to have the soil quite acid. Acidity is measured on a scale of pH, with 7.0 being neutral, and 1.0 being extremely acid. Blueberries do best with a pH of 4.5, but do fine in the range of 3.5 to 5.5, which is more acid than many soils. You can adjust the pH of your soil by adding an acid fertilizer or digging in acid soil amendments when you plant, things like peat moss or sawdust. Get your soil tested, or better yet, learn to do it yourself so that you can monitor the soil pH once a year.

Blueberries are heavy feeders and benefit by being fed each year with an acidic organic fertilizer such as Holly-gro or Holly-tone, both of which are sold for feeding rhododendrons and hollies, as well as blueberries. Composted manure is also good. The best time to feed them is when they are blooming. In our cold climate it is important not to feed them in the late summer or fall, or it may stimulate them to grow new shoots that don't have time to get hardened up before winter. If you give your blueberries a heavy dose of nitrogen, you may get lots of green growth but few berries, which is yet another reason for using organic fertilizer—it is released slowly. You should pull back the mulch when fertilizing so that it can easily get to the roots. Don't try to work the fertilizer into the soil as the roots are right at the surface.

I recently visited two octogenarian friends, Mayme and Lafayette Noda, who maintain 1,600 blueberry bushes in their "pick-your-own" blueberry farm in Meriden, New Hampshire. Amazingly energetic people, they do almost all the work themselves, from pruning bushes in the spring to weeding under the bushes. They grow three varieties of blueberries: Berkeley, Bluecrop, and Patriot. They like Patriot bushes best, as these seem the most resistant to disease. Blueberries need to cross pollinate, so you need to plant at least two different varieties in order to get berries. Buy bigger plants if you can afford them, as they will produce berries sooner. Three-year-old plants are fine.

The biggest problem the Nodas have is with the birds. Birds love blueberries. They discourage the birds in a number of ways. They hang big eyeball balloons from tall stakes. They have a "squawker," which runs on a car battery and emits the sound of a robin in distress. The scariest for me is the propane-fired cannon, which automatically fires off a very loud bang every few minutes. I'm just glad

I don't live next door. But the average gardener will not find any of these methods satisfactory. You will need to cover your berries with a fine bird netting to keep them away from the fruit.

This year I developed a system for putting up bird netting which I like a lot. If you just drape the netting over the bushes it gets caught on twigs, and is hard to remove when you want to pick. And besides, birds will reach in through the netting unless you use something like cheesecloth, which is more expensive than netting.

Jim Phelps of Windsor, Vermont, and I built a simple structure for supporting bird netting, and it seems to work very well. His row of berry bushes is 65 feet long and about 5 feet tall. We used 120 feet of half-inch plastic electrical conduit (pipe), available at local building supply stores, to support the netting. First we cut four 10-foot lengths in half and glued a 5-foot section onto each of the eight remaining pieces of conduit. After the glue was thoroughly dry we bent these 15-foot lengths into hoops to go over the bushes at 8- to 10-foot intervals. Jim had some thin fiberglass rods used for supporting electric horse fencing, and cut them into 2-foot sections. He pushed them halfway into the ground at a slight angle (leaning away from the bushes), and then we slipped the conduit over them. It worked "slick as a bean," as some Vermont farmers say! The hoops stood up without any further support. We then unrolled an 80-foot length of 17-foot-wide bird netting he had purchased, and it slid up and over the hoops with no snags. The great thing about this support system is that there are no corners for the netting to catch on. This allows you to slip it off, pick, and slide it back up.

The birds defeated us by the next day, of course, so we had to modify the system slightly. They all sat on one section of netting to weigh it down, which allowed them to reach through the net and steal some berries. Who says birds have teeny-tiny brains? We slid off the netting, and I ran a string from hoop to hoop at the very top. At each hoop I ran the string around the conduit in a Boy Scout clove hitch. When the netting went back up it was able to withstand their weight. We'll be fine as long as wild turkeys don't show up, in which case it's back to the drawing boards!

The other line of attack that the birds employ is to go under the netting. Jim had lots of scrap lumber around, so we just placed boards along the ground on top of the excess netting. You could use string, or tie-wraps from store-bought broccoli, or even hair clips, to fasten the netting to the bottom of the hoops. And who knows,

Karen's Ten-Cup Blueberry Pie

This pie uses any standard two-crust pie recipe, such as Fanny Farmer's. The filling is much less sweet than the average pie, as it uses only 1 cup of sugar for 10 cups of berries. This allows you to taste the fruit better, in my (biased) opinion. But see for yourself.

In a bowl combine the following:

> 1 cup sugar
> ½ cup flour (more if using very juicy berries)
> ½ teaspoon cinnamon
> ½ tsp nutmeg

In a large mixing bowl combine dry ingredients with

> 10 cups blueberries, washed and drained

Place a crust in a 10-inch glass pie pan, and add berries. Getting this many berries in the pie is tricky. As the pile gets higher, smooth out a flat place or a crater to hold more berries, slowly adding them a few at a time until it seems impossibly tall.

Add top crust, and bake at 425°F for 20 minutes, then reduce heat to 375°F and continue for almost another hour. Check every 10 minutes toward completion. Test for easy penetration with a wooden skewer, and look for the juice beginning to ooze out around the edges. The quantity of berries makes this pie a longer bake than usual.

maybe the birds will show up with little pairs of scissors to get in. But for today, anyhow, we have them beaten.

Gardening: The Slowest of the Performing Arts

It is commonly accepted that gardening is America's number one recreational activity. It is ahead of snowmobiling, raising goldfish,

and bowling. Biking, boating, and beekeeping have their proponents. But a little gardening is done by most of us outside the cities, whether to garner a few tomatoes, or to decorate our yards or tables with flowers. Why is gardening so popular? Much of it is hard work, and the results are unpredictable. Perhaps part of it is an innate desire to create beauty. Try as we might, most of us cannot transform ourselves into the media-defined image of beauty. But we can grow a perfect flower that pleases us greatly just by planting a few seeds or a nursery-raised seedling.

Most children want to grow things. There is something inherently fascinating in planting a tiny seed, and watching it grow and develop over the course of a summer. Most of us started out that way. As adults we develop more sophisticated tastes and have more complicated plans. The simple bed at the front of the house soon is not enough. We plan more beds, buy shrubs and flowering trees. We start to notice what the neighbors are growing. Sometimes we want to grow those same flowers, and other times we want to do something absolutely different. We want to create our own style of garden, find new and unusual plants that the neighbors don't have.

Ultimately, the serious gardener becomes a conductor for the symphony of growing flowers. We plan our gardens, we dream, we imagine. Much of what we hope for happens, but each year some of our plants surprise us, no matter how long we have been gardening. Perhaps it is that element of surprise that brings us back to gardening each year.

This year my always reliable dahlias have refused to bloom. The plants are healthy and big, but the buds are still small, and so far I have not seen a single bloom. They were planted a little late, but not a month late. On inquiring, I found that others in Cornish Flat have had a bad year for dahlias, too. We can only hope for a late frost so we can enjoy their blooms. Dahlias like moist soil, and this summer's drought is probably the cause. If you tried dahlias for the first time this year, you should know that we need to dig up the tubers after the first frost, put them in a brown paper bag with the tops cut off, and store them in a cool basement until next spring.

Phlox, on the other hand, have been spectacular, and healthy. Often the tall late-summer phlox gets a white mildew growing on it, but there has been little of that this year. That is understandable to me, given that we have had so little rain. My phlox is also helped by growing in rich, organically prepared flower beds. Healthy soils grow stronger, healthier plants, which resist diseases like mildew better.

As I look around my property I am struck by the fact that the flowers that I usually count on for September and October bloom are mostly done blooming. That is a function of the hot, dry summer, I suppose. Only my tall asters are yet to bloom, as stubborn and set in their ways as a bachelor uncle.

One of my favorite fall flowers is sneezeweed (*Helenium autumnale*). It is a tall flower in the aster family, along with black-eyed Susans and sunflowers. It usually grows 3 to 4 feet tall. Their blossoms range from pure yellow to mixtures of orange, red, and yellow with bronze stripes. It is distinguished by petals that bend back from the center button of the flower. If you want to try some, plant them toward the back of the flower bed as their lower leaves turn brown early on, giving them "bad legs." They last very well as cut flowers, and have nice stiff stems that won't flop in an arrangement. Plant them in full sun (six hours per day or more) in moist rich soil. Despite its common name, sneezeweed doesn't seem to generate anything that causes sneezing. Perhaps it was used as a cure for sneezing in some distant past.

As you try to create a mural of colors, shapes and forms, one flower that is almost always predictable is the wonderful fall chrysanthemums that are currently available in my part of New Hampshire. Granted, they were ready earlier this year, and will be done blooming a little earlier than other years, but what you see is what you get. Choose colors that please you and fill in those bare spots in your fall flower beds. Mums are perennial in warmer parts of the country, but here I treat them as annuals. Even if your mums winter over, they will never look as good the second year. Growers of mums go to a lot of work to pinch back their buds in June, and again in July, to create the plants that are covered with as many as 200 blooms.

Many mums are grown in peat pots, but you should not plant the peat pots in the ground. It is true that the pots will eventually decompose, but in the meantime they will dry out your plants. The peat acts as a wick, drawing the moisture out of the soil. Before you plant your mums, submerse the peat pot in a bucket of water and hold the mum down until it stops sending up bubbles. You might have trouble getting the mum out of the peat pot. If so, take a sharp knife and slice from the bottom, which is softer, up to the lip of the pot, and tear it away. And you don't need worry about the quality of the soil, or the amount of sunlight you give your mums. As long as they are kept moist they will bloom nicely.

A plant that pleased and surprised me this year, and that has been blooming constantly for over two months, is Datura or angel's trumpets. It is not hardy here, but was well worth the two or three dollars I spent per plant in 3-inch pots back in June. It produces beautiful white, trumpetlike, 6-inch flowers, which usually open in the late afternoon and which are almost irridescent at dusk. Very striking. It is in the potato family, but both the seeds and the flowers are poisonous to eat, so it may not be a good choice for families with small children prone to munching on plants.

A gorgeous vine with brilliant orange flowers and edible beans is the scarlet runner bean. If you haven't tried it before, you may want to plan on it next year. It is fast growing with wonderful foliage that will quickly and efficiently cover a trellis. We eat the beans when they are small, or let them dry and use in chili. They will grow 10 feet or more in a season, and we plant them at the base of a bentwood arched trellis that serves as the entrance to our vegetable garden. So far they have never let us down. But who knows, maybe next year the chipmunks will get them.

Gardening is a bit like opening a birthday present. You might think you know what you are going to get, but it doesn't always work that way. The surprise is part of the fun. You may choreograph your oriental poppies to bloom with your Siberian iris. Maybe next year they will perform together, but then again, one may miss its cue and wait off stage like a dancer at a bad dress rehearsal.

Savoring and Saving the Season: Red Rocks, Pickles, and Pesto

Tomatoes! I'm eating them fresh from the garden for breakfast, lunch, and dinner. I admit to being a bit of a fanatic when it comes to tomatoes, but I am not alone. Many gardeners have a vegetable garden primarily for that special taste of a freshly picked tomato. One that has never been transported by truck, nor put in a refrigerator. One that has been grown in that portion of the property that gets the most sun, one that has been watered and protected from bugs and weeds. We are now eating tomatoes that have been coddled and loved. And it all seems worth it.

Unfortunately, the tomato season is short in New England. Frost seems unthinkable in August, but in a month we will be listening to the weather guys with increasing anxiety. Will there be an early frost, or will we still be picking tomatoes in October? How can we make those summer flavors linger?

Many of us remember our

Karen's Bean Salad

1 quart frozen garden beans
1 small onion, red if available
1 clove garlic
⅓ cup chopped almonds
a sprinkling of Marukan brand seasoned gourmet rice vinegar

Defrost a quart of frozen garden beans. Dice up one small onion, red if available. Crush one clove garlic, and mix in with the chopped almonds. Sprinkle with rice wine vinegar. One bite, and you are back in summer!

mothers or our grandmothers slaving over a hot stove to preserve tomatoes or can tomato sauce for the winter, usually doing so on a hot August day. I've done my share of that myself, but in recent years I've taken a couple of short cuts that I like: red rocks and "sun-dried" tomatoes.

Red rocks are simply whole frozen tomatoes. Toss them in the freezer, but be careful when you open the door, they do feel like rocks if they land on your toe! Once they are frozen solid, put them in a Ziploc bag, and they will be ready to use in a sauce or stew next winter. They will be mushy when defrosted, but taste better than canned tomatoes, and you know they have no chemicals or preservatives in them. If you have a good-sized freezer you can put up a year's worth of cooking tomatoes without the fuss of canning.

Sun-dried tomatoes are readily available in the supermarket, but their price has always seemed exorbitant to me. Some years ago a friend gave us a simple Mr. Coffee brand food dehydrator for Christmas, and we have been using it to make our own "sun-dried" tomatoes ever since. It consists of a heating element and a small fan in the base of an appliance that has five stacking 12-inch-diameter drying racks. It uses 250 watts of electricity per hour, that means that a batch of dried tomatoes that takes 10 to 12 hours costs 25 or 30 cents to prepare. These dehydrators are locally available, and cost thirty to forty dollars. Larger sizes are also produced, taking up to twelve trays at a time.

During the tomato season we have our dehydrator going almost all the time. We package the dried tomatoes in Ziploc freezer bags, keeping one in the fridge, and the rest in the freezer. The dried tomatoes are wonderful in a sauce or stew, in a pasta salad, or on a pizza. The flavor seems concentrated, giving a burst of summer in the dead of winter. If you want to soften them up before using, cover them with a little hot water for a few minutes. Cherry tomatoes dry very well if cut in half; full-sized tomatoes can be sliced about a quarter of an inch thick.

Pesto is another of my favorite foods prepared with fresh summer herbs. It is simple, tasty, and keeps well all year round. Although pesto will keep fresh for a long time in the fridge, we like to freeze some for use in the winter. We put it in ice cube trays, and when it's frozen we put the little green chunks in a Ziploc bag, each one just right for a dinner's worth of pasta and pesto for the two of us.

The basil in pesto is definitely a "renewable resource." Cut the top leaves and buds back severely and it will bush out and grow lots more leaves. Try to do this before the basil produces flowers, as it gets a little bitter then. The more you use your basil, the more it will produce.

Bread-and-butter pickles are an old family tradition for me, but I have made some modifications that I like both for flavor and as a way of using up zucchini and other garden runaways. You can use the basic recipe from *Joy of Cooking*, but substitute zucchini, patty pan, and other summer squashes for some of the cucumbers. I also add in sweet red peppers, some spicy peppers, and broccoli side shoots. For the first time ever I will reveal the spice that makes my pickles special: I add a teaspoon of ground cardamom to each batch. I also reduce the sugar by one third, and use cider vinegar instead of white vinegar. There you have it, my special, prize-winning pickle potion.

One last thought about preserving garden produce: Do a little at a time, so that it is not an overwhelming task. Fresh frozen green beans are wonderful later on, especially in a bean salad. It is easy to do one package of beans after dinner, rather than trying to do a dozen all at once.

Bring a pot of water to a boil, drop in the beans, and after they come back to a boil, cook for sixty seconds, then remove from the heat. Put them in a pan of water and ice cubes until cool. Place the beans on a tea towel to dry, then put in a freezer bag and freeze.

My garden gives me pleasure all year. I love puttering around in

Pesto

In a blender or food processor put the following:

2 cups fresh basil, well packed
½ cup fresh parsley
½ cup olive oil
2 heaping tablespoons pine nuts, walnuts, hazelnuts, or almonds
4 cloves garlic
½ cup grated Parmesan or Romano cheese
a handful of sun dried tomatoes (optional)
salt to taste

Blend until an even consistency. It is a great alternative to tomato sauce on pasta.

the garden at dusk, watering or weeding, and watching bats skim over my head as they eat those malicious mosquitoes. I love looking out to the snowy garden from indoors in winter, enjoying the lines of my homemade garden arbor and dreaming of fresh beans. And I love eating healthy organic foods from the garden throughout the year.

Late Summer Flowering Plants

As summer winds down, most common flowers tend to be big, bright, and cheerful. Bee balm, phlox, asters, daisies, black-eyed Susans, and daylilies are everywhere. They are all great plants, but I think it's also nice to have some other flowers that are different and unusual. I'd like to share with you some thoughts about some plants for the season that are less common, plants I grow and love.

Most gardeners know an annual flower simply known as lobelia. Its masses of small intense purple (or occasionally white) flowers have made it a favorite in window boxes and along edges of flower beds. Its Latin name is *Lobelia erinus*, and it is just one of over 200 species of lobelia that carry the name of sixteenth-century botanist and doctor Mathias de l'Obel. I grow two other lobelias, perennial ones, that I consider wonderful.

I first saw cardinal flowers (*Lobelia cardinalis*) while paddling down the Connecticut River some years ago. Even from a hundred yards away I could see a splash of intense fire-engine red on shore, and changed course immediately to investigate. This native wildflower grows in tall spikes 2 to 5 feet tall, and likes moist soil. I like people—and flowers—that will look me in the eye. Cardinal flower does that for me, as I grow it in full sun in moist, rich black soil. It will do all right in drier soil if it gets some shade, particularly from the hot afternoon sun. In either case, amend the soil with lots of organic matter. The individual flowers are an inch or so long, tubular blossoms with three lower lips and two less prominent upper petals. It is the number and intense color of the blossoms that make it so striking. If you have a wet spot on your property, the cardinal flower should definitely be planted there.

Great blue lobelia (*Lobelia syphilitica*) is another cousin that provides nice bright color, this one an intense blue. It grows 2 to 3 feet tall in nice tight clumps that never flop over for me. My books tell me they do best in rich, moist soil, but right now mature specimens in my garden are sending up thirty or more stems with blue blossoms even though they are in a dry, sunny location. Of course I've been adding organic matter to my soil for a long time, which helps. This plant drops seeds all over the place, and consequently new clumps turn up every year. But I don't consider it invasive because it is easy to weed out, or give away, and doesn't spread by lateral roots. Individual plants are not long-lived, but it doesn't matter since babies show up every year. Both of these lobelias are native plants, have a long bloom period, and are readily available in plant nurseries.

Meadow rues, or Thalictrums, are great plants that grow with a variety of sizes, colors, bloom times, and growing requirements. They are stately, airy plants with small blossoms in white, yellow, and a variety of purples, mauves, and lavenders. Some grow wild, even appearing by the side of the road. As I write this, there is a meadow rue outside my window that is over 9 feet tall, *Thalictrum rochebrunianum*, probably Lavender Mist. (It was given to me, so I can't be sure of the variety name.) The stem of this specimen is bare of leaves for distances of 18 inches or so; then it has a cluster of compound leaves, then more bare stem, and so on, which gives it a unique look. The stem is stiff enough and the blossoms small enough—a scant half inch or so across—that it doesn't need to be staked. There are clusters of lavender blossoms at the top of the plant and on side shoots near the top. Lavender Mist doesn't always grow so tall, only reaching 4 to 5 feet in other places on my property. It seems happiest in full sun in rich, well-drained soil, but I have one growing in almost full shade under an apple tree.

Thalictrum delavayi, Hewitt's Double, is similar to Lavender Mist, but is more delicate, shorter, and has tiny double blossoms that look like miniature peonies! Wonderful! Amazing! In my experience Lavender Mist is hardier than Hewitt's Double, but both self-seed if you let them. I consider Hewitt's Double a Zone 5 plant. All the meadow rues have delicate, handsome foliage that looks good throughout the growing season.

If you like the sparse airy stems of meadow rue, you will love the annual flower Brazilian verbena, *Verbena bonariensis*. It has a stiff stem with small clusters of light purple flowers, each with five tiny petals. It seems to float gracefully above other flowers, reaching 3 feet or more in height. Although it is technically an annual in New England, it will self-seed, and shows up wherever it pleases—but I predict that it will always please you when it does. It has the added advantage of being quite frost hardy, persisting well into the fall. The more you cut it, the more it produces flowers.

Culver's root, *Veronicastrum virginicum*, is a plant I like very much, but it is rarely seen in the gardens I've visited. It is definitely a full-sun plant, as it will flop in shady sites. Although it prefers moist, well-drained soils, I've seen it flourish in quite dry locations. It grows 3 to 5 feet tall, with narrow leaves whorled around the stem in groups of five, which I find handsome in their own right. In time, they form clumps 3 feet wide. It has delicate white spikes, each made up of many tiny flowers. Although it doesn't have a long bloom season, you can extend the season by cutting part of it back before bloom, causing it to branch out with later—but smaller—flowers. Doing this also makes it branch, producing four or five flowers for each one you cut off.

Japanese anemone (*Anemone* × *hybrida*) is another late-season bloomer that starts blooming for me in late August. They have white or pink flowers above handsome dark green foliage on branched stems, standing 2 to 3 feet tall. It is a bit of a fussy plant, but worth trying, even if you lose it once or twice before finding the right home. It will grow in full or light shade, likes moisture in summer, but hates it in winter. Don't go out and buy some now—it needs a summer to settle in before winter, so buy it next spring. It is in the buttercup family.

It's my theory that June gardens are some of the best looking because that is when people have the most enthusiasm for gardening, and when they spend their money on plants. By late summer many gardeners have run out of energy, and their gardens reflect that. We need so many different species of flowers in order to have something blooming all the time that some folks get discouraged. Don't be. Try one or two new things each season, and before you know it your gardens will overwhelm you—with their beauty, their surprises, and with the joy they will bring you.

Building a Garden from the Ground Up

I remember when teenage girls used to swoon over the Beatles. Well, I nearly swooned recently when I put my hands in the soil of Gardener extraordinary Sydney Eddison. There had been no rain in six weeks, yet beneath a layer of leaf mulch the soil was dark, fluffy, and slightly moist. It looked good enough to eat with a little vanilla ice cream. Really.

I had traveled to Newtown, Connecticut, to meet Mrs. Eddison because I like her gardening books, and because I wanted to see the gardens she has been working on for forty years. And I knew I could learn from her. The design and layout were wonderful, the plants were exquisite, and the soil was incredible.

Obviously, I wanted to know how she made her soil so wonderful. In a word, the answer is this: leaves. For the past twenty years or more Mrs. Eddison has been mulching with leaves. In the fall her husband runs over them with the lawn mower; she bags them up (dry) for the winter, and then spreads a 3-inch layer in the spring.

As they break down, they enrich the soil. Their gardens are surrounded by forest, and so their lawn gets covered with leaves each fall.

Leaves are a wonderful source of organic matter. Trees transfer minerals from the soil to the leaves, sometimes mining them from deep in the earth, releasing them to your soil as they break down. Earthworms love to munch on them, breaking them down and moving around this nourishment for plants.

Sydney Eddison's gardens are beautifully laid out, full of diverse plant matter, and they made me feel rested and calm as I walked around (despite her little dog, Chloe, who zoomed around at a high rate of speed, and who has bitten her way through two vets and is working on a third).

I asked her for tips about designing such a wonderful outdoor space. She told me that it was important to create a long axis for the garden. Her lawn extends back from the house perhaps a hundred yards, and perennial beds surround it and extend into it. She has made islands of vegetation that follow the contours of the land rather than imposing rectangular beds on it.

She also explained that a good garden evolves. She didn't start with a master plan, but let the land speak to her over a long period of time. As she worked on it, clearing trees, digging out roots and rocks, she developed her ideas.

The land is full of stone outcroppings, which dictated the location of some of the islands of vegetation. She uses shrubs, particularly rhododendrons, to give the beds height and texture all year round, and to hide rocks too big to move. At first she made lots of little flower beds, but eventually she joined some together, with each bed becoming perhaps 60 feet long and 10 to 15 feet wide.

There is very little space between plants, a luxury that many of us cannot afford in a new flower bed. She knows her plants and has divided and propagated them over the years. I also reminding myself that she has been working on these beds for forty years. Good gardens take time. Time, persistence, and hard work.

She said that it was important to enjoy what you are doing. Sydney and her husband bought their house when she was a young woman. "I was twenty-nine years old, strong as an ox, and I loved physical labor." Using a mattock and a lawn mower she cleared space out of "the jungle" that they had purchased. Later she added that "When I feel bad, I go dig up a rock." For her, as for many

serious gardeners, working the soil is a source of joy and feelings of great accomplishment.

Mrs. Eddison was refreshingly candid about the mistakes she has made en route to the spectacular gardens she has created. She said that they had some site work being done and decided, on an impulse, to have a swimming pool put in. It turned out to be a waste of money and space, and not something they really needed, so they eventually had it removed. Even great gardeners make mistakes.

Clearly Mrs. Eddison is a woman who has a great sense of design. She has created gardens that could (and do) grace the pages of the most elegant gardening magazines. She is a self-taught gardener, and has better gardens than you or I probably will ever have, even if we try for forty years. I highly recommend her book *The Self-Taught Gardener*, (Viking Penguin, 1997). It is full of good advice for not only the beginning gardener, but any gardener.

We can't all visit Mrs. Eddison's garden, but there are lots of local gardens that are open to the public each summer. I highly recommend visiting as many as you can. We can all learn much from seeing what other gardeners have done with their corners of this world. Many of the tours are fund raisers for good causes.

As a serious gardener I am always intrigued to see another's garden. There is always something to learn: new plants, or a different combination of plants, or unique combinations of color and texture. Each year I work on my gardens, and each year they please me a little more. Someday, perhaps, I will decide they are finished, but I doubt it. I think that even after forty years I'll be like Sydney Eddison, trying to perfect them. But that's part of the fun of gardening.

Chapter 7

September

Summer Is Over

Summer is over. Okay, it's not over officially, but it is for me. I've never admitted this publicly before, but I have a mild addiction to soft-serve ice cream. And the Dairy Twirl closed its doors, as it always does, on Labor Day. This is almost as traumatic as the first killing frost, which always sends me into a deep—but brief—funk. And although this particular summer has not been much in terms of heat and tomato production, it was all the summer we are going to get, and it's (nearly) over. Here is a preview of what is ahead for the gardener.

First, what about tomatoes? September is the month when we should be harvesting and processing tomatoes, preserving them for winter. But most gardens I've seen recently are barely producing enough tomatoes for salad and sandwiches. What's a gardener to do?

For starters, don't let your vines produce any more foliage. Pinch back or trim off the growing tips so that the plants will put their energy into producing tomatoes, not new growth. Second, take off some of the existing leaves so that the sun we do get will hit the fruit, encouraging ripening. Some people pick off small tomatoes so that the bigger ones will develop more quickly, but I have a hard time doing that. As an eternal optimist, I always think they will have a chance to grow up and ripen.

Tomatoes, eggplants, and peppers get set back in their efforts to produce ripe fruit by nights that dip below 50°F. Traditionally I cover my tomatoes at the end of September when the humidity is low, the sky clear, and the dinner-time temperature a mere 50°F. Those conditions portend frost. This year, I've started covering my precious tomatoes even when the weather guys predict a night in the forties. Not because of frost, but because I want my fruit to stay warm, and to ripen up. I am using Remay, a spun agricultural fabric that keeps things a little warmer. I'm also trying some big pieces of the bubble wrap I got from a furniture store—it's lightweight, free, and should be a good insulator. I tried leaving some of my plants covered during the day, but found it didn't help. They stayed warmer, but some of the sun's ultraviolet rays were blocked, and ripening was slower.

If you do get hit by an early frost and haven't covered your plants, all is not lost. Get out at dawn with your hose and wash off the frost. You will still lose some squash leaves, perhaps, but your plants will be less damaged, and if it's just a light frost, they will be okay.

As your garden winds down, don't let it go to weeds. Weeds are trying very hard, right now, to set seeds and get them scattered so they can come back to humbug you next year. Don't give an inch. You've worked hard all summer trying to keep the weeds down. Don't stop now. When you walk around your property and see a weed that has set seed, pull it! Even if you just wanted to grab a cuke to take to work and are in your go-to-work clothes. Pull that weed, you'll be glad you did.

Pumpkins are traditional fall crops, which, this year, are far behind schedule where I live. A couple of weeks ago, in mid-August, I started cutting off the ends of the vines. No point in wasting energy producing something that can't produce a crop. Now I should pick off blossoms and small pumpkins that don't stand much chance of reaching maturity.

I was thumbing through a book on cold-weather gardening recently and saw an interesting picture of a tomato patch. The gardeners had set a row of tall cedar poles on either side of the garden, perhaps 8 feet apart, and strung clothesline between them. This made it easy to put up plastic sheeting on those cold night without snagging it on tomato cages. Although there were no instructions on how to set this up, I envision the gardeners using clothespins to keep the plastic from blowing away. Nifty. I may try this when Jack Frost gets ready to poke his nose into my garden.

Now is the time to get ready to plant bulbs. You can plant bulbs from now till the ground freezes, but if you are ordering bulbs, you should do it soon! Planting in September is good; it gives the bulbs time to set out little roots and establish themselves before the ground freezes. If they send up a few green shoots, don't worry, it won't cause any harm.

Fall is also the time to plant trees and shrubs because most root growth occurs in the fall. You are also less likely to lose plants from dehydration as it is generally cooler, and more rain falls in autumn. You will still need to water your new plantings, but the season is more forgiving than summer. Take a walk around your property and see where you might like to have a new tree, or a nice flowering shrub. Planting now is better than later.

Pruning hardwood trees and shrubs is another autumn activity— one that most gardeners prefer to avoid, it seems, but an important one. Don't think that after the leaves are raked you have a vacation. Nope. That is the time when you can see what your trees and shrubs look like without the clutter of leaves, and it is a good time to prune. So put it on your calender, right after getting that root canal, perhaps.

Lawns this year have stayed pretty nice all through August, and into September. They will soon start to slow down, giving you a little reprieve from mowing. But don't cut your lawn really short—it will do better if you leave it a little longer than you kept it all summer. If you have some bare spots, fall is a good time to replant. Try to make a spot on your calender to do it in September or early October, so that it can get established before winter comes. Last year I planted some grass seed in late October, and it succeeded nicely, though I was lucky to get some warm weather.

There is really very little rest for the serious gardener. January and February are our vacation months. And even when the heavy snows fall, we will be planning what we will do next year. The leaves haven't turned and fallen yet, but I'm already thinking about next year. And I can't wait to see how this year's new plants will do next year!

Organic Farmers Steve and Nancy Clark

Steve and Nancy Clark of Charlestown, New Hampshire, are organic farmers. This means that they use no chemicals to control weeds, or to kill insect pests or treat diseases. Like this author, they believe that growing food need not—and should not—require the use of toxic chemicals. They run a small farm stand, they sell produce at Cornish and Charlestown, New Hampshire, farmers' markets, and they sell poinsettias to a local grocery store. Steve and his grown son, Hank, also run a sawmill, which helps them make ends meet, particularly in the winter months. They have chosen a lifestyle—and a way of farming—that suits them well, and that allows them to be true to their views of how food should be produced. But it is not always easy.

Steve and Nancy grew up in rural Charlestown and rode the same bus to school every day. Steve was twenty when they married, Nancy even younger, and they have been happily married for thirty-four years. They became organic farmers after reading *Organic Gardening* magazine, over thirty years ago. Except for a couple of lean years when raising their four children, they have subscribed ever since, and saved every issue.

All farmers are subject to the whims and vagaries of the weather. Being organic means that if they are subject to an invasion of insects that can ruin a crop, they don't run for the sprayer. They have learned ways to combat them without chemicals, generally by prevention. Being organic doesn't mean they suffer heavier crop losses. They believe that their plants are healthier, more resistant to disease and insect attack, because the balance of nature has not been skewed

with chemicals. Insecticides kill not only pests, but also the predator insects, those that kill pest insects.

For example, Nancy told me how she keeps striped cucumber beetles off her vine crops, and I will try it next year. She interplants cukes and squashes with nasturtiums, which she believes has reduced losses considerably for her. Of course one never really knows which of the many tricks used by organic farmers really cause the beneficial changes observed unless scientific tests are done with controls and repeated trials. But Nancy reads *Organic Gardening* magazine, notes the good ideas, and tries them herself.

Another way of baffling bugs that Nancy got from *Organic Gardening* magazine is to mix crops like onions with cabbage, or lettuce with broccoli. She has noticed that a large area devoted to one crop is more liable to insect damage than one that is interplanted with different crops.

Steve and Nancy are not hung up about weeds. In fact, some weeds Nancy considers her friends. She told me that Queen Anne's lace (that tall, lacy white wildflower that is in bloom right now) harbors a small parasitic wasp that attacks cabbage loopers and other destructive pests.

Because the Clarks do not use herbicides, and because they don't hire any outside labor, their field of vegetables gets pretty weedy. They put down black plastic under their vine crops, and mulch heavily with hay if they can get it at the right price. Sometimes Steve uses his string trimmer to cut down the weeds. He also plants his rows quite far apart so that he can cultivate with Pat and Mike, his big Belgian horses. Running the sawmill and going to farmers' market takes up much of his time, and the weeds do get ahead. But that is not all bad. Steve has observed that they get much less deer damage when the fields are left alone. "If we weeded our garden, the deer would get everything," he said. "We weed a row of beans, and the deer come right in and eat it down to the ground. So we don't weed much."

For their cash crops Steve and Nancy have a four-acre field that is located down the road from their home. They raise tomatoes, squashes, melons, peas, beans, and other vegetables.

Because of the field's location, they don't grow corn anymore. There are too many raccoons and deer competing for the corn. But perhaps it's just as well. I recently talked to a corn farmer who told me that customers won't buy corn unless he sprays it regularly with chemical pesticides. Apparently some customers don't want to buy corn with even a possibility of corn borers, he said, and won't come back if they find them. Three sprayings of the pesticide Sevin are needed after ears start to form in order to prevent borers, and some farmers spray within three days of harvest. I think I'd prefer borers, thank you very much.

The Clarks also have two greenhouses for starting seedlings, and for raising cash crops like poinsettias, pansies, and petunias. They are always looking for a way to bring in a little extra cash, and poinsettias have been a help these last few years. A friend has connections with a greenhouse in Massachusetts, and gets them free poinsettia carcasses that have had all their stems cut off for propagation. Nancy coaxes them back to life, and by Christmas they are big, bushy, and gorgeous. She feeds them fish emulsion and seaweed extract, which they seem to love. Or perhaps it is her captivating smile that they respond to.

The Clarks grow many of the standard tomatoes like Jet Star, Roma, the heirloom Brandywine, and Sweet 100s, a very sweet cherry tomato. They also spoke highly of tomatoes I didn't know but will try next year. They grow Amish Paste, a large canning tomato with lots of meat and very little juice. Another one they suggested is Mountain Gold, a 3½-inch yellow-tangerine tomato that they described as very tasty, and not so acidic as some others. They get these seeds from Totally Tomatoes (phone 803-663-0016; website www. totallytomato.com), and I think I'll try ordering some seeds from them next year.

Steve loves his draft horses, Mike and Pat. He plows with them in the spring, occasionally cultivates with them, and will use them to haul logs out of the woods for customers who want low-impact logging done. But most of all, Mike and Pat are his pets. His face lights up when he talks about them, and although they are an expense, he gets great joy from them. He showed me his plow rig, a John Deere plow that is perhaps seventy-five years old. With Pat and Mike he can plow "side hills" that no tractor would attempt. Just as Steve and Nancy believe that using chemicals is not something they want to do, plowing with horses just feels right to Steve.

We all know that the life of a farmer is not easy. This summer's weather has been cold and wet. Last summer there was a drought. But no matter what Mother Nature deals them, Steve and Nancy Clark have smiles on their faces and something positive to say when I see them Saturday mornings at the Cornish farmers' market. So they truly are rich people—rich in happiness and healthy, home-grown produce.

Planting Bulbs

I love the changing seasons in New England. Each season has its own joys and special surprises in the garden. Autumn brings beautiful foliage and crisp, clear days. But it also brings touches of wistfulness for me as the flowers of summer dwindle and disappear. The morning of the first frost each fall is a sad day for me. Cosmos and dahlias are blackened, squash vines turn brown and limp, and the basil I so love in salads and sauces is gone for another year. If I have been industrious my tomatoes were covered the night before, and will continue on a little longer. With the frost comes the knowledge that winter is on the way, and that until spring work in the garden will not be part of my daily life.

Planting bulbs is a sure cure for any autumnal melancholia for me. I love to plant bulbs. Gardeners are essentially incurable optimists. We plant things with the belief that they will grow, and bring beauty or food into our lives. Of course, that is not always the case, as we all know. But we do it again and again, whether or not our expectations are fulfilled. Planting bulbs, however, is an activity for even the most skeptical and jaded gardener, because with some bulbs you are almost guaranteed success.

Daffodils are sure winners. Chipmunks and voles treat them much as the first President Bush treated broccoli. Deer won't eat the flowers. Plant daffodils and you surely will be rewarded for your efforts. The classic pure yellow trumpet of a King Alfred is a sight to behold. An excellent cut flower, it stands tall and proud. I never tire of it. About the only thing you can do to cause a daffodil to fail is to plant it in heavy clay that never dries out, where water accumulates and keeps the soil soggy all fall, winter and spring. And even then, you might succeed.

Planting bulbs does require considerable effort, especially if you are going to plant lots of them. I planted over 3,000 one fall and have developed some techniques that will perhaps make your job less arduous. I have also learned that bigger *is* better. Buy larger, more expensive bulbs for bigger, more numerous blooms.

First, forget about planting bulbs individually, each in its own little hole. You could spend a day just planting a hundred. The best way is to excavate a space that is big enough for twenty-five or more bulbs. Ignore the directions on the package, which generally tell you to space bulbs 6 inches or more apart. That is fine if you are planting for a nice look in five years. Daffodils and most other bulb flowers look best massed together. Yes, they will eventually produce offsets, little bulblets that will develop into blooming bulbs. And yes, eventually they can begin to compete for nutrients and become less vigorous bloomers. But I plant for immediate results and like the results. Plant your larger bulbs a couple of inches apart, smaller bulbs closer.

The package will say plant these bulbs 6 inches deep. But your daffodil bulb is big, an inch and a half long, perhaps, or more. Do you dig the hole 6 inches deep, or deeper so that the bulb is covered with 6 inches of soil? Deeper is generally better, unless you have a heavy clay soil. Shallower will probably bloom a little earlier, and you can experiment if you want. I always plant tulips a little deeper than recommended as a hedge against rodents.

Choose a location where your flowers will be visible to you in the spring, but keep in mind that you will have to live with the foliage for weeks, even months after the blooms have faded and gone. And if you plant them in your lawn you won't be able to mow that spot until the foliage has turned brown and dried up, or your bulbs won't be able to renew themselves.

As a boy growing up I lived in a house that had a nice open hardwood forest with footpaths throughout. Someone had planted daffodils along the paths, and it produced a terrific effect in the spring. Nobody cared about the dying foliage afterward, and we had plenty of flowers to cut and enjoy all spring.

Another technique for hiding the bulb foliage is to plant bulbs in and around plants that start off slowly in the spring but develop lots of foliage later. Mature hostas are great for hiding declining daffodil foliage, for example.

Dig a hole in a shape that pleases you, perhaps an oval, a circle, or even an eye-shaped space. Instead of putting the dirt on the lawn, put it directly in a wheelbarrow or on a tarp, thus keeping the job tidier. If your soil is rocky or a heavy clay, you should figure on throwing away some of it and mixing in lots of compost with the dirt before you use it to cover up your bulbs.

Although most gardening centers and catalog bulb vendors want to sell you "bulb booster" to put in the hole with your bulbs, it is very expensive and I don't use it. A good organic fertilizer such as Pro-Gro will be just as good and costs a fraction as much. Do not use standard 10-10-10 chemical fertilizer as it can burn, and because it is more water soluble than organic fertilizer, it washes away too quickly. So scratch in a handful of Pro-Gro and you are ready to plant.

Place your bulbs in the hole, and be sure to put the pointy end up. For round bulbs, look for little roots to indicate the bottom. Gently cover the bulbs with good soil, press firmly, and water them if the soil is dry. Mid September through October is the ideal time to plant bulbs, as they will send out roots and establish themselves before winter sets in. But you can plant bulbs until the snow flies if you want to.

Tulips are lovely, but do have their problems. Rodents like to eat them from below ground, and deer from above. The fancier tulips don't usually last very many years, they tend to fizzle out after two or three years. If you buy tulips marked "Darwin hybrids" they should naturalize, blooming and increasing in number for years to come, especially if you add organic fertilizer, scratching it into the soil every year or two. The books suggest doing this is the fall, but who knows exactly where their bulbs are then? Plant labels tend to disappear, even in the best managed gardens. If you plant a few grape hyacinths (*Muscari*) with each bunch of bulbs, they will mark the places where your bulbs are, as they send up some foliage in September.

As for the underground marauders, I sprinkle cayenne pepper in the hole along with my bulbs. It seems to work in the short term, though probably it will not in the long run. Sprinkling dried blood meal on the surface also acts as a squirrel repellent, though this also is a short-term help, and may attract your Labrador retriever.

For me, planting bulbs is a bit like putting money in a piggy bank. Unless a squirrel gets there first (or a sibling raids the piggy bank), you are bound to have something wonderful when you need it most.

Fall Is a Good Time to Plant Trees and Shrubs

Killing frosts have come to my part of New Hampshire, and most gardeners are taking a much-deserved break before cleaning up their vegetable gardens, raking the leaves, and doing other fall chores. Some might even forget about gardening long enough to watch a postseason baseball game on a sunny afternoon without feeling guilty. But don't get too relaxed: This is an excellent time to plant trees or shrubs.

Trees planted in the autumn benefit in several ways. First, the majority of root growth occurs from September to December. Second, the soil is generally more moist in the fall, which helps forgetful gardeners who miss their watering days.

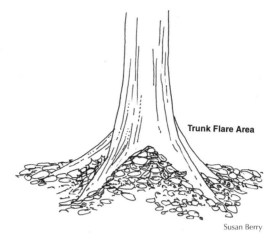

Trunk Flare Area

Susan Berry

Temperatures are lower, which reduces water loss, and leaves will soon be gone, reducing water loss further. We can't see our tree roots, but the scientists have determined that they continue to grow until the ground is frozen.

An important factor for tree success is choosing a species of tree whose needs can be met in the environment where it will be growing. You might not kill your new sun-loving shrub by planting it in the shade, but you probably won't see many flowers, and it won't grow as nicely as you might have expected. Before buying a tree, you need to learn about its requirements, something any good nursery should be able to help you with. Then comes the hard work: planting.

Many a tree has failed to thrive because of efforts made based on good intentions and assumptions. I have an apple tree that I planted years ago that never has produced more than an apple or two per year. I did a number of things wrong when I planted it, and I hope to help you avoid my mistakes.

First, I assumed that I should dig a deep hole and fill it with rich, improved soil. Wrong on both counts. Trees should be planted in holes that are just the depth of the root ball, so that the roots sit on undisturbed soil. And the soil that goes back in the hole should not be amended.

If your tree is purchased with its roots wrapped in burlap, you need to unpack it carefully and gently loosen any soil that is covering up the "trunk flare." This is critical for tree health. Go look at mature trees in the woods. Look at the base of the tree. Normally the trunk widens and spreads out, and you may be able to see the beginning of the roots above ground. This area is called the trunk flare. You want to expose this same portion of your young tree. Covering the trunk flare area with dirt or mulch often leads to fungus rot, which is eventually lethal. If you dig a deep hole, the soil will settle and your tree may end up planted too deeply. Measure from the base of the trunk flare to the bottom of the root ball, and dig a hole that is just that deep, or even an inch or two shallower.

The tree you purchased has probably been harvested mechanically by a big machine with jaws that simultaneously severe the roots and dig it up. In the process, extra dirt gets packed on top of the trunk flare. If it has been at the nursery for several months, secondary roots have started to grow in that dirt around the trunk flare. If you were to plant the tree just as it came out of the burlap, these secondary roots would continue to develop and could eventually girdle or strangle the major roots, which supply the tree with water and nutrients. They also waste energy that could be used to extend their existing roots. Take a sharp knife or pruners and cut off these secondary roots.

You might think that fertilizer and manure or compost would make your tree grow better. But instead, it encourages the roots to stay right there in the hole you dug, and never venture farther away. The roots of a healthy tree extend far beyond the area immediately below its branches, so you don't want them to stay in the little bathtub you dug for your new tree. Keep the soil you have removed to plant the tree, remove any large rocks, and use it to fill the hole back in. If you need more soil, use soil from a nearby area.

Do not add chemical fertilizers, as they can burn the roots. In fact, this is not the time to give your tree any sort of fertilizer with nitrogen because you do not want to stimulate new growth of leaves or branches. I give new trees some rock phosphate and a little green sand, both staples for the organic gardener. Rock phosphate provides phosphorus to promote healthy root growth and good fruit or flower production, but it becomes available to the plant very slowly. Greensand provides potassium for growing good thick cell walls, which will resist the effects of cold or drought. It also provides lots of trace minerals. I sprinkle in a cup of each in the hole, and scratch it in a little, but neither can burn even fine roots the way a chemical fertilizer could. After the tree is established you can top-dress it with a little organic fertilizer from time to time.

When you handle your tree, do so by the root ball, don't pick it up by the trunk. Be sure to remove all the burlap and wire, which may be tough for a large tree. You can tip it on its side in the hole to do so if necessary. For plants grown in pots, make sure that the roots aren't circling around or tangled up. Tease them out if need be, and be sure the root flare is exposed.

The width of the hole you have dug should be at least three times the diameter of the root ball, and four times is even better. Soil near your home has probably been compacted in the construction process, and digging a wide hole just makes it easier for the roots to penetrate the soil. The sides of the hole should curve gently up and out. Stand back and look at your tree from a distance before you begin to refill the hole. Check to see that the trunk is straight, and that the best side of the tree is facing the side where you will see it the most. Rotate as needed.

If you are planting in a dry time, you should stop and water well when you have filled the hole half way. Let it drain, then continue filling. Work out air pockets by poking the soil with the shovel handle. Do not tread heavily on the new soil.

If you think the wind may disturb your newly planted tree, you may steady the trunk with two or three ropes and stakes, but leave them loose so that they encourage the roots to grab on and take hold. Cover the rope with cloth or garden hose so it won't chafe at the trunk and damage it. The ropes should only be 18 inches above ground, as this allows the trunk to flex in the wind, which will encourage it to build lignin, making it stronger. It's kind of like exercising your muscles to make them stronger.

Watering is key to tree success. You should apply about an inch of water over an area twice the tree's height in all directions with a sprinkler each time you water. This needs to occur twice a week for the first eight weeks, and then in lesser amounts for two years, making sure that the soil does not dry out. Overwatering can be bad, too, so use common sense. Trees don't generally do well if their roots are in soggy soil. You should water even after the leaves have fallen in the autumn, right up to the time that the ground freezes if the soil dries out.

Do not plant grass or flowers under a newly planted tree. Bark mulch can be helpful in retaining moisture and preventing weeds. It is essential to keep the mulch away from the trunk flare area by at least four inches. Never mulch right up to the trunk—this can lead to fungus rot. Check your existing trees for overexuberant mulching, and pull back mulch as necessary.

A few final words of advice: Remember that the cute little pine tree you buy will eventually be 40 feet tall and 15 feet wide. Try to picture it full sized before you plant it. Keep any shrubs back far enough from the drip line of your roof so that winter snow and ice will not land on them, even ten years from now when they are much bigger.

Think of planting trees as your legacy: A tree planted properly this fall will be there to provide shade or fruit or flowers to your grandchildren. Consider planting trees to celebrate life's great moments, or to honor loved ones. It maybe harder work than planting pansies, but hopefully the results will please you for decades.

Planting the Smaller Bulbs

Some days summer still feels present. The afternoon sun can be strong against the back of my neck as I get my gardens ready for winter. But the leaves are beginning to turn color, especially on trees under stress, and a taste of fall is in the air. Before we know it, snow will be on the ground and we will trade in our garden rakes and shovels for roof rakes and snow shovels—which is nice. For a while, that is. But I do get tired of cold weather by mid March, and it is for that reason that I plant bulbs in the fall.

I need flowers to grow and bloom in the spring, and I need flowers well before warm weather arrives. To me it is a real gift to be able to go outside and pick flowers while snow is still on the ground. To fill bouquets on days when frost is a certainty at night. So each year in the fall I plant as many as time and budget permits. And in April when those gloomy mud-season days of drizzle appear, I go outside and pick flowers, enough to have vases on all the flat surfaces of the house. I pick things like crocuses and snowdrops that most people consider too small to be of consequence. I appreciate the small flowers as much as the big ones, particularly since they grace our table before their showier cousins.

Most everyone knows the crocus as one of the early harbingers of spring. There are actually some eighty species of crocus, and hundreds of varieties. They originate in eastern Europe, the Mediterranean, southwest Asia, and China. They actually grow from corms, or hardened underground stems, not bulbs, but they look like "bulbs" to most of us. The spice saffron is actually the dried stamens of the *Crocus sativus* flower. (Stamens are the male reproductive parts of flowers, consisting of a stem and the anther, which contains the pollen.)

Most garden centers have only one or two species of crocus, and generally they sell those which have the largest flowers. If you want something unusual, how about a *Crocus chrysanthus*, variety Blue Pearl: "Soft lobelia-blue outside with a bronze-yellow base, lighter inside with a deep yellow throat." And it is hardy to Zone 3, or temperatures of minus 30 to 40 degrees. Or perhaps try Crocus *korolkowii*: "This species is named for a Russian general who found it in Turkestan. Hardy and floriferous, the bright golden-yellow flowers, tinged green, open flat in the late winter sun like shining varnished stars." Zone 3, 2½ inches tall. I'm ordering some, even knowing that people like me (plant fanatics with a tendency toward exaggeration) write the descriptions. Both descriptions are from the catalog of McClure and Zimmerman, available by calling 1-800-883-6998, or on the web at www.mzbulb.com.

My favorite bulb blooms for me in early March. It is the snowdrop, *Galanthus nivalis*. It is small and white, with its little face down turned, perhaps against the cold March winds. Delicate in appearance, sometimes it literally pushes its way through snow and frozen ground. Plant it on a south-facing slope where the snow melts first, and it will provide you with some very early blooms. This year I've ordered some *Galanthus elwesii*, or "giant snowdrops," which allegedly will grow twice the size of mine, up to 11 inches tall, and are hardy to Zone 4 (−20 to −30°F).

An interesting plant that resembles the snowdrop is the giant snowflake, *Leucojum aestivum*. This blooms much later, generally in June, and stands 12 to 20 inches tall, with two to nine flowers per stem. It has lush green foliage. I was delighted to find it for sale at my local feed and grain store, not just in the catalogs. It is touted to like sandy, well-drained soil full of organic matter, but I have also seen it do well in rich moist soil. Sun or light shade, hardy to Zone 4, but just barely.

While the snowdrops are still blooming, along come some wonderful small purple and blue plants. Scilla is one of those plants with no commonly used English name: Even though my plant books list "squill" as the common name, everybody I know calls it scilla. I grow *Scilla siberica* for its deep blue or purple, down-turned, half-inch-wide flowers, and for its ability to grow in tough spots. It will grow in sun or shade, even under evergreen trees where little else wants to be.

Glory of the snow, *Chionodoxa luciliae,* is another lilliputian blue flower that blooms very early in the year. But unlike scilla and snowdrops, it turns its blossom upward, showing off its face. It likes good, well-drained soil in full sun or part shade. If well satisfied with its location it will increase in number nicely, which is good, as one needs quite a few blossoms for a good display.

The allium (or onion) family has many wonderful, underutilized members, both big and little. *Allium giganteum* is a show stopper: Its 4- to 5-inch purple blossom sits atop a stem 3 to 4 feet tall. Similar to it, and much less expensive, are common leeks. If you grew some this year, leave a few in the ground, and they will blossom next year and be very handsome. Garlic chives are useful in the kitchen, have nice foliage all summer long, and are blooming right now with nice white flowers a foot off the ground. *Allium senescens*, variety *glauca,* is also in bloom now above short blue-gray foliage which is nice at the front of a border. Nurseries often sell this growing in pots. *Allium sphaerocephalum* is another favorite, with reddish purple blooms on stiff stems. It is a great dried flower, keeping its color for a year or more.

Some people sprinkle commercially prepared ground oyster shells in the hole with their bulbs to deter rodents, but I don't know that it helps. Having cats helps a lot, particularly cats like my Winnie, who brings me a small rodent almost every day. I trade her a cat treat for the rodent to discourage her from actually eating them. Kind of like the gun or needle exchange programs in the cities. Turn in a rodent, get a reward.

There is no such thing as having too many tulips, or any of the spring-blooming bulbs. Select your bulbs to get a wide range of bloom times, from early to late. Plant in masses. Plant big ones and little ones. And don't forget the fragrant ones. Their blooms are your reward for planting them, and for surviving another New England winter.

Pruning Shrubs

I love to prune. On a crisp fall day there is little that I'd rather do than work on trees and shrubs, sculpting them into clear, clean shapes that will stand out nicely against the inevitable winter snows. Fall is the best time of year to prune deciduous trees and shrubs. As the leaves fall to the ground it becomes easier to see the individual branches or stems that give a tree or shrub its shape and character. I particularly like to transform shapeless shrubs into sharply outlined forms that please the eye. It isn't really hard to do this, and if you keep a few simple rules in mind, you really can't go wrong.

Pruning does two things: It allows you to shape the tree or shrub into a pleasing form, and it promotes healthy growth. Shrubs are a bit like teenagers—they need some guidance. If you don't help them develop in appropriate directions, most will never reach their full potential.

Start by standing back and looking at the shrub you wish to prune. Can you see the individual branches, or are there so many that it is just a cluttered mess? Does the shrub have nice "legs"? Most shrubs look better if they have a clearly defined base, with their lower branches exposed. Is the shrub the right size for the space it is in? Many people plant shrubs too close to the house, a walkway, or another shrub. If it is getting too big, try to visualize the size you want it to be when you are done pruning.

I like to prune on a dry day because I generally start to work on a shrub by sitting or lying on the ground at its base, and working my way up. First I cut off sprouts that have grown up from roots. Many (but not all) shrubs spread laterally by sending up new shoots from an ever expanding root system. Others spread when branches droop down to the ground, form roots, and send up new shoots. If you don't remove these new branches every year or two, your shrub will get away from you, and soon be large and unsightly.

Once I have exposed the base, I look up into the interior of the shrub and look for dead branches. Often branches are shaded out by new growth and so die back. You can tell if a branch is dead by rubbing it gently with your fingernail. If it shows a green layer beneath the bark, it is still alive. Dead branches are generally inflexible, snapping easily if you bend them.

Next I look for what I call "invaders." These are very vigorous newer stems that have shot up willy-nilly through the shrub, reaching for light. They often cross older branches, rubbing and injuring them as the wind moves them. They need to be removed at their point of origin, either the base of the shrub, or from a large branch. Once they have been removed, stand back and look at your shrub to decide how much more you need to remove.

Keeping a shrub from getting too tall is often difficult, as your idea of the "right" size may not correspond with its natural inclination. Electric hedge trimmers are often used by gardeners who want to keep evergreen hedges under control, but I don't recommend them for most shrubs, as they leave gaps in foliage and stubs of leafless stem. Follow the tallest branches back to their points of origin. Wiggle them to see how many side shoots or branches are attached. If taking out the entire branch will create too big a gap, cut it back to a spot where there is a bud or a twig. For many shrubs, cutting back a branch will cause it to grow two or more new shoots from the incision point. Stagger your cuts so that not all the branches are the same height, and cuts are hidden. This will produce something like a layered haircut instead of a buzz cut.

Many trees and some shrubs send up "water sprouts," which clutter up the interior of the plant. These are shoots that grow straight up from a branch in an effort to increase leaf surface area. Often they end up shading out mature branches and totally filling up the interior. Snip them off before they turn into full-sized branches. They are never anesthetically pleasing, so get rid of them!

It helps to know if your tree or shrub blooms on last year's growth, or if it blooms on new growth each year. Many viburnums, lilacs, forsythia, and most early-blooming shrubs bloom on branches that grew the year before. Pruning them now won't do any harm, but it will reduce the number of blossoms you get, so many people prefer to prune right after blooming. I like to do major pruning now anyway, as you can see what you are doing better without leaves present, and I generally have more time for pruning now than in gardening season. Do not prune your roses now, as the cold winter winds can damage their freshly cut branches and the new growth that may occur in response to pruning.

Much of the pruning I do is strictly for looks. I don't like clutter (though my work desk often belies this statement), and pruning allows me to give a tree or shrub a look that seems so much nicer to my eye. Most trees and shrubs benefit by some pruning, and there is little you can do that will cause harm. So give it a try yourself— you might find that you'll like it, too.

Chapter 8

October

Putting the Garden to Bed

When I was a young boy my grandfather would ride the train for three hours to visit us every fall when it was time to rake the leaves. He would create huge piles of crisp red and yellow maple leaves, then stand aside to let me jump in them. After I'd had my fill, he would lay down a piece of cloth he'd sewn together from old bedspreads, rake the leaves onto it, then take them away. Autumn was a joyous time.

By the time I got to high school, fall cleanup meant extra work for me. Not only did I help my grandfather clean up our yard, I had a job raking leaves for Mrs. Wetzel, an antique dealer who lived nearby. She was a wonderful lady, but was absolutely obsessed with getting every single leaf and every last fallen crab apple off her lawn. She would have me rake leaves once a week until the last one was gone, and would inspect the work at the end of the afternoon. I remember picking up leaves and crab apples during inspection and sticking them in my pockets. This colored my view toward fall clean up to this day, and I must admit that I am not very enthusiastic about it. However, there a number of fall chores that we should do soon. Here is my list.

First, you need to pull up and bring in any tender summer tubers or bulb plants like dahlias, gladiola, sword lilies (Acidanthera), or Crocosmia. These should be put in paper bags or wooden boxes and stored in a cool, dark place. Label the bags for colors if you can. They will not survive freezing. It's fine to leave the dirt on them, it will keep them from drying out too much. If you planted your amaryllis outside for the summer, it should be ready to bloom again this winter after a suitable rest. Dig it up, put it in a bag in the basement, and it will be ready to be repotted in forty-five days.

If you have a vegetable garden, it is time to get the carcasses of your tomatoes, potatoes, and vine crops hauled away. You shouldn't put them in your regular compost pile, but burn them, send them off to the landfill, or put them in a spot away from the garden. You want to avoid reintroducing insects or plant diseases into your garden next year. I suspect that Colorado potato beetles will find my potatoes no matter what I do, but if there are eggs on the dead plants, I don't want them hatching near next year's plants.

We are still harvesting a little broccoli, and brussel sprouts, carrots, and beets can take even colder weather. Late lettuce, Swiss chard, and leeks are still growing lethargically, so there will still be cleanup to do for another month or more.

You are *not* going to like this next suggestion, but it is important. And if you do it, you will be rewarded with less work next summer. You need to weed your gardens, both the vegetable and flower gardens. It is easy to let the weeds get away from you at the end of the season, and they will take advantage of your lackadaisical attitude by producing seeds for next year when they think you aren't looking. We had a very dry summer, hence fewer weeds, but the fall rains have allowed them to grow and to produce a late crop of seeds.

The flower beds are now full of tall perennial flower stalks and spent flowers. You may leave them if you like to look out in winter and see them nicely contrasted with the snow. Purple cone flowers, teasel, ornamental grasses, and plants with stiff stalks are often left for winter viewing. Most others will not stand up to the weather and may as well be cut down to the ground now. I use old-fashioned hedge clippers as they do the job much faster than scissors or pruning shears. A small pruning saw can be used very efficiently to slice through fleshy stems of plants like hostas. Dead annuals should be pulled up and composted. Any flower that showed signs of disease or mildew should not be composted.

If you have blackberries or raspberries, this is a good time to cut back the canes that produced berries this year. If you have fruit trees, you should consider putting wire mesh around the bases to keep rodents from chewing on the bark under the cover of deep snow. Ask for quarter-inch-mesh "hardware cloth." Wear gloves when you cut it—it's lethal to hands. I don't recommend wrapping trees with those plastic strips sold as protection against rodents, as the wrapping can harbor insects or strangle your tree if you forget to take it off.

This is a good time to divide daylilies if you need more, or to give to friends who don't know how to garden. If you can't easily pull clumps apart, feel free to hack them apart with a shovel or machete. You can't kill a daylily no matter what you do, so it's a great gift for new gardeners. Iris can be divided now or in the spring.

Fall is the best time to feed the lawn, even though most people do it in the spring or summer. Most years I don't bother, but I've already spread some organic fertilizer over one part of the lawn that surrounds a big old maple tree that has seen better days. The organic fertilizer is a 5-3-4 slow-release fertilizer, which will provide some extra nutrition to the tree and will feed the lawn as well. I just broadcast it by hand onto the lawn surface, and will let the fall rains do the rest.

Even after your lawn stops growing topside, the roots don't. Roots particularly benefit from phosphorus, which promotes good root growth. If I haven't converted you to the use of organic fertilizers, please be advised that this is not the time to use a chemical fertilizer that is high in soluble nitrogen. You can't hurt your lawn with an organic fertilizer, properly applied.

Fall is a good time to feed flower beds and spring bulbs. I try to find time to spread some sheep or llama manure over the flower beds, just throwing on an inch layer or so with a shovel. Over time it will break down and feed the microorganisms that help make my soil such a wonderful place to be a plant. Any pelletized manure is good (rabbit, sheep, deer, goat); it won't burn the plants, and generally is weed free. Cow and horse manure will help your soil a lot, but if applied fresh can bring unwanted guests—weeds. If you don't have a farm source for manure, it is also available by the bag at garden centers as Moo-Doo, or just plain compost.

I highly recommend spreading some organic slow-release fertilizer on the surface of your flower beds. The plants use up the nutrients in your soil to help build their bodies, and eventually they will deplete all the good stuff if you don't replenish it. If you notice that your iris, for example, have an empty spot in the middle, it is because the plants have used up the nutrition and grown toward the outside in search of food.

It is important that your newly planted trees and shrubs go to sleep for the winter with well watered roots. If the fall is a dry one, it is important to water them well before the ground freezes.

Don't forget to drain your hoses, roll them up, and put them away for the winter soon. Empty out clay pots, and wash them out before you put away the hose for the season. When you are done with your hand tools, clean off any dirt, and wipe down the wooden handles with boiled linseed oil on a rag. A little machine oil will keep the metal surfaces from getting rusty in the winter.

The last thing on my list is to clean up the leaves, and now I only do it once, after they have pretty much all fallen. Leaves are wonderful nutrition for your soil, as they contain minerals that the roots have mined from deep in the earth. I run over the leaves with my lawn mower (with the blade set at 3.5 inches) to break them up, then rake them onto a blue plastic 8 × 12 foot tarp, and drag them to the vegetable garden. You can work them in now and they will start the decomposition process. I prefer to to wait until spring, as they help to keep down the early weeds.

Mrs. Wetzel, wherever you are, there is a lot more to fall cleanup than keeping the lawn perfectly free of leaves. And although I never have planted a crabapple tree for myself, one day I just might. If I do, I'll leave a few on the ground for little animals and birds to enjoy. Who knows, maybe this year I'll even jump into a pile of leaves.

Growing Garlic

Aaaah, garlic. From Chaucer to modern times, garlic has been celebrated in literature and life. Some people believe it prevents illness, others that it keeps away vampires. Although I once was given a T-shirt with the inscription "Garlic is as Good as Ten Mothers," I retired it several years ago after getting glares in the supermarket. I think it is wonderful stuff, garlic, but make no claims about its special powers. I love to cook with it, eat it, grow it. And this is the time to plant garlic for next year's harvest.

Garlic is probably the least labor-intensive crop I grow. More importantly, I grow it because grocery-store garlic is not nearly as tasty as the stuff you can grow. I doubt that anyone would challenge the statement that home-grown tomatoes are light-years ahead of "store-bought" tomatoes in taste, but most people figure that garlic is garlic. Wrong. Do not pass go, do not collect $200. There are many different types of garlic, and many different tastes and potencies. You can grow garlic that is rich in flavors you never imagined, but rarely is the good stuff for sale.

There are two major categories of garlic, soft-neck and hard-neck. Soft-neck is what you find in the grocery store, and it is the type that is made into those great-looking braids hanging on the walls of Italian restaurants. It has a longer shelf life than hard-neck garlic, which is why it is sold commercially. Hard-neck garlic is what I grow. Yum.

Hard-neck garlic has a stiff, almost woody neck. People who grow hard-neck garlic like to pass it around, to share with other gardeners, so much of what I grow is an unnamed variety I was given some years ago. Recently I visited organic gardeners John and Jean Sibley in Etna, New Hampshire, who are the best organized gardeners I've ever met. They knew the name of every variety they grow, and gave me samples to try. These included Porcelain, which produced their biggest bulbs, and which Jean likes the best. Others were Marino, Kearney, and Dominic. This year I will label each, so I will know which do the best for me.

I asked Jean Sibley where she bought her garlic, and she gave me several sources. Johnny's Select Seed in Maine is at 207-437-4357. Seeds of Change in Sante Fe, New Mexico, waxes almost poetic about its garlic, and can be reached at 505-438-8080. Hillside Organic Farm in Troy, New York, is at 518-279-9637. Of course, most of what the Sibleys plant each year is started from their previous year's crop. They sacrifice the biggest and best for starting their next crop.

Garlic likes a rich, sandy soil. My garden borders a stream, so the soil is good alluvial soil to begin with, but is a little heavy on the clay for garlic. In a bed about 3 feet wide and 8 feet long I add

Betty Woodbury's Garlic Bread Spread

1 stick butter, warmed to room temperature
2–3 cloves garlic, pressed though a garlic press
3 tablespoons grated Romano cheese
½ teaspoon dried tarragon

Mix and mash the ingredients, and it's ready to use. Cut a loaf of good Italian bread lengthwise, lather on the garlic spread, and heat for 10 minutes in the oven at 350°F.

a large wheelbarrow load of coarse sand and three wheelbarrow loads of composted manure. I sprinkle on two one-pound coffee cans of Pro-Gro organic fertilizer, and a can each of rock phosphate and green sand. Then I work it in well, until thoroughly mixed. I grow a lot of garlic, 100 heads or more, so you probably should scale down your efforts proportionate to your garlic needs.

The added ingredients have made the garlic bed a raised bed, which gives it good drainage. This is important as I am planting now, and wouldn't want my garlic to rot by sitting in wet earth all winter and spring.

Take a head (or bulb) of garlic and separate it out into the individual cloves. Each head will give six to ten cloves, and each will produce a new head by next July or August. Plant the cloves 6 inches apart in rows 8 inches apart, pointy end up. They should be planted 2 to 3 inches deep. Firm the soil with your hands, and water. For best results, plant garlic between September 15 and October 15, though I have planted as late as November 1 without problems.

The next step is the key step. Garlic will not compete with weeds. It likes it cool in the summer, and wants to be kept moist but not soggy. The solution? Mulch it with 12 inches of straw or mulch hay. The garlic will grow right through the mulch, but weeds won't. Depending on the weather, your garlic may even send up leaves this fall, but that is not a problem.

I recently read that by cutting off the flower scapes in July you can get heads that are 25% bigger. I've never done this, but will experiment with this next summer. When the leaves start to yellow, it's time to harvest. Dry your garlic by hanging in a cool dry place with the leaves on. Apparently, some of the nutrition in the leaves will travel back to the garlic bulbs during the curing process, which takes about three weeks. Store in a cool, dark place. Hard-neck garlic will last from harvest till spring, when it will start to sprout. Soft-neck garlic is said to last up to a year.

I predict you will be delighted with the results of your efforts growing garlic. And if you grow as much as I do, you'll rarely get a cold—because most people will stand back three paces!

The Wonderful World of Hydrangeas

In my experience, most of us like what we know. I find mashed potatoes and gravy comforting because I grew up eating them. This may account for the love so many people have for the hydrangea, an old-fashioned shrub or small tree that has decorated the New England landscape longer than any of us now living. Along with the lilac, it is a fixture. It may also be the reason that many people are starting to ignore them. They are looking for new, exciting plants. Be the first on your block to own a *Heptacodium miconioides*. Which is fine by me, I love trying new trees. But the hydrangeas still have much to offer.

There are several different species and many different varieties or "cultivars" that grow here. The most common is the Pee Gee hydrangea (*Hydrangea paniculata Grandiflora*). It is that wonderful old tree we see in our graveyards, vase-shaped and loaded with white pompoms that slowly fade to pink, and then brown up after frost. Introduced from Japan in 1862, it has had a long and distinguished career. I find it handsome in winter with its textured bark and some flowers still hanging on. It may come into bloom in late July or early August and stay handsome for months. Michael Dirr, the guru of woody trees and shrubs, calls it "difficult to blend into the modern landscape because of its extreme coarseness," thinks it is "totally disgusting in late fall and winter," and believes it has been "over-planted". (This from the *Manual of Woody Landscape Plants*, my tree bible.) Usually I agree with his comments, but here I take exception. And obviously, so do many others.

Unfortunately, Pee Gee hydrangeas are not usually available as good-sized, nicely shaped trees. If you want to buy one, you have two choices. You may buy a 2- to 3-foot-tall, multistemmed plant, which, despite its fast growth rate, will take ten years or more to get to the point where it starts to look like those old beauties in the graveyards, and will require some pruning to get in that shape. Or you can buy a "standard," a tree that has a single bare stem rising 3 to 5 feet from the ground, then a top that was grafted on and has a dozen or so branches popping out near the top of the trunk. They are handsome, but will probably never have that old-fashioned look. We Americans are generally in a hurry, so this new format has become very popular—it's instant tree. They do best in full sun or partial shade, and are not fussy about soil.

Often the flowers on hydrangeas are so big that rain weighs them down to a point where branches bend severely, and even break. I recently learned a neat solution to the problem. Take your pruners and cut off the tip off the blossom. It still looks good, but weighs less. And don't fertilize your hydrangeas. The richer the soil, the bigger the blossoms will be. The blossoms do make great dried flowers; just place them in a dry vase, and they will please you all winter.

Another nice cultivar is the *Hydrangea paniculata Tardiva*, which blooms a month or so after the Pee Gee. It is not quite as flashy as the Pee Gee. They both have their blossoms arranged in panicles (the pompoms that most people would call "blossoms"). The Tardiva panicles are longer, narrower, and a more delicate mix of showy sterile and less conspicuous fertile florets. The Tardiva is less likely to flop on wet days.

I've had good luck with a third variety of panicle hydrangea, the Unique. It will accept more shade than the others mentioned, and is very vigorous. The panicles are not nearly as big as those of the Pee Gee.

The grocery stores often sell potted hydrangeas with bright blue flowers, the bigleaf hydrangea, *Hydrangea macrophylla*. These are not supposed to be hardy here (though I've seen exceptions), so if you put them outside, think of them as annuals. They are fascinating to people because the color of their flowers depends on the acidity of the soil. It is actually affected by the availability of aluminum ions in the soil, but making the soil more acid makes aluminum more available to the plant, turning the blossoms a deeper blue.

The climbing hydrangea, *Hydrangea anomala*, subspecies *petiolaris* is one of my favorites. It is a clinging vine that can attach itself to a brick wall with little rootlike holdfasts. It blooms in late June or early July, and has wonderful flat-topped arrangements of flowers with showy outer flowers and subtle inner ones. It is slow getting started, but after a few years it can really take off. It has handsome, dark green shiny foliage, and the thick vines are shaggy and interesting in the winter. Professor Dirr, cited earlier, admits it is "the best vine" and that the flowers are "magnificent."

If you have a steel roof, you know by now that the snow comes off in a big "whoosh," and has the potential to annihilate any shrubs or trees growing beneath it. This has lead to the increased popularity of the smooth hydrangea, *Hydrangea arborescens*. This shrub dies back to the ground every fall, but bursts forth in the summer with an amazing spurt of growth, producing plants that are 3 to 5 feet tall. Depending on the variety, it can produce blossoms that are as big and showy as those of the Pee Gee hydrangea. Not only that, they will do fine on the dark north side of the house!

There are two common varieties of smooth hydrangea, Annabelle and Grandiflora, also called Hills of Snow. Annabelle has huge panicles of white flowers, often so heavy that they bend over and hit the ground, even on dry days. The Hills of Snow has a much more upright format, and smaller blossoms. Both will spread by root, sending up shoots in an increasingly large area unless disciplined by you, the gardener. It prefers some shade, and if you plant it in full sun it will not do well in dry soil. You can cut back all the stems right to the ground in the fall or early in the spring. I favor leaving the stems and spent flowers on till spring, as they do provide a reminder of summer when it's 20 below zero out.

I've planted several hydrangeas recently and have one last bit of advice. Be sure to tease out the roots from the root ball or pot. They often have such vigorous root growth, even at the nursery, that the roots get tangled, or they grow up the side of the pot. Try to spread them out in the soil as you plant. I find soaking the plant in a bucket of water first helps, as the roots tend to be a little brittle when dry.

Fall is a great time to plant trees and shrubs; this is the time when their roots do the majority of the year's growth. So take a look around you, and think what might be nice to add to your landscape.

Hydrangeas may be old-fashioned, but they are tough plants, very adaptable and hard to kill. And I think they are wonderful.

Pruning Deciduous Trees and Shrubs

Most people look forward to pruning their trees and shrubs about as much as they look forward to going to the dentist. As a result, many planted trees and (especially) shrubs are formless, messy, and cluttered. I love to prune. It is an opportunity to create sculpture, but without the tedious chipping away of granite or wood with a chisel. I think most people don't prune because they don't know just what to do, and they are afraid of doing something awful, something irreversible to their precious tree or shrub. Better to leave it till next year than make a mistake now, many think. And anyway, it's football season.

Most gardeners have a feeling that March is probably the best time to prune apple trees, and they are right. Few gardeners would pick fall as a good time to prune deciduous trees (those that that lose their leaves) and shrubbery, but it is. Once they have lost their leaves, it is easy to see their form—and the problems they are suffering from. Insects and diseases are dormant and less likely to attack an open wound now. So get your saw and bypass pruners, and get to work! Please note that the time for pruning coniferous trees and shrubs has passed. They should be pruned mid-summer, after new growth.

A word or two first about tools to use: The technology has changed in the last twenty years, so you should think about getting some new tools. Sharp is important. That rusty old-fashioned bow saw you've had hanging in the garage for years is not what you want.

Pruning saws now have tricut blades with teeth so sharp that they go through hardwood like the proverbial hot knife through butter. This is good. A sharp saw gives a clean cut and doesn't tear. The new saws can't be sharpened, or not by most of us, but they are worth the price, and will last for years if you keep them clean and don't misuse them.

Pruning shears come in two styles: bypass and anvil. The anvil shears are the type that has the blade come down on a flat surface on the other side. Bypass shears work like scissors, and they are what you need for good pruning. Anvil shears, especially after they get dull, tend to mash branches, leaving raw ends that are more susceptible to disease.

Before you begin pruning, it is important to know where to make your cuts. Although trees vary considerably in the shape of their branches, most have a swollen area called the collar where the branch meets the trunk. Often you will see wrinkled bark at the outer edge of the branch collar. It is important not to cut into the collar, but to prune just beyond it. The collar produces protective barriers against invading disease. A flush cut tight to the trunk removes this important area and opens a large area up to disease. In past times we were told to make flush cuts, and to paint them with tar. Now research indicates that these are not good practices.

If you are cutting a branch of some size, you need to make three cuts in order to remove the branch without risk of damaging the collar. First, make an undercut on the branch to be removed. It should be made about 12 inches from the trunk on the branch you want to remove. Cut about one third of the way through the branch. This will prevent a tear from extending into the collar. Then make a top cut that will sever the branch, a little farther out the branch. Finally make a cut to remove the light-weight stub that you made by severing the branch.

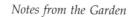

Do not remove the collar, but be sure that you trim off the stub tight to it.

Now you are ready for surgery. Stand back and look at the tree or shrub. Is the form pleasing to you, can you see strong lines? Is it the shape you hoped for when you bought it? Keep these thoughts in mind as you get to work.

The first step is to remove all dead wood. This might seem

tricky without leaves to guide you, but it isn't. Dead branches don't usually have the buds that will produce leaves or flowers next year. They are brittle, their color is different, and often their bark is flaking off. You can remove deadwood at any time of the year.

Next look for branches that are crossing or rubbing, and prune out the smaller or least desirable branch. If the branches have fused, you may decide to eliminate them both.

Then look for branches that are damaged, cracked, or in poor health. A tree in good condition shouldn't have too many of these. Cut them back to healthy wood, or remove totally.

Fourth, look at branches that are competing for the same sunlight. Sometimes two branches will grow parallel to each other. One will shade out the other, so remove one of the two. Leave the strongest, fullest branch.

Fifth, eliminate the "invaders." These are branches that spot an opportunity to catch some sunlight, and reach out for it like a teenager going after the last cookie on the plate. Invaders ignore the basic branching patterns and clutter up the interior of your tree or shrub. Often they become problems, rubbing or crossing branches. They don't contribute much to the tree for the amount of energy they use up by reaching across the tree.

Last, prune out water sprouts. These are small branches that tend to shoot straight up from larger branches. They are often a response by a tree in stress. They are a tree's way of producing extra leaves, and thus additional food. Many apple trees produce numerous water sprouts every year. In the heat of the summer the leaves at the top of the tree become somewhat dormant due to the heat. The interior part of the tree is cooler, and remains better able to produce food. Instead of eliminating all of them, try training a few to fill in the interior of the tree. This should slow down the annual production of water sprouts.

For years I followed the rule that it was all right to prune out up to one third of a tree each year if necessary. Current research indicates that it is better to cut out only 20% to 25% of the live branches on any given year. Cutting off branches may make your tree look better, but you are also reducing its ability to produce food. So take out all the deadwood, but be moderate in eliminating healthy branches. Some shrubs will withstand severe pruning without suffering. When thinning multistemmed shrubs, cut back the oldest branches all the way to the ground. This allows younger, more vigorous stems to predominate.

Pruning can make a scruffy shrub a thing of beauty. Don't be afraid to try your hand at it; almost anything you do is fixable. Trees and shrubs will respond to pruning by becoming healthier and more vigorous. If you take off a branch in an "ooops!" procedure, another will eventually take its place. Take your time, especially at first, and step back often to look at the entire plant. You will be rewarded with not only a more handsome plant, but also a better appreciation for its form, texture, and personality.

A Visit to the White House Gardens

When I was a young boy my family took a trip to Washington, D.C., to see the cherry blossoms in bloom. It was quite a sight, especially when the wind blew, and a rain of pink petals filled the air. We walked around the town, visiting all the tourist spots, and I remember well walking past the White House.

"That's where Mr. Eisenhower lives," said my father. Having worn an "I like Ike" button to school for weeks, I felt a certain responsibility for his election, and was delighted to see what a big house came with the job. We didn't get to tour the White House back then, so it was a real treat for me to visit the White House grounds recently with the chief horticulturist, Mr. Dale Haney.

The grounds of the White House are full of history. Every President except George Washington lived in the White House, and many left their mark on the landscape. President Jefferson had thousands of carts of dirt brought in to create two huge mounds on the south lawn of the White House, giving him a little more privacy and allowing him to create a more pleasant setting than the flat, barren space he moved into.

John Quincy Adams, inaugurated in 1825, was an avid gardener. He not only employed a full-time gardener (probably not at taxpayer expense), he took an active role in designing and planting. An Amer-

ican elm Adams planted survived until 1991, and a cutting from that
tree was grafted onto an elm planted by First Lady Barbara Bush.
Two towering Southern Magnolias planted in 1830 by President An-
drew Jackson in memory of his wife shade the White House.

The area that intrigued me most was the Rose Garden. For the
last four decades it has been a formal garden, though Mr. Haney
explained that it had been used in a variety of other ways. It sits just
outside the West Wing of the White House, bordering the Oval Office
and executive offices, and it was originally a horse pasture. This explains, in part, the good soil there. President Grant used the space
to grow vegetables. In 1913 President Wilson's first wife, Ellen, grew
the first roses there, and it has been a flower garden ever since.

The Rose Garden is a formal garden in the European tradition
surrounding a lawn that measures 125 feet by 50 feet. President Kennedy had it designed by a family friend, Mrs Paul Mellon, after he
visited the gardens at Versailles.

I was surprised to see that there are only sixty roses planted in
the ground, although others in pots are brought in for important
occasions. The sixty roses are only planted along the two long sides
of the lawn, which means that they are spaced about 4 feet apart. A
few were still in bloom when I visited in mid October, mainly a
white floribunda rose known as Iceberg.

The roses are really only a very small part of the plantings in the Rose Garden. Bordering the lawn are low boxwood hedges. Next to the boxwood are the roses, which are complimented with other flowers that change with the season. Beyond the roses are crab apple trees, a cultivar known as Katherine, which were planted in 1961 at the request of President Kennedy. Unfortunately, the crab apples have gotten so large that they dominate the garden space, casting shade over the roses and sending roots into the garden beds. They probably will have to be replaced in the next decade, perhaps a few at a time. Dale Haney told me that the variety Katherine is no longer available through the nursery trade.

Every time I talk to another gardener I learn something, and talking to Mr. Haney was no exception. He explained to me that each fall they plant thousands of tulips among the roses. I noticed a healthy gray squirrel population on the White House grounds, some brazenly cruising the Rose Garden while we stood there talking. I asked him how they protected these delicacies from rapacious rodents. He explained that they plant in large groupings, and bury chicken wire over the bulbs but below the surface of the earth. And they provide the squirrels with an adequate supply of corn so that they need not eat tulips to survive. A kinder, gentler solution than I would have anticipated.

The gardeners at the White House plant some three dozen varieties of tulips, including many parrot tulips, orange, black, and blue ones. Tall White Triumphant tulips (28 inches) are planted, as well as red and yellow Oxfords, Sweet Harmony, and the JFK tulip, which is a buttercup yellow with touches of red. One new variety of tulip they will plant this fall is not available to the public yet. It is a pink one, the Hillary Rodham Clinton tulip, and I wonder how it will be received by President and Mrs. Bush.

In the spring after the tulips have put on their display, they are removed and replaced with a mix of annual flowers and showy perennials like Oriental and Asiatic lilies, and hollyhocks. Dusty miller, santolina, salvias, and white begonias are interplanted with the roses. A particularly nice salvia they use is called Blue Giant. Later chrysanthemums are installed for the autumn. All the flowers they plant are grown in greenhouses offsite by Park Service personnel, and all are treated as annuals since they yank one display to install another. I'd love to have some of their rejects. Perhaps they have potential as fund raisers!

Mr. Haney brought me to see the Jacqueline Kennedy Garden, which is outside the East Wing of the White House. Like the Rose Garden, it is a formal garden surrounding a lawn. Interspersed with ornamental trees are sculptural works of American artists. Displays are changed for each new First Lady. The current show features works inspired by Rodin including those by Willem de Kooning, Bryan Hunt, Malvina Hoffman, and Louise Bourgeois. Three pieces by Rodin, who was French, were slipped into the show. The garden was begun by Jackie Kennedy but finished under the eye of Lady Bird Johnson after JFK's death.

I asked Mr. Haney if the White House grounds were maintained with only organic pesticides and fertilizers, and was not surprised to learn that they are not. They use organic controls whenever possible, but if Arafat or the Queen is coming, THERE WILL BE NO JAPANESE BEETLES ON THE ROSES. They do use Safer Soap for soft-bodied pests, and Rose Defense, another organic product, for powdery mildew.

The grounds of the White House are open to the public two weekends per year, once in April and again in October. The dates are not fixed very far in advance, but you may call 202-208-1631 for information. In my experience, when you call the White House, someone answers by the third ring. No machines. Twenty thousand people filed through this October on a first come, first served basis.

The grounds of the White House really are the backyard for the President and his family. Eisenhower had a golf putting green installed. Nixon had it taken out, thinking perhaps that it sounded too elitist, just as he wouldn't let his wife, Pat, wear a fur coat. The grounds crew were instructed to build one for President Clinton, and were delighted to find that the infrastructure for the original green was still functional (drainage, in-ground watering system, etc.).

Amy Carter had a treehouse designed by her father built in a Blue Atlas cedar (*Cedrus atlanticus*). It was bolted together so it wouldn't damage the tree.

It suddenly hit me that I was in the Clinton's backyard when I met Socks, Chelsea's cat. Socks is a big, friendly, black and white cat, who was enjoying a warm sunny morning outside the Oval Office. He was wearing a harness and was attached by a long length of ordinary clothesline to a big tree. He came right up for an ear rub, and I asked him several questions. But being the cat of politicians, he made no comment.

Ginseng

Asian Ginseng *(Panax ginseng)* has been used in herbal remedies for at least two thousand years in China, perhaps for as long as four thousand years. Its close American relative *Panax quinquefolius* is a highly valued root that grows wild in New England. It can be started by seed and grown in the woods, but not without some difficulty.

There has always been a mystique about ginseng, and what it can and can not do. It is said to prolong life and increase vitality by restoring "chi," the vital life force which is said to affect all our systems, helping the body to heal itself.

In some cultures ginseng is thought to affect male potency, which may account for its high price. It is consumed as a tea, roots are chewed, and extracts are now commonly found at health food stores and pharmacies. Its effects are not immediate, but build up over a period of weeks.

Ginseng is a slow-growing plant that takes at least six years to reach the stage at which it can be harvested. Unfortunately, the root is the part of the plant that is used, so once it is harvested, the plant is gone. In some areas this means that the plant has disappeared, or is in very short supply.

The scarcity of ginseng plants is exacerbated by the fact that dried wild roots can be worth up to four or five hundred dollars a pound (150 to 300 plants are needed to produce a pound of dried roots; about 3.5 pounds of fresh roots make a pound of the dry).

Growing ginseng successfully in your woods depends on many factors. I am planting seeds and rootlets now, as fall is the time of year to plant, right up until the ground freezes. Location is critical to success.

Ginseng grows best in fertile soil that stays moist but is not soggy. Look for a north-facing hill that has a mature stand of sugar maples, black walnut, yellow poplar, or white ash trees growing on it. If the average circumference of these trees is 60 inches or more, this is a big plus. The slope of the hill should be from 10% to 35%, and the soil deep and fertile. The fewer stones the better.

Ginseng grows best in 80% shade. An excellent location for growing ginseng will have maidenhair fern, rattlesnake fern, goldenseal, wild ginger, or ladyslipper orchids already growing there. Almost as good are environments that include Christmas fern, blue cohosh, baneberry, trillium, jack-in the pulpit, and bloodroot.

There are several ways to plant ginseng seeds. The technique I favor is to grow it in the woods, as it would grow naturally. First rake away the leaves in the fall and loosen the soil. Some growers just lay seeds on the ground and then cover them with leaves or forest duff. Others plant the seeds from ½- to 1-inch deep, while still others plant them even deeper. Young plants are susceptible to drought, so it makes sense to me to cover them with soil.

Scott Harris, a grower in New York State, advised me to add gypsum to the soil as a source of calcium, which he deems critical for success. Bob Beyfuss (of the Cornell University extension system) agreed, saying that 5 pounds per hundred square feet applied annually is good.

Commercial growers plant 8 to 10 seeds per square foot. Beyfuss explained that ginseng is self-thinning, and that by planting 5 or more seeds per square foot, you will end up with about one plant per square foot after three years.

Young seedlings may have a hard time fighting through a thick layer of leaves in the spring, so some growers rake off planted areas in the spring before the seeds sprout.

Ginseng seeds are expensive, but there are 350 to 400 per ounce. It is important to buy seed from a reputable source, and preferably from a source as close to local as possible. The seeds need to be stratified, so freshly harvested seeds do not grow until the second year. Organic seeds generally have higher germination rates, because commonly used fungicides can adversely affect the seeds.

Most ginseng products come from Wisconsin, where it is farmed as a cash crop under shade cloth, but it is generally heavily treated with pesticides.

Some ginseng growers sell two- or three-year-old rootlets or plants. The New England Wildflower Society is a reliable source of plants, starting April 15. They can be reached at 508-877-7630.

Scott Harris of Sylvan Botanicals in Cooperstown, N.Y., sells a minimum order of two ounces of organic seed for $16, or $105 for a pound, plus shipping. He also sells plants, both two- and three-year-old rootlets. He can be reached at 607-264-8455, or by visiting his website at www.catskillginseng.com.

Bruce Phetteplace, of Chenago County, New York, sells both seeds and seedlings. Seeds are available at about $16 per ounce plus shipping. He can be reached at 607-334-4942.

If you are serious about wanting to earn an income growing ginseng, you can apprentice at the National Center for the Preservation of Medicinal Herbs in Meigs County, Ohio. This is a nonprofit organization that does research on how best to grow wild herbs like ginseng and that teaches cultivation techniques. They offer a one-month apprenticeship program in the fall and a two-month program in the spring for $135 or $235, respectively, which includes room but not board. Apprentices work 26 hours a week in the woods, and attend classes 10 hours a week. For information call 740-742-4401 or visit their website, www.ncpmh.org.

"Wild simulated ginseng" is the term in the ginseng trade for ginseng that has been planted and grown in the woods. It brings a slightly lower price than true wild ginseng, but root buyers generally know the difference. Wild ginseng roots are often twenty years old, even as much as fifty. The older and gnarlier the root, the higher the price.

If you find ginseng in the woods, I advise against harvesting it. Harvest and plant the seeds before the chipmunks or wild turkeys eat them, and wait some years to let the population build up. Most states have laws protecting wild ginseng, which is endangered.

My father often told me, "There is no such things as a free lunch." Growing ginseng sounds like easy money, but I am not counting on it to support me in my retirement years. There are lots of things that can go wrong. If the soil is not deep and well drained, roots can rot in a wet year. If there is a blow down of trees, lack of shade can kill it in a few days. It can be ruined by disease or insects. Poachers can steal it all in one night.

Heck, if everybody who reads about ginseng starts growing it, we may flood the market in ten years, causing the price to plummet. So, on second thought, don't bother trying. In a decade I'll let you know how I did.

Chapter 9

November

Attracting and Feeding the Birds

As I write this a cold wind is blowing, the sky is gray, and snow is forecast for tomorrow. I should be outside raking leaves, but the woodstove has made the house a much more inviting place to be. Earlier I heard the call of Canada geese as they headed south, and I ran outside to see them, as I always do. There is something primal in the call of the geese, and I respond to it at a level I don't fully understand. It makes me look at the woodpile with concern; it makes me glad I have 100 pounds of home-grown potatoes in the cellar. Winter is coming.

With the migrating geese comes the realization that it is time to get out the bird feeders. I love seeing birds coming to the feeder, and for years have used a feeder I got from the Audubon Society. It is a box that fits into my double-hung window and features one-way Plexiglas sides. I can see my cardinals up close and personal, but they can't see me. Recently I've wondered about birds becoming too dependent on us. So, although I'll feed birds in our feeders, I've also been planting shrubs that allow them to feed themselves. A food-for-work program, if you will.

Our local naturalist, Ted Levin, told me that I shouldn't worry. He says bird feeders only supply a small fraction of the food consumed by our bird population. And they connect us with nature. Planting shrubs with berries can attract birds to your yard, and many of these shrubs are pleasing to look at on a snowy day.

Birds are a bit like like unsupervised kids. They eat what they like first. If they get hungry enough, they'll eat almost anything. Research has shown that birds first eat the berries with the highest lipid content—which means they like berries with fat. Pepperoni berries would be popular, no doubt. If you want to plant trees or bushes for birds, you need a variety of plants, so that they will have treats in all seasons.

One of the first blooming trees in the spring is the shadbush (*Amelanchier arborea*), a white-flowered, gray-barked understory tree. Weeks later they produce bluish berries, which I've read are tastier than blueberries. But they are never available to us because they are so highly prized by birds that they are eaten immediately. I plant shadbush because of its early blooms, and because its multistemmed form is beautiful to my eyes. It is living, growing art if pruned well.

At the other end of the scale are the fruit of the staghorn sumac (*Rhus typhina*). These are still on the bushes when the robins return in the spring, and are an important food source for robins when the earthworms are still hiding deep inside the frozen earth. Sumac berries are high in sugar content, preserve well, and stay on the tree. I would never plant a sumac as they are a dreadful nuisance: They spread aggressively by roots, and will take over a landscape. It is almost impossible to rid yourself of sumacs once they have established themselves. They often send up new plants from their roots 20 feet from the mother tree.

Two vines providing early fall berries for birds are Virginia creeper (*Parthenocissus quinquefolia*) and poison ivy (*Toxicodendron radicans*). Their foliage turns bright red, serving as "foliar fruit flags" for migrating birds. The bright leaf color gets their attention and tells them to stop for a quick snack, kind of like those golden arches. McBerries. I don't recommend planting either, but maybe this will make you feel better about having poison ivy on your stone wall.

A nice understory shrub that grows well here is the pagoda dogwood (*Cornus alternifolia*), a native dogwood that bears lovely blue berries. They grow at the edge of the woods, and have subtle white flowers in the spring. The birds just finished stripping the berries off one growing outside my window. The red stems of the berries are still attached. The form of this shrub or small tree is pleasing to me, especially in winter.

Another great group of shrubs are the viburnums, and they all have nice berries for birds. The most commonly planted native viburnum is the American highbush cranberry viburnum (*Viburnum trilobum*). Its red berries are prominent now, but the birds usually eat them all before the winter is half gone. They are tough plants that will grow in full sun or in part shade. Arrowwood viburnum (*Viburnum dentatum*) is a multistemmed shrub that the birds like. It is very hardy in sun or part shade, and tolerates salt quite well. Its berries are blue.

Birds are very attracted to the berries of the American elder (*Sambucus canadensis*), a 5- to 12-foot-tall shrub. Do not confuse it with the boxelder (*Acer negundo*), which is a weedy maple-family tree that gets to be 30 to 50 feet tall. The elder berries ripen in fall and are important food for migrating birds. Elder will grow in wet places, spreads quickly by suckers, and is not a decorative shrub as far as I am concerned.

A number of invasive plants are very popular with birds. The seeds pass through the birds and are deposited widely—along with a little deposit of fertilizer. In this group are the barberry (*Berberis* spp.), autumn olive (*Ealeagnus umbellata*), and many honeysuckles (*Lonicera* spp.). Burning bush (*Euonymus alatus*) is certainly an invasive shrub in southern New England, but does not seem to be in the northern parts.

Inkberry (*Ilex glabra*) is an evergreen holly with black berries that persist well into winter, and sometimes until May. Like its cousin common winterberry (*Ilex verticillata*), it will do well in wet places and tolerates shade. The winterberry is one of my favorites with its masses of bright orange-red berries, which look great against the snow. The berries are often gone by the end of January, however. Hollies are dioecious, which is to say there are male and female plants, and you need both to get berries. One male will pollinate several females, but they should be "within sight" of each other.

Shrubs and trees are also important in the urban and suburban landscape because they provide places for birds to rest and nest. It allows them to catch their breath or spend the night in a cat-free zone. Pruning shrubs this fall I have found many nests tucked inside shrubs right near houses.

I admit it. I haven't finished cleaning up my garden for the winter yet. When I clean up my flower beds, however, I will leave plants with good seeds for the birds, and cut the stalks down next spring. We leave our sunflowers up for the birds, who love them, and they help us by letting a few self sow. Black-eyed Susans (*Rudbekia* spp.), purple coneflower (*Echinacea purpurea*), and various ornamental grasses provide food for birds in the winter. Hey! Maybe that gives me an excuse for leaving some weeds. Bird food! On the other hand, it might be better just to buy some extra black oil sunflowers, and pull the weeds. I'll try to get to those weeds. But if I don't, and the weed police show up at my door, I've got an alibi.

Fall-Blooming Crocus and Other Bulb Wonders

I would like to start out by apologizing to most of you. I am going to write about some absolutely gorgeous flowers that are blooming in my garden now. Others have just bloomed, or will bloom soon. And if you are reading this now, in November, you can't have any this year. Most of us "serious" gardeners see something wonderful, and immediately go buy one—or many. Sorry, you will have to wait till next year to get them. I'm talking about fall-blooming bulb plants.

Like many gardeners, I always knew there was a fall-blooming crocus, and another, bigger bulb called the colchicum that resembles the crocus but is in the lily family (crocuses are in the iris family). But in the past whenever I thought of bulbs, I thought of masses of spring bulbs, daffodils and tulips and all manner of lovely things that I plant. So I ignored the fall bloomers till this year when I saw some for sale in a shop, and bought a few on impulse. And, *wow*, was I delighted with what I got. At this time of year there are few things blooming for most of us, so even a few blossoms can be uplifting. I planted two species of crocus and one type of colchicum.

I planted my bulbs in mid August, and could have planted them in September and still have seen blossoms this fall, I've read. Being unusually cautious with my dollars, I only bought one colchicum, as it cost me $4.95 and I wanted to "test drive it" before buying others. What I didn't know was that it would not give me just one blossom, but a succession of magnificent blossoms, six in total. Apparently if it is happy where it is, I could get up to twenty blossoms from that one bulb in future years.

The variety I bought was a hybrid form called Lilac Wonder. It produced lovely vase-shaped lilac colored flowers 2 to 3 inches in diameter. My colchicum was a delightful surprise for me because it bloomed without warning: It had no stem, and no leaves. They produce leaves in the spring, which disappear by midsummer. They can be grown in sun or partial shade in fertile, moist soil. My books tell me they need to be fertilized heavily for maximum bloom.

My catalog for rare and wonderful bulbs, McClure and Zimmerman (1-800-883-6998), lists the Lilac Wonder colchicum as a Zone 4 plant (able to withstand 20 to 30 degrees below zero in winter). Some of my plant books list all colchicums as Zone 5 plants, only able to withstand minus 10 to 20 degrees. When the ground is well frozen I'll throw some bark mulch over it to protect it. And if this one survives the winter, I'll try some other varieties next year, such as the variety Waterlily, a double variety that looks like a real waterlily hovering above the fall leaves. (P.S.: My colchicum *did* overwinter, and produced thirteen blossoms in its second year.)

Next to bloom for me were some *Crocus speciosus*. Like the colchicum, they have spring foliage, and just pop out of the ground unannounced. Mine were light lavender flowers perhaps 3 inches tall and wide when open. They stayed lovely for days, as they only opened on warm sunny days and closed up on gray days. Discouraged by not getting to see them much, I cut one on a rainy day and brought it into the house. It opened up the next day on a sunny windowsill, and stayed open for another two days before wilting. It was a real treat at this time of year. And then, that same bulb sent up a replacement blossom a week later! Smaller, but nice. Two for the price of one is always delightful.

The true fall crocuses are small, very hardy, relatively inexpensive bulbs (30 to 70 cents per bulb). And if you believe the catalog, they will increase in number, as they produce cormlets that break off and start new plants. (Crocus produce corms, not true bulbs). One book even recommended stirring up the soil with a garden fork to help spread them next year.

The *Crocus sativus* bulbs I planted showed their leaves on November 6 for me, short striped leaves that look just like the spring crocus leaves, but they didn't bloom for me this year. These crocuses are purple with yellow anthers (the male portion of the flower which produces pollen). For well over 2,000 years this species of crocus has been an important cash crop in other parts of the world, as it is the source of saffron. However, lest you think it might be a good supplement to your income in retirement years, you should know that it takes 7,000 plants to produce three ounces of this spice.

Early last summer I planted some tubers of another fall-blooming flower, the hardy cyclamens (*Cyclamen hederifolium*, sometimes called *Cyclamen neapolitanum*). Having learned about them from writer Jamaica Kincaid, I ordered some from Dutch Gardens (1-800-818-3861), which listed them as Zone 4 plants. In other sources they are listed as Zone 5 plants. They took forever to send up their leaves, but they are now displaying gorgeous variegated green and silver ivylike leaves that look marvelous against the drab fall leaves surrounding them. Reading up on them, I've learned that they will send up tiny pink or white flowers much like those of the well-known houseplant, but that they flower before the leaves appear. It may take another year or two before mine are big enough to bloom, but the leaves are a delight on their own. They like to grow in dry shade. I'll mound leaves over them just before the snow flies.

When I planted the cyclamen tubers it was not at all clear to me which end was up. This can also be a problem with some anenomes (*Ranunculus*). They are black and knobby and flat, but have no obvious roots or sprouts. I know that a bulb planted upside down uses up much of its energy getting its flowers and leaves to the soil surface. So I planted my cyclamen on their sides, like pancakes planted vertically. This allowed them to sprout from either side without too much trouble. And it worked. Of course I kept thinking that they were never going to grow because they took two months to send up leaves.

Fall is a time of both melancholy and hope for me. I will miss my gardens these next long months. I hate the gray drizzly days of autumn, but rejoice on the sunny ones, and plant hundreds of spring-blooming bulb flowers on the good days. Late next summer I will plant more fall-blooming bulbs for this last gasp of color before the snows come. The crocus and colchicum were such a delight this fall, they almost felt like my garden was sending up one last message.

Planting Bulbs for Forcing

I once knew a dog with great foresight. She would catch a woodchuck and bury it till it was good and ripe, then dig it up and roll in it. Now this didn't endear her to anyone, but she considered it great fun, and it did show that she could plan ahead for those days when she really needed a pick-me-up.

Likewise, I have been burying things for some much-needed lifting up of the spirits later this winter. Although it has been suggested that I exhibit many characteristics of Labradors, woodchucks are not my thing. I have been planting bulbs in pots to force in February and March.

Many garden centers have put their spring-blooming bulbs on sale now, as the ground is freezing up. If you haven't already bought some, it's a good time to buy a few and try your hand at it.

Before you buy the bulbs, you might want to see if you have a good spot for storing the pots of bulbs. In order to succeed you will need a cold dark place. Forty to 45°F is ideal. Anything over 50°F is too warm, and anything below freezing is too cold.

If you are looking though bins of bulbs and selecting your own bulbs (as opposed to buying bulbs in sealed packages), take time to select good ones. The warm dry climate of a store does not offer ideal storing conditions. Avoid the ones that have already sprouted long green leaves. A hint of growth is fine. Pinch the bulbs. Are they firm? If they feel as if they are made of paper, put them back in the bin.

Having bought my bulbs, I make an effort to plant them right away. The first thing I do is go out to the driveway and rake up some pebbles to place in the bottom of the pots. A single layer of stones is fine. It is important that your bulbs have good drainage, so always select a pot that has drainage holes.

Bulbs sitting in waterlogged soil will rot or suffocate. Plants get their oxygen through their roots, so it is important that your soil be porous and well drained. After you water, the soil should drain, allowing air to fill the spaces in the soil. Keep this in mind if you are digging up garden soil for your pots, as heavy clay is not a good growing medium.

I generally mix up a wheelbarrow of soil for bulbs and indoor plants toward the end of the growing season, and store it in a big plastic bin in the basement. I put two shovels of garden soil, three shovels of good fluffy compost, and one shovel of coarse sand. And I mix in a couple of cups of a good organic fertilizer, a 5-3-4 or something similar.

If you don't have compost, substitute a commercial "potting mix." In fact, a 50-50 mix of garden soil and potting mix will work fine. And don't be discouraged if the ground has frozen: Put your weight on the shovel, and you will get through the thin frozen layer that has formed over garden soil in most places by now.

Daffodils and tulips are both great for forcing. Read the labels on the tulips, however. Some say "good for forcing"—many do not. Darwin tulips generally are fine for forcing. Narcissus or daffodil varieties are not usually labeled for forcing, but those marked "early" are better for forcing than later varieties.

Some bulbs can be forced in as little as six to eight weeks, notably crocus, hyacinths, and *Muscari* or grape hyacinths. Although some books indicate eight weeks of dormancy is fine for daffodils and tulips, I recommend twelve to fifteen weeks. This gives them time to develop a good root system and to have adequate rest before starting their bloom cycle. If you rush them, you risk getting foliage with no blooms, so be patient if you can. In my experience, tulips will never bloom if you bring them in before February, no matter when you start.

And beware of mice: They will dig up your tulips or crocus while in the basement if you don't take precautions. Rodents! They like my bulbs inside or out. You can place some wire screen called hardware cloth over the pots, or perhaps a board. Maybe I should let Winnie the Hunter Cat into my basement.

I have lots of those black plastic pots that came with perennials in the summer, so I use them for forcing bulbs. A good size is 7 to 8 inches deep and almost that wide at the top. Once I bring them into the house for display, I place them in baskets. Alternatively, you can wrap them in colorful paper or cloth. Clay pots are fine, and some people prefer shallow, wide ones.

I like to plant two layers of bulbs in an 8-inch-deep pot. In the bottom of the pot I put a layer of small stones, then an inch of soil. I arrange five tulip or daffodil bulbs on the soil, and next to each I stand up a broom straw as a marker. Then I add more soil, and plant a second layer of bulbs so that their pointed tips are an inch below the soil surface. The straw helps me avoid planting one bulb over another. Pat the soil to firm it up. Leave half an inch of space below the lip of the pot so you won't make a mess when you water. The two-layer system results in blossoms at staggered intervals.

Water well, then water again every few weeks. You do not want dry soil or soggy soil.

Tip your pots on their sides and look for roots poking through the drainage holes before you bring them into a warmer location. If you see roots, they are certainly ready.

Your bulbs should be awakened gently from their dormancy. No blaring alarm clocks. They should start out where it is still cool, say 55 to 65 degrees, and out of direct sunlight. Once their shoots are green and growing nicely, put them on the warmest, sunniest window sill in the house. Rotate the pot daily.

Having gone through all this work to get flowers, you can prolong their blooms by keeping them in a cool spot with indirect light. My mudroom is cold, near freezing during the winter, and I often move flowers (especially purchased cut flowers) there at night to prolong their blooms. You will be delighted at how much this stretches their useful life.

I keep something blooming in my house every day of the year. I buy cut flowers in the winter, but there is still something special about forcing bulbs. It presages spring. Forced flowers remind me that spring and summer are coming, no matter how far away they may seem. And often I need that pick-me-up during mud season. Especially if my dog has dug up a woodchuck.

Goldilocks and the Three Soil Types

We gardeners don't get much time off from gardening, which suits most of us just fine. By now, in late November, there isn't much to do outside, so I spend more time reading about gardening than I do in the summer. It is also a good time to reflect on the past gardening season, to think about what worked, and what didn't.

In my part of New Hampshire we had a relatively cool, wet summer, which meant that newly planted flowers and shrubs did well. Few gardeners are as conscientious as they need to be about watering, so dry summers are tough on new plants. If you read a gardening book about what the average plant wants, it reads something like this: "Plant in full sun in rich, moist, well-drained soil." This summer, at least, most of us got the moist part right.

Rich, well-drained soil is something everyone can have. People tend to classify themselves as gardeners into one of two categories: those with brown thumbs, and those with green thumbs. What they really are is this: those who don't have good soil, and those who do. Being an organic gardener, and working to feed your soil, will lead you toward the elusive Green Thumb Award.

Chemical fertilizer sales reps to the contrary, the soil is not just there to hold onto your plants and keep them from blowing over. Nourishment for your plants should not just come from a bag. The soil should be full of living things: bacteria, fungi, earthworms, and lots of others. These organisms process minerals and organic matter, making them available to your plants as needed. Organic growers help to provide their soil with compost and manure to feed these little critters, which also help your soil to have good texture. A healthy soil tends to be rich, moist, and well drained.

There are three basic soil types: sandy soil, loamy soil, and clay soil. And just as Goldilocks found two out of three beds were uncomfortable, your plants—in general—will find two out of those three soil types to be less than ideal. But you can make yours into a nice loam with work.

Sandy soils are com-
posed of large soil particles, and consequently water flows through them like
a hose placed in a wire
basket full of golf balls. If
you add compost and ma-
nure, you fill up some of
the spaces, and provide ab-
sorbent materials to hold
the water like a lot of little

sponges. The compost also attracts the microorganisms that can re-
lease nutrients to your plant's roots. They can dissolve minerals,
making them into a soluble form.

Clay is made of microscopic particles. Think of a wet clay as
being like uncooked bread dough. It's moist, but more water can
puddle on top, and it won't drain off. The individual bits of bread
dough—or clay—are so close together that roots would have a hard
time pushing through it. If your soil dries out, it turns to rock, and
a quick summer shower won't get down to your plant's roots. You
can improve it by adding lots of compost, manure, leaves, or any
organic matter.

A good loamy soil is like Goldilocks's favorite bed: not too soft,
not too hard. It has some sand, some clay, and plenty of organic
matter. It also has plenty of room for the air and water it needs.
Plants need oxygen, and they can only get it through their roots, so
they must get it from the soil. A waterlogged soil can suffocate your
plant. But without some moisture, your plants can't get the nutrients
they need from the soil, and the tips of their roots will die back. It's
a balancing act. "This flower bed with heavy clay soil is too wet, this
sandy one is too dry . . . and this nice loamy organic flower bed is
just right," says Goldilocks.

Your plants make their food by photosynthesis, combining carbon dioxide from the air and water from their roots to make carbo-
hydrates. Most stomata (the pores that allow plants to "breathe" in
carbon dioxide and release oxygen) are on the underside of leaves.
A good, working soil full of living organisms generates carbon dioxide, which can be absorbed by the leaves. Carbon dioxide levels
produced by poor, inert soils are inferior.

Most people are surprised that a good loam is only about 45%

minerals by volume. It should contain about 10% organic matter (stuff created by living plants and animals, their by-products, and dead bodies). The rest is air and water, 20 to 30% of each, making up about half the volume of your soil.

A clay soil has much less space for air, and holds onto water and nutrients tightly. Without getting too technical, let me explain that clay has strong positive charges that hold onto ions of certain elements like nitrogen, phosphorus, and sulfur, which your plants need as building blocks.

My grandfather, John Lenat, was an organic gardener and a great intuitive gardener. I grew up helping him make compost and manure tea. I don't believe Grampy ever had a soil testing kit, but he did know soils, and he had the best vegetables and flowers in Spencer, Massachusetts. Consequently, much of what I have done as a gardener has been intuitive. But there are times when intuition is not enough.

Even if your garden has done well, you should think about sending off a soil sample for testing this spring. For a fee, your state extension services will test your soil for you. A basic test gives you soil pH and minerals. They can also measure organic content and analyze your soil texture. Order your kit now, because you'll be so busy in the spring you might not get around to it.

I would recommend getting all three tests done at least once. The lab will explain what the results mean, and your extension agent can give you some good suggestions on what to do if you need extra help. If they only give you recommendations for chemical fertilizers, call back and ask for recommendations for organic soil improvement.

Nitrogen levels are not usually given with soil test results, as nitrogen levels can vary radically from day to day depending on temperature and moisture levels, but a soil rich in organic matter is a good indication of adequate nitrogen.

If you don't want to spend the money on a soil test, you should at least buy a kit that will allow you to test the pH of your soil. The pH of your soil is an important measure of your soil quality. A neutral (7.0) or slightly acidic pH (6.2–6.9) is important for the health of the microorganisms in it, and also determines if key minerals will be in a form that is available for your plants for use. You can have plenty of phosphorus, for example, but if your soil is too acid, it can be insoluble and unavailable to your plants. Adding wood ashes or agricultural limestone will help your soil become less acid. Our New England rain is acidic, so untreated soil generally is, too.

Last, but not least, you should know that a plant needs sixteen elements to grow and be healthy. Thirteen of these come only from the soil. If even one is missing, or rendered inaccessible, a plant will suffer. It may not die, but it will be more susceptible to disease and insect infestation. A bag of 10-10-10 has only three of those thirteen elements. Of course, many of those elements are present in your soil.

Bagged organic fertilizers are made from natural ingredients like seaweed and compost, so they have many of the micronutrients not present in bags of 10-10-10. Organic fertilizers are also slow-release fertilizers, so their ingredients do not wash away as quickly as chemical fertilizers.

By adding organic matter every year, and supplementing with a bagged organic fertilizer from time to time, you will certainly build a healthy soil. And before too long, you will have soil that the mythical gardener Goldilocks will pronounce to be "just right!"

Jean and Weston Cate, Growers of Heirloom Vegetables

Those of us who have reached the age of maturity—whatever that may be—can remember when vegetables tasted better. Or is it the rose-colored glasses we wear to look at our past, those simple days before the advent of cell phones, VCRs, and call waiting?

I remember eating corn and tomatoes Grampy grew in the 1950s, the tastiest ever grown. So I was delighted to find the Golden Bantam corn he grew available in the *Seed Savers 1999 Yearbook*. I don't remember which tomatoes he grew, but I'll bet they are somewhere in that book, too, and if I read it all, I may remember. At least now I'll be able to take off the rose-tinted glasses, and grow some of that corn. I hope it's as good as I remember.

I'd been meaning to find out about the Seed Savers Exchange for a long time, so I was delighted when a friend of mine mentioned that his parents were members of the exchange, grew heirloom veg-

etables, and would be willing to talk to me. So I went to visit Weston and Jean Cate at Fox Run Farm, in East Montpelier, Vermont.

Mr. and Mrs. Cate live in a trim red New England farmhouse, and have been serious gardeners for more than fifty years. Their son Paul and family live next door, and together they have a 5,000-square-foot vegetable garden, raise some chickens and hogs for meat, keep bees, and make maple syrup. They have berries and fruits for their own use, and in the year 2000 they sold 269 jars of jams, pickles, and relish at the farmers' market in Montpelier. Wes Cate turns eighty soon, a time when many people are settling into rockers by the woodstove. But the Cates are not slowing down much; they continue to enjoy raising and preserving their own food, and growing new vegetables varieties—new to them, but mostly they try antique varieties.

In this age of genetically engineered crops and "terminator seeds," it is refreshing to learn that there are lots of people who are continuing to grow old varieties of vegetables, and saving and sharing seeds, so that genetic diversity is not lost. There is a whole system in place for sharing seeds. For $30 a year, one can become a member of the Seed Savers Exchange, and receive their annual catalog of seeds available from other members. For $1 to $4 you can get seeds that have been grown every year for many decades, thereby keeping antique strains alive. This system is decentralized: You don't order seeds from the exchange, you order directly from the gardener who grew them. I like the concept.

Mr. Cate gave me a package of heirloom squash seeds that the Cates grow, the Boston marrow. He said that in 1850 it was the most commonly grown squash in America. It is a winter squash similar to a hubbard, but bright orange, and is a great "keeper." At some point it fell out of favor, and I (for one) had never heard of it. He recounted the tale of giving a talk about heirloom seeds, and passing out little packages of seeds to everyone attending. He told people that in the fall they should cure their squashes outside for a few days, then bring them upstairs and store them under the bed. "I got a call one night," he said. "A woman told me that she had done everything right, but now she had a problem. She said they had done so well, they wouldn't fit under the bed!"

Not all heirloom vegetables do so well. In fact, breeders have worked hard to develop varieties that are resistant to diseases, and others that will travel well to markets across the country. Most heirloom varieties are not disease resistant, which may be one reason why commercial growers have given up on them. For the average gardener, heirloom vegetables do just fine, and they certainly provide unique flavors.

As gardeners taste the advantages of antique varieties, some commercial seed growers are now selling the heirloom varieties, particularly for tomatoes. Fedco, Johnny's, Pinetree, and The Cook's Garden are just a few of those selling them. Locally, the Cates get heirloom seeds from High Mowing Seeds, run by Tom Stearns, 802-888-1800.

Looking through the Seed Savers catalog, I did learn that there are many hundreds of varieties of heirloom vegetables. For example, I've been growing an heirloom tomato called Brandywine, which is now commercially available. In the Seed Savers Exchange there are many different Brandywines, and people are allowed to impart a few words about their particular variety, so one could spend the next few months just reading this catalog, which is nearly 500 pages long! The 1999 catalog has 11,520 different varieties of vegetables listed, and 989 members supplying them. To join the Seed Saver Exchange, send $30 to it at 3076 North Winn Rd., Decorah, IA 52101, or $25 for persons on a "fixed income."

Cornell University was one of the first agricultural schools to start encouraging gardeners to save old vegetable varieties from extinction. Wes Cate gave me a copy of a leaflet produced by Cornell called "The Heirloom Vegetable Garden," which was full of quotations from nineteenth-century gardening pamphlets. One of my favorites was from 1860 that explained that when vinegar was scarce, "We used to get two gallons of whiskey, and put four gallons of water with it, put it in the pickle barrel and fill the barrel with cucumbers as fast as they grew." This kind of pickle could make for some very interesting picnics.

As the Cates have gotten older, they have looked for ways to save labor. They have done two things that I find very interesting. They have created a number of raised beds that are contained by big logs, planed flat on top. This allows them to sit down comfortably to weed their vegetables. The beds are about 3½ feet wide, and from 10 to 16 feet long.

But Jean said, "The magic word to me is leaves." They collect their leaves in the fall and store them in bins made of 4-foot-tall sheep fencing. Their son Paul also collects leaves from Montpelier folks who bag them up for removal. After banking the house with the bags for the winter, they put them on the garden in the spring. They have essentially developed a no-till system. They part the layer of leaves to add compost and plant their tomatoes, for example. Once the plants are tall enough, the Cates pull the leaves back close to them. Earthworms digest the leaves, dragging good nutrients down into the soil. And the weeds just don't have much of a chance.

The Cates have been gardening for a long time. Jean has a set of 5-by-7-inch index cards dating back to the late 1940s on which to record the food they have "put by." Some years it has reached 500 jars on the cellar shelves—more recently, perhaps "only" 200 or so. They are not only growing antique vegetables, but they are also computer literate, and e-mail connected. They are growing and learning as they get older. I hope I have their energy and enthusiasm when I reach their age.

Steps to Take That Can Save the Life of a Newly Planted Tree

Have you have cleaned up your garden and put it to bed, planted your spring bulbs, and pruned your hardwood trees and shrubs? Have you raked all your leaves, put away the hoses, and oiled all your tools? If so, you may be feeling that there is nothing left to do until spring, and you might be right. And you certainly are very unusual, as most of us gardeners still have chores on the "to-do" list. In fact, my to-do list is like a Mobius strip: it is endless. On the other hand, if you have planted some trees in recent years, there just might be one more chore for you.

This would be a good time to tour your property and look at the way trees have been planted, as a commonly made mistake can be corrected. And this just might save the life of some of your trees.

What you need to look for are trees that have been planted too deeply. Sometimes people plant trees the way they plant tomatoes in the spring: They bury some of the trunk. This is good for tomatoes, but not for trees. The bark of a tree is designed to shed water and resist pests above ground, but not below it. Rot may develop, and plant health will decline.

Signs of poor tree health are numerous. Are upper branches or their tips dying? Did your trees show signs of changing color earlier in the fall than others of the same species? Are they wobbly if you wiggle them?

Look at trees that grew of their own accord. You will notice that at their base they widen or "flare out." You will see major roots that head away from the tree above ground, then disappear.

Now look at the trees you have planted. At ground level does the trunk resemble a telephone pole (which stays the same width) at ground level? If so, your tree is headed for trouble. Unfortunately, most people don't recognize the cause-and-effect relationship between planting trees too deeply and their demise six to ten years later. A strong wind comes along and the trunk, which has rotted just below the ground, snaps off. The wind is blamed, when the person who planted the tree should be blamed. Bark mulch piled up against the trunk can be just as lethal.

I recently noticed a municipal tree planted a year or two ago that has had 2 feet of bark mulch piled up against the trunk. I could see roots trying to grow in the bark mulch. The tree is struggling to survive, and expending energy building a second set of roots because it is suffocating. Trees get their oxygen through their roots, not their leaves. Just as you can drown a tree, you can suffocate it by planting it deeply and overmulching it in such a way that air can't get to the root system.

If your trees have bark mulch touching their trunks, you need to remove it. There should be no mulch within 4 inches of the trunk all the way around the tree. And bark mulch never needs to be more than about 4 inches deep. If there are roots growing in the mulch, snip them off gently with a pair of pruners. But be careful not to damage the bark, which will be tender from staying moist all the time.

Don't get me wrong: Mulching around your trees is good. It keeps down competing weeds, and keeps away potentially lethal string trimmers and lawn mowers. If you didn't mulch a recently planted tree, you should do so now. Before winter. It will keep the soil above freezing for a few more weeks, allowing more time for root growth before hard freeze.

Beware of dyed or stained "bark mulch" in plastic bags. It may not be bark mulch at all, but ground up pallets that once were placed beneath any sort of materials, possibly even leaky chemical containers. Read the bag carefully to see what it claims to be.

If your tree is planted too deeply, you can help it by removing the soil around the trunk until you expose the trunk flare area. If it has been in the ground for a year or more, it may have started sending roots out from the trunk above the flare, and these need to be snipped off. Work carefully with a small hand tool (I like a soil scoop available from Gardener's Supply, 1-800-863-1700). Create a ring a foot or more wide all around the trunk. If you don't like the looks of the depression created, you can regrade the area.

When I was a boy, nurseries grew trees in their own fields, dug them up at an appropriate age, and wrapped them in burlap. Many trees now sold in nurseries are grown by wholesalers far away and harvested mechanically by machines. In the process, dirt usually gets heaped up against the young tree's trunk before it is shipped to the nursery.

If you ask how deep to plant your tree, many nurseries will tell you to plant the young tree so that the top of the root ball is at ground level. Unfortunately, that usually means you will plant the tree too deeply. You need to remove all the burlap (and wire basket if used), and then expose the root flare. This usually means removing 2 to 6 inches of dirt that has been placed over the flare. Then plant the tree with the flare above ground level. If you do this, you will have a healthier tree. If you didn't, a little excavation around the trunk flare area will help it considerably.

Another note of caution the next time you buy a tree: Some nurseries may tell you not to worry about planting the tree in the burlap, saying that it will decompose quickly. I disagree. First, these days plastic "burlap" is replacing real fiber burlap, and that stuff never breaks down. Second, even real burlap can restrict root growth for a number of years before it breaks down, depending on soil conditions and moisture. I don't know about you, but I want my trees to get big fast. And removing the burlap is no big deal.

Nut trees generally send down deep taproots, which means that they are tough candidates for transplanting. This fall you might want to play squirrel. If you would like a black walnut tree, a hickory, an oak, or a chestnut growing on your property, think about getting a few nuts and planting them. You can do this now. If you get nuts from a neighbor's tree you will see what a mature tree looks like. Plant several where you want one. If more than one grows, yank out the weaker of the lot next spring. Use plant labels to mark the spots where you plant so that you won't mow them over.

I think there is great satisfaction to be had by planting trees by seed, particularly if you plan to stay put for a long time. Young trees grow faster than you might think. If you plant two trees by seed at hammock distance, think of the satisfaction you could have in your retirement years, resting in your hammock with a grandchild in your lap. I better go find some nuts!

Chapter 10

December

Holiday Gifts for the Gardener

Thanksgiving is over, and the holiday shopping frenzy is fast approaching. Some would say it has already ground to a halt, as they bemoan traffic snarls and parking-spot deficiencies. A few friends tell me they have stopped going out to shop. They are shopping on the World Wide Web. Not me. You won't find me surfing the Web for www.SantaClaus.com. I believe in buying locally and supporting our area merchants and farmers. Why buy a new gizmo off the Web, when we can get lots of things for the gardener in our own backyards?

This may not sound romantic, but the best gift for your loved one—if she or he is a gardener—is a truckload of aged manure. Now don't start with the jokes already. I'm serious. Call around to the local dairy operations and ask a few questions. Will they deliver a load of barn scrapings? Do they have any aged manure? Do they have any that has been turned and aerated to encourage hot composting?

Cow manure and (especially) horse manure can be full of weed seeds, but seeds can be killed if the manure pile has been "worked," so that it reaches a temperature of 140°F. If a pile just sits, it eventually turns to compost, but some seeds in it may remain viable. So, if possible, buy composted manure that has been hot composted. But no matter what style/color/model number of manure you buy, it always helps. And you don't have to drive to the mall to get it.

Magazines are wonderful gifts for gardeners. We keep sane all winter reading them, drooling over the pictures, and dreaming of spring. I recently discovered a gardening magazine produced for New England gardeners. It's from Maine, and is called *People, Places, and Plants*. I like it because it is organic, and because it has lots of in-  formation relevant to New Englanders: public gardens, garden tours, interesting gardeners, and plants that work here. If truth be told, they have hired me to be their Vermont and New Hampshire editor, but I would have told you to look at this magazine anyway. Honest. It comes out six times a year. Call 1-800-251-1784 for subscription information.

Every year at this time I remind gardeners that *Organic Gardening* magazine is a wonderful gift for any gardener. My gardening grandfather started subscribing in the early 1950s, and the one issue of his that survived is still good reading, just as is every issue today. It covers growing vegetables and flowers, with tips on composting, fighting insect pests and weeds organically, and all sorts of useful, practical tips. I learned how to make my "mole mix" from it, for example. This is a concoction I brew to repel moles. The magazine is published six time a year. Contact it at PO Box 7736, Red Oak, IA 51596-2736.

For the serious flower gardener I like *Fine Gardening* magazine. Unlike many of the flower magazines, this isn't just gorgeous pictures of gardens (without any weeds) full of things we'll never find for sale. The magazine is technically good. It will introduce you to new flowers, ways of growing them, and new design ideas. And it will give you enough information so that you can do it, too. To subscribe, call 1-800-888-8286. The magazine is published as six issues a year.

If you are helping your kids to select a present for a grandparent, I think a gift certificate is great. I'm thinking of a nicely made card with a coupon for three hours of help in the garden. There is probably nothing nicer for a grandparent than spending time with a loved child, and where better than in the garden? And this gift, too requires no time in traffic.

All right, books are a great present for the gardener, but buying them can take you out into the real world. I only buy books from local, nonchain bookstores. You can go to a chain, I suppose, or buy off the Web. But I, for one, like to be helped by people I see year after year, people who know their books and can make good recommendations. You can't get that on the Web. And if we all buy off the Web, or from the big chains, we might save a dollar, but one day those friendly little bookstores will be gone. I'll make a few recommendations here, but a good bookseller will have lots more ideas.

Every gardener should own Barbara Damrosch's book *The Garden Primer*. It is an excellent reference book that give you the basics on everything from berries and bulbs to beets, bark mulch, and bouncing Bet. From garden gear to making compost to dealing with pests, it's all there, packed into 673 pages (Workman Publishing Co., 1988, paperback).

Ed Smith's *The Vegetable Gardener's Bible* (Storey Books, 2000, paperback) is a great resource for anyone who wants to grow vegetables well. I agree with just about everything he says. He is an organic gardener who uses most of the techniques that I recommend. He uses lots of compost and raised, wide beds. Excellent illustrations.

There are lots of coffee-table books about flowers. I recently bought Allan M. Armitage's *Armitage's Garden Perennials* (Timber Press, 2000, hardback) and felt it was a good investment. It's much more than just a pretty face. I usually judge a book by reading a section about something I know to see if I agree with the author, or if I learn something. I also want a book that is well written and interesting. This book got an "A" from me on all counts.

Professor Armitage is highly opinionated about the merits of various flowers, which I like. And he illustrates the book with 1,500 color photographs, showing many named cultivars of species, so you can see their differences. He has good growing tips, too. Pricey, but worth it. I hope to read it cover to cover this winter.

Most people don't need another houseplant. But you can buy a cyclamen in bloom very reasonably and give it as you would a bunch of cut flowers. Cyclamens don't need a lot of sunshine to be happy, and will bloom nicely for much of the winter with very little fuss. Just water them once a week from the bottom, letting them draw up water from a saucer, and keep them out of west-facing windows.

Are you looking for an inexpensive present to give all those people at work? Instead of giving unneeded calories in the form of cookies or candy this year, how about making up little packages of Pro-Gro (or the organic fertilizer of your choice)? Help your friends discover the benefits of organic gardening.

A fifty-pound bag of Pro-Gro costs under $20, it's Vermont made, and you can make ten nice presents from it. Fill up plastic milk jugs with it, wrap them handsomely, and show you care—not only about your friends, but also our environment. And who knows? If Santa is watching, he might just reward you with a truckload of manure!

Bonsai

The ancient Japanese art of bonsai is becoming increasingly popular with Americans, despite the fact that it demands much of those who grow them. Bonsai in Japanese means "to cultivate in a tray." It is the art of growing miniaturized plants as living sculpture. It is appealing because these miniature trees are so simple and beautiful. Bonsai allows the grower to mold and form a work of art even if the person could never do so with an artist's brush or chisel. This is not an activity for someone who just wants a handsome or unusual houseplant. It is a slow process to create good bonsai, and they are not forgiving if you ignore them.

People who are bitten by the bonsai bug often take this "hobby" to great extremes. I talked to one man who twice a year takes an extended sales trip, leaving home for two or three months at a time. He takes his favorite bonsai with him in a special glass box that sits on the passenger seat. His cat travels with him, too, though his wife stays at home. Another bonsai buff had an addition built onto his house to accommodate his passion for bonsai (and to appease his wife, whose kitchen had been taken over by his plants).

Retired geology professor Bob Reynolds of Hanover, New Hampshire, explained to me that when one looks at a well-groomed bonsai, one should have the feeling of looking at an outdoor scene—that it might conjure up feelings of an ancient tree seen from a distance, perhaps perched on the edge of a cliff.

Bonsai trees are groomed to be small, and it is not uncommon for a thirty-year-old tree to be just 12 inches tall. This is accomplished by careful pruning, not just of the branches but of the roots as well. If you have ever seen the low-growing, bent, and windswept look of evergreens at the top of a mountain, you have seen trees growing as "natural bonsai." Those mountaintop examples are eking out an existence at the very limits of where they can survive, often where there is little soil to nourish them. Bonsai trees grown for their looks depend on their human caretakers for their survival, and would perish quickly without regular care.

The most important care needed by a bonsai in a pot is regular watering. The frequency of watering varies considerably depending on on the species, time of year, size of the container, and wind and sun conditions. For some that means watering once a day during the spring, two or three times a day during the summer if the plant is outside, once a day in fall, and once or twice a week in winter. For others, a watering every three days is fine. Because bonsai are grown in diminutive containers with little soil, there is very little water in reserve. Humidity is also a factor. Hot dry homes during a New England winter are very tough on some bonsai.

Given the water needs just described, do bonsai collectors give up their vacations in perpetuity? No. There are a number of ways to deal with bonsai if you are going away. Bob Reynolds puts his in the bath tub with wet newspapers beneath and the shower curtain closed. The humidity and lack of direct sun reduce their needs for water and allow him to leave for a few days. A plastic tent around a bonsai will usually hold in the moisture enough to survive a week or so. Bill Smedley, a nationally known bonsai expert living in the Spofford, New Hampshire, area, has someone come in to tend his plants while he is away. Some plant nurseries or bonsai growers will take back your plants and, for a small fee, take care of them while you are away. Since bonsai trees can become very valuable with age, it is important that you not entrust your best bonsai to a neighbor with a busy schedule or a failing memory.

Bonsai trees whose native habitat includes a winter every year need a dormant period in order to survive. They will not survive outside unprotected in their bonsai pots, so serious bonsai people often dig pits for their plants to live in during the winter. A typical winter home for bonsai is dug into a hill three or four feet deep, and covered with plywood and insulation. Even a dormant plant will die if it dries out totally, so it has to be watered every couple of weeks. Bob Reynolds is lucky: His garage stays at about 40 degrees all winter, which is perfect for his dormant plants. Another bonsai friend of mine keeps his in an unheated room in his house. Light is not needed for the plant once it goes into dormancy.

Tropical bonsai do not need a dormant period, so you should find out if the bonsai you are purchasing requires a dormant period. Buy from a reputable, knowledgeable dealer who can answer your questions. I was told that some stores sell bonsai that need a dormant period but that haven't gotten it. They will then die in the fall . . . and you will blame yourself, but shouldn't. So ask if it has had a rest during the winter.

Bill Smedley recounted to me the story of a street vendor hawking bonsai on the streets of Miami. "Come buy your 'lucky' tree," the man shouted. Bill, the former president of the American Bonsai Society, stopped and explained the difficulties of growing bonsai to the vendor, adding that most uninformed people would indeed be "lucky" if their bonsai survived the first year. Bonsai are not just fancy houseplants.

Root pruning is important to keep your bonsai healthy and its roots active. Plants become pot bound and need to be root pruned and repotted. Older conifers might only need root pruning every three to five years, deciduous trees every year or two, and active young trees might need it more than once in a year. The soil mix is very important, and is sold commercially. It needs to be very porous with lots of gravel, so that it drains quickly. This helps to prevent root rot, which might occur if the plant sat in a wet medium all the time. Most bonsai growers water by submersing the plant, pot and all, in a basin of water or diluted fertilizer such as Miracle-Gro.

There are rules about how a bonsai should look, and unless you are willing to pay a hefty sum for a well-trained tree, you will need to learn how to train your tree. Unlike a painting or sculpture, your creation will change as time goes on, so you may wish to have a plan for it. Common bonsai styles include upright, slanting, cascading, forest or group plantings, and clump style. Each of those styles is further divided into straight, curved, or windswept. The bottom third of a bonsai is generally kept free of branches. This allows one to observe the trunk, which will thicken with age.

Some bonsai trees have some of their bark removed, then are treated with a lime sulfur solution to make them look old and weathered, or as if the tree had been struck by lightening. The semblance of age is important for good bonsai. There are bonsai that are over 300 years old and are passed down from one generation to the next. Sometimes in Japan a bonsai is a person's inheritance. Just think of it: all those years without forgetting to water! Harvard's Arnold Arboretum has several locked behind bars that are over 200 years old. Bonsai increase in value with age.

Copper or aluminum wires are sometimes used to bend branches to achieve a certain look. The wire is wrapped around the trunk, then around the branch to hold it in position until it will stay put. It must be removed before the tree engulfs it the way trees grow over barbed-wire fences outdoors.

Potential bonsai plants can be collected in the wild, but beginners should not try this. There are strict rules against collecting them on mountaintops in state parks. Some people find plants that have been mowed over by road crews year after year, and that have developed a low, gnarly form that could be trained, over a period of time, to live in a pot as a bonsai.

There is only so much you can learn from books about bonsai. The bonsai people that I talked to all felt passionate about bonsai, and were ready to share with me whatever they knew. So before you buy a bonsai, find someone who is willing to teach you a little. If you sign up for a correspondence course on bonsai with the American Bonsai Society, the group will assign you a mentor, who will be on call to help you. Any bonsai greenhouse has a vested interest in helping you to succeed and will be very helpful. See addresses in the sidebar.

As much as I love the stark beauty of bonsai, I do not plan to get started with bonsai. I know myself and my limitations. At this point in my life I do not need a plant that needs tending to as often as a bonsai. Talking to Trudy Anderson at Mill Brook Bonsai I explained this, saying I understood that one couldn't go away and leave one's bonsai unattended. "That's right," she said, "no more than you could your children!"

More Books for the Gardener

There are few sure things in life. But buying a gardening book for a gardener is a pretty sure bet. Most gardeners like books on gardening, and most of the time most of us never have the time to read them cover to cover. But, like peonies, poppies, or posies, we often think one or two more would be nice. Since December is a time when many of us are buying presents, I thought this list might be a nice supplement to the books I mentioned earlier. These are all books I own, like, and use.

Organic Gardening Books

Four Seasons Harvest, by Eliot Coleman, Chelsea Green Press, paperback, 1999. Coleman explains how he grows vegetables in Maine all winter long in an unheated greenhouse. Coleman actually makes his living as an organic gardener in Maine. Anyone can use his techniques for a few inexpensive fresh vegetables.

The New Organic Grower, by Elliot Coleman, Chelsea Green Press, paperback, 1995. This is a good book that will tell you how to become an organic gardener. It also gives good info for those who want to garden commercially.

The Vegetable Gardener's Bible, by Ed Smith, Storey Books, 2000, paperback. Described earlier, page 186.

Rodale's Pest and Disease Problem Solver, by Linda Gilkeson, Pam Peirce, and Miranda Smith, Rodale Press, paperback, 1996. As with anything Rodale Press does, this is well done. Good photos and recomendations.

Start with the Soil, by Grace Gershuny, Rodale Press, paperback, 1993. This is a very readable basic text on organic soil preparation. I learned some very interesting things reading this.

General

The Garden Primer, by Barbara Damrosch. Described earlier, page 186.

Cold Climate Gardening, How to Extend Your Growing Season by at Least 30 Days, by Lewis Hill, Stovey Books, 1987, paperback.

Flowers

My basic reference, the one I use every day when planting, is the *Manual of Herbaceous Ornamental Plants* by Steven M. Still, Stipes Publishing Co, 1980, 1993, paperback. The 814 pages here give you all you need to know about almost any flower, giving great specific info on what any plant likes and needs. It has a few photos in the back.

Rodale's Illustrated Encyclopedia of Perennials, by Ellen Phillips and C. Colston Burrell, Rodale Press, hardback, 1993. Another *great* Rodale book, with lots of tips on growing plants, and with good photos, too. I carry it with me in my van when I go to work in other people's gardens.

The Well Tended Perennial Garden: Planting and Pruning Techniques, by Tracy DiSabato-Aust, Timber Press, 1998, hardback. I think every serious perennial gardener should have this. It tells you when to cut back, how to get a second bloom out of perennials, and lots of other good cultural information. I use it often.

The Self-Taught Gardener, Lessons from a Country Gardener, by Sydney Eddison, Viking Penguin, 1997, in paperback. A good book to read from cover to cover this winter. She is a delightful writer, and gives good, sensible advice.

Armitages's Garden Perennials, A Color Encyclopedia, by Allan M. Armitage, described earlier, page 186.

Trees and Shrubs

Manual of Woody Landscape Plants, Their Identification, Ornamental Characteristics, Propagation and Uses, by Michaael Dirr, Stipes Publishing Co., paperback or hardback, 1975, 1990, and later. This is the "bible" of woody plants. I couldn't live without it. It tells you everything you need to know to succeed with woody ornamentals. Dirr has *very* strong opinions, and generally I agree with him. Over 1000 pages, no photos in my edition, but newer ones may have them.

The American Horticultural Society's *Pruning & Training* by Christopher Brickell and David Joyce, DK Publishing, 1996, hardback. A well-illustrated book on pruning with plant-by-plant information.

Forever Green, The Dartmouth College Campus, An Arboretum of Northern Trees, by Mollie K. Hughes, Enfield Publishing, 2000, paperback. It is great to have a book that tells you where to find mature specimens of trees, so that you can see them, not just little ones in nurseries. This is good for anyone who can go to Hanover, New Hampshire, to look at trees.

Other Garden Books, Nontechnical

A Place of Beauty, The Artists and Gardens of the Cornish Colony, by Alma A. Gilbert and Judith B. Tankard, Ten Speed Press, 2000, hardback. This is a lovely book about the gardens in my hometown, illustrated nicely with old and new photos.

Deep in the Green: An Exploration of Country Pleasures by Anne Raver, Vintage Books, 1995. It is one of my favorites, even though it doesn't tell you how to garden. It uses the garden, and gardening, as a backdrop for thinking about life. Anne shares her experiences in the garden and her encounters with unusual gardeners.

My Garden [Book], by Jamaica Kincaid, Farrar Straus Giroux, 1999, hardback. This is a literary gem, an intensely personal and complicated book of essays. I love Ms. Kincaid's fiction, and found this a delight, too. Full of Latin names and complicated thoughts.

Indoor Plants

Making Things Grow, A Practical Guide for the Indoor Gardener, by Thalassa Cruso, Lyons & Burford, 1969. The best book I've seen on this topic. Interesting and informative, you can read it straight though, cover to cover. Out of print, but worth looking for.

My Friend Emily, a Very Determined Gardener

I love the holiday season. I love the bright lights on trees outdoors that outline ordinary shrubs, giving them a month of glory—even if they are badly pruned and look scraggly the rest of the year. I love the cookies, the parties, the music. But sometimes it gets to be a bit much, and it's easy to forget what all the activity is supposed to be about. So every now and then I like to take some quiet time to reflect on how lucky I really am, how blessed my life has been.

I was thinking about this recently, and thinking how much richer my life has been because of being a gardener. It also occurred to me that most of my friends are also gardeners, and that many became my friends because of our common love of growing things. Gardeners love to share gardening stories, our successes and our failures. I love writing a gardening column because it allows me to share not only my ideas, but those of my friends, and of readers who write me. And over the past year I have gained some new gardening friends though this column.

One of my new gardening friends, Emily, is one of the most determined gardeners I have ever met. Emily is a handsome woman in her early forties with short, dark hair and an engaging and frequent grin. She uses a wheelchair to get around because she suffers from a rare autoimmune disease that has destroyed her sense of balance and made her unstable on her legs. Her indomitable spirit has not been affected. And she is a remarkable gardener.

Emily was trained as an engineering geologist, and was devastated when her disease made it impossible to drive a car or to hike around the work sites as she needed to. Several years ago she lost her job, her marriage fell apart, and she realized she was going to be disabled for life. She felt herself sliding into a depression with no apparent way out. So she decided that she would devote her energies to gardening. Gardening had always been something that made Emily feel good, it always picked up her spirits if they lagged.

The first thing Emily did was to give up on any pretense of keeping clean. She made raised garden beds by crawling through the

How Emily Grows Potatoes

Emily grows potatoes above ground by creating bins 36 inches in diameter with galvanized welded steel fencing. She leaves an 18-inch opening so she can access the potatoes when sitting on the ground. Each bin is tied to bamboo stakes driven into the soil. She lines the bins with a thick layer of newspapers, then adds 4 inches of soil, upon which she puts her potato chunks. Each chunk gets two tablespoons of a 15-15-15 slow-release fertilizer mixed into the soil around it. Emily covers the potatoes with 1 to 2 inches of soil mix, and after they have started growing she mulches them with leaves. She fertilizes again with a 5-5-5 fertilizer when they are in blossom.

Soil Recipe for Potato Cages

Emily mixes her soil for container gardens and potato bins in batches, from the ingredients listed below, in a 5-foot plastic toboggan sled. She premoistens the dry soil with water from a garden hose before filling the potato cages. Each potato bin uses about eighty quarts of soil mix.

  3 parts bagged, sterilized topsoil
  1 part peat or similar organic material
  1 part compost and/or well aged horse or cow manure
  1 part clean, "traction" sand (play box sand is too fine)
  1 cup dolomitic lime, per potato cage
  1 cup bone meal, per cage
  (optional) worm castings, greensand

garden, using a hand trowel to move the earth and to dig out unwanted shrubs. She had time, and determination. She used her engineering background to find ways to do things as efficiently as possible. She devised a watering system that she can activate with a valve under the kitchen sink. She designed a wheelchair ramp wide enough for pots on the landings, and with rails that would accommodate planters. Instead of looking at the disadvantages of container gardening, she points out that slugs can't reach her bok choi and beets on the rails of her ramp.

Tomatoes are planted in big pots on the edge of the driveway where Emily can reach them from her wheelchair, thirty-five plants in total last year. Always the engineer, she figured out ways to keep the top-heavy plants from blowing over. Instead of feeling sorry for herself for leaving a career she loved, she points out that she uses engineering principles every day of her life. The tomatoes in pots are grown on her asphalt driveway, and the added heat from the black-top gave her an excellent harvest last summer, despite the lack of heat in general.

Potatoes were a challenge for Emily. She loves everything about them, from planting them to eating them, but she has found the traditional method of growing them in the ground increasingly difficult. So three years ago she built wire cages to grow them above ground. The first year she got nothing. Two years ago she modified the soil and the mulch, but only got a tiny harvest. This past summer Emily tried some new techniques and got a great potato harvest. As she points out, there is no success so sweet as one after many failed attempts. And eventually, Emily succeeds.

Growing plants in pots is different from growing them in the ground, but has its advantages. Each day in the summer when her beans are ripening, Emily picks them as she goes to get the mail: They grow up the rails of her ramp. Those that elude her eye going down, she sees coming back up. Emily always tries to see the positive in every situation. Traveling slowly gives her time to really enjoy what she has grown, and to observe the daily changes in her plants. Miracles happen every day, she says, if you open your eyes to them.

Low-maintenance plants went up the hill, farther from the driveway. She planted blueberries and raspberries there even though she doesn't eat them herself. She wanted to grow plants her friends and neighbors would enjoy.

Emily's success with plants has given her a new outlook on life. She has gotten to know her neighbors, who have come to depend on her for a supply of seedlings in the spring, and fresh vegetables in the summer. It is one way she can pay them back for all the kindness they show her in the course of a year.

And she has realized that she should not limit her aspirations. Growing up, Emily was trained as a classical musician. She thought her days on the piano were over when she could no longer use the foot pedals. But her success in the garden, overcoming the many difficulties she faced there, has helped her to believe that she can take on any new challenge. Emily is enrolled in a program studying to be an accompanist for baroque music, which doesn't require the use of the piano's foot pedals.

Although she was already an excellent gardener, this last year Emily successfully completed the nine-week course held by the University of New Hampshire Extension Service, and is a certified Master Gardener. She loves being able to help others who want to garden, particularly those with disabilities. She is an aspiring writer who just sold her first article on gardening with disabilities, and hopes to reach a wide audience this way.

Having Emily as a gardening friend has taught me much. Since Emily lives in the Concord, New Hampshire, area, I can't drop in to say hello as often as I would like, but we keep in touch by e-mail. I never cease to be amazed at her upbeat attitude, her courage, and her determination. She's a friend who teaches me more than just new gardening techniques. I count Emily's friendship as one of my blessings.

Growing Shiitake Mushrooms

I first heard about growing shiitake mushrooms from a friend who is always looking for ways to eke out a living from the land. He explained that innoculated logs will produce mushrooms on and off for three to five years. Since these mushrooms are expensive at the grocery store, it seemed like something worth trying. So I did. And although I have decided that raising mushrooms is not going to be my ticket to riches, it *is* relatively easy to grow your own mushrooms.

In order to grow shiitakes, you need some 4- to 6-inch-diameter hardwood logs cut in 3- to 4-foot lengths. Oak will yield the best results over time, but poplar (*Populus grandidentata*) will produce a little more quickly. Other good tree species include chestnut and ironwood (also known as hophornbeam, *Ostrya virginiana*). Most other hardwoods are good, but avoid fruit trees, walnut, elm, red maple, and all conifers. If you don't have trees and a chain saw, contact your local firewood dealer and explain what you need. Never use dead or fallen trees, and avoid those with badly damaged bark.

Order plug spawn from a mushroom dealer (see sidebar). These are $5/16$-inch-diameter plugs of hardwood that harbor the shiitake fungus. Get a sharp $5/16$-inch drill bit to make the holes that will accept the spawn plugs. I found a "twist bit" better than a spade or paddle bit. You need to drill holes $1\frac{1}{4}$ inch deep, so wrap your drill bit with a little tape at the appropriate place to show you how deep to drill.

For a 4-inch log, I use about fifty wooden spawn plugs, which cost me about $3. I start at one end and drill holes every 6 inches in a straight line to the other end. Then I drill a new row about 2 inches from the first, but stagger the holes so that they don't line up with the first row. I continue drilling rows of holes until I have gone around the log. Some growers space out the holes more, leaving 8 inches between them, and 3 inches between rows. I am impatient, so I use more spawn plugs to hasten the harvest.

Next, I insert the spawn plugs into the holes just drilled, tapping them in with a hammer. Finally, I seal the plugs from contamination with hot wax. The supplier of shiitake spore plugs will also sell you food-grade wax. I bought a used electric frying pan for under $10 at a junk store. I set it at 300°F, and it kept the wax just right. I applied it with an inexpensive foam paint brush. Two people working together can inoculate three or four logs in an hour.

A new development introduced from Korea involves "thimble spawn." The plugs are larger, thimble sized, and come embedded in a plastic sheet. They are installed without using wax. The have a styrofoam cap attached that keeps out stray fungus spores, instead of the wax. They are a little less expensive, and are said to to produce mushrooms sooner. I tried them and found the styrofoam caps were not well attached, so I sealed them with wax anyway.

You can inoculate logs at almost any time of the year if you follow a couple of commonsense rules. The spawn plugs should not be exposed to extremes of hot or cold. Work in the shade, as spawn is sensitive to ultraviolet radiation. Work in the cellar or the garage if it is very cold and windy. Shiitake fungus is inactive when the logs are frozen, so you may want to keep them in the cellar for a few weeks to give them a good start if you are doing this in the dead of winter.

The logs need to be stored outdoors in the shade and preferably

Tuscan Style Shiitake Mushrooms

2 tablespoon olive oil
½ cup chopped onion
½ cup water or broth
8 ounces fresh shiitake
  mushrooms
1 teaspoon sugar

1 teaspooon salt
1 tablespoon soy sauce
½ teaspooon dried savory
  (or thyme)
2 teaspoons cornstarch in ¼ cup
  cold water

Prepare mushrooms by removing stems, then tearing (not cutting) into bite-size pieces. Discard the stems, which are very tough, or use to make soup stock.

Place oil in skillet over medium heat. Add onion and sauté until slightly browned, 2 or 3 minutes.

Add liquid, then add mushrooms and cover skillet. Simmer for 30 minutes at low heat, stirring occasionally.

Mix the cornstarch in water with the salt, sugar, soy sauce, and savory. Add to skillet and stir while simmering for another 5 minutes.

Serve on a bed of freshly cooked pasta.

out of the wind. But they should not be left in contact with the earth. Put a couple of ordinary logs on the ground, and then stack your inoculated logs on top of them. Some people prefer to lean them against trees instead.

Most people are afraid of picking wild mushrooms for fear of getting poisoned. Hardwood logs that have been inoculated with commercially prepared shiitake spawn almost never grow other types of mushrooms. Most poisonous mushrooms grow in the soil, and the two common poisonous ones that will grow on wood look nothing like the shiitake. But if in doubt, go to the grocery store and buy a couple of shiitakes to bring home for comparison, if it will ease your mind.

Shiitake mushrooms have a unique flavor, unlike other mushrooms I have eaten. See above for one of my favorite recipes.

Shiitakes appear mysteriously, when they are ready and not until. The literature says they will appear "six months to a year after inoculation." You need to keep them from drying out, so you should spray or soak them if you have a prolonged period of drought.

Sources of Shiitake Spore Plugs

I got my spawn plugs from Mushroom Harvest, PO Box 5727, Athens, OH 45701. George Vaughan, the owner, is very knowledgeable and helpful. Contact him by e-mail at mushroom@frognet.net, or by phone at 740-448-6105. My 150 plugs, enough for three or four logs, cost $9.00

Hardscrabble Enterprises, Inc., PO Box 1124, Franklin, W V 26807. Paul Goland, the owner, is very helpful, and his prices are the same as given above. Contact him by e-mail at hardscrabble@mountain.net, or by phone at 304-358-2921. He supplied me with the thimble spawn.

Spring and fall are when I have harvested shiitakes. Sometimes all the logs will bear profusely, and at other times only a few mushrooms will appear. Each log should produce 2.5 to 4 pounds of shiitakes over its useful life, but this varies considerably. It's a bit like fishing: You never know what you are going to catch, nor when, but it's always a treat.

Composting: Facts or Fiction

Once upon a time there were three little pigs. One was fairly lazy, built his house of straw, watched a lot of TV, and had just six tomato plants but lots of weeds. One was your average pig, who built his house of sticks, kept the lawn looking pretty nice, had a few flowers, and grew nice veggies. Then there was the compulsive pig. He built his house of bricks, had no weeds, canned lots of tomato sauce, and made great compost in no time flat.

When it comes to a compost pile, I've generally fallen into the first category. Throw weeds and kitchen scraps into a pile and leave it to rot. Period. After an indeterminate number of years (two? three? four?) when it has all rotted, I use it. But I have lots of land, and good places to hide compost piles in various states of decay. This year I decided to become a Category III pig and build a compost pile that "cooks." And I can see why I never did it before. It's hard work.

Here is the theory of how compost piles work: If you create a nice mixture of brown and green vegetable matter, a little dirt, and just the right amount of moisture, and if you make sure there is adequate air, you will get a compost pile that is "working." Which is to say, your pile heats up enough to kill weed seeds and quickly turns kitchen scraps into fluffy, dark brown compost.

This all happens compliments of bacteria that break down organic matter. As they break down your waste, they generate heat. The more bacterial activity, the more heat. A compost pile that is working well can reach temperatures in the range of 140 to 160 degree Fahrenheit. My books tell me that weed seeds are killed by temperatures of about 140 degrees.

I started my new compost pile this summer by laying down a 3-inch layer of hay. Hay or straw is said to be good for a compost pile because the hollow stems contain air. The breakdown process is an aerobic one, requiring oxygen.

Then I layered on some sod I had removed when planting trees. Sod has the advantage of contributing both green material (which contains the nitrogen needed by the bacteria) and dirt (which contains a good supply of bacteria).

I kept layering on fresh material and hay or other dried material. Dried plants contain lots of carbon. Carbon is what is broken down and used by the bacteria as their source of energy.

Then, like the Category I composter that I really am, I turned to other tasks and let the bacteria do their own thing. But nothing happened. I waited two weeks, checking the temperature regularly with a 3-foot-long soil thermometer, but it wasn't heating up. I thought maybe it was too dry, so I hosed it down. I added more material to see if that would help. Still nothing. Hmmm. I aerated it by turning the pile, flipping it over onto a new spot next to the first. No action.

Grass clippings are said to be good for a compost pile, so I mowed the lawn and raked up a large wheelbarrow of grass, which I added to the compost pile, mixing it in carefully. This started things cooking, but it didn't last long. I had temperatures of 100 to 120 degrees for a few days, but only in the center of the pile. This wasn't working the way it was supposed to, according to the gardening books.

Everybody says manure is good for a compost pile, so I got a couple of wheelbarrows full of llama droppings and turned the pile over again, mixing in the manure and more grass clippings. Now it cooked! The temperature soared to 155 degrees! But after a few days, the pile started to cool down again, and I wasn't looking at the rich dark compost I'd been promised. Only the center of the pile got really hot.

In the course of experimenting with making good compost I learned several things. First, the bigger the pile, the more likely you are to get it cooking. My first piles were pyramidal, but I progressed to larger cylindrical piles, which heated up better. A good size for a compost pile is 3 feet high and 4 or 5 feet wide. To keep it cylindrical I surrounded the pile with posts and sticks (more work!). The outer edges never heat up very much.

You need either manure or grass clippings to get a hot compost pile, and you need a lot of it if you want to get it working for more than a few days. But even so, it is very tough to keep a pile hot. Recently I got a couple of pickup trucks full of fresh cow manure and straw that I mixed in. It heated up some, but I did not record any temperature above 115 degrees.

A hot compost pile will definitely kill seeds. I made little sachets of old pantyhose and put annual grass seeds in them, and placed them in various places in the compost pile. After a week I took them out and tried to germinate them. Those that were in a cool part of the compost pile actually started growing *in* the compost pile! But seeds that had been at 140 degrees (or higher) even for a couple of days would not germinate. Of course, this does not necessarily mean that tough weed seeds would not survive, and I still think it's a good idea to keep all seeds out of compost piles, especially as it's so hard to get the entire pile hot.

I bought a special harpoon-shaped gizmo touted as a compost-aerating tool. Don't bother. It's hard work, and I never saw the compost pile heat up after using it. A pitchfork is just fine if you want to fluff it up.

Here are a few other rules for composting: Do not add meat scraps, grease, or oil to your compost pile. Do not put dog or cat waste into it, as they can carry diseases. Whenever possible, chop up the materials to a small size to promote faster decay. I found a machete handy for chopping up big pieces of sod and tall weeds.

I am going to go back to my old way of composting. It's true that it was possible to achieve temperatures high enough to cook an egg, but unless your compost pile is your obsession, hot composting is not practical for the average gardener. The books lied to me when they made it sound easy.

Please don't get discouraged about composting. By all means do collect your leaves, grass, and other garden by-products. Pile them up, add your kitchen scraps, and eventually it will turn into great compost. You just shouldn't expect it to happen fast or count on it to kill all weeds and seeds. I think it's okay if you don't want to struggle to have a compost pile that really cooks. I'm a Category I piglet myself.

Chapter 11

January

Winter Mulching: Save Those Christmas Trees

I like keeping my Christmas tree up well into January. Its lights spread a kind of pagan cheeriness long after the holiday itself has passed. As a gardener I realize that, properly used, it is worth its weight in gold, as it can be used to protect some of my most delicate plants.

I have an English tea rose that is in its sixth winter, despite the fact that everyone I know says that "they definitely are not hardy here." Most people here treat them as annuals, and they are wonderful as such. But they can be wintered over, as can many other plants that are successful in Connecticut and points south.

After Christmas each year I take my pruning shears and cut all the branches off the tree, then use them as mulch. I bend the branches of the rose to the ground, and place a thick layer of Christmas tree branches over the rose. Then I put some hay over the branches, which further protects them from the cold and the drying effects of the wind.

Use your Christmas tree branches over any species of plant that you have had to replace after hard winters in the past. Lavender is a plant that I often lose to the cold, as I never seem to get around to covering it. I should remember to cut branches and layer on some hay after the ground freezes, but before the snows arrive each year. You don't have to have evergreen boughs; any kind of branch would help to keep the hay from matting down with rain. A thick mat of waterlogged hay can suffocate your plants and kill them as easily as the cold. Plants need oxygen even when they are dormant, and water will drown them.

This year I planted a mountain laurel (*Kalmia latifolia*), a plant I grew up with in Connecticut, but that is a little far north for its comfort here in New Hampshire. I planted it out of the wind, protected by the house. Mountain laurel doesn't lose its leaves, so it is subject to drying out if it is planted in a windy spot. I could wrap it in burlap, or Remay (spun agricultural fabric), which is the same as moving half a USDA zone to the south. I hate to pamper plants too much, but maybe if the weather guys predict a cold snap I'll relent. After all, this is its first winter. It's still a baby!

Unfortunately, I don't have enough branches to save every delicate plant, so a few disappear each year. Snow is a great insulator, but alas, we can't always depend on it. After a few nights of 20 below zero without snow cover I may lose some plants unless they are protected one way or another.

If you want to help your perennials to survive the winter, you can mulch them well with bark chips, leaves, or hay. This mulch helps to prevent the freezing and thawing that can push a plant up out of the ground, especially one planted this year (which hasn't developed an extensive a root system). The timing for doing this mulching is always tricky. For best results, let the ground freeze solid before adding any supplemental mulch. Of course, by then there may be a foot of snow on the ground, and you can't do it. Once the January thaw comes and the snow disappears, your tender perennial is vulnerable.

But don't despair if your Christmas tree has already voyaged to the great compost pile in the sky. Losing a few plants isn't all bad; it gives us a good excuse to go out and buy some new plants. Things we didn't have space for last year, but that we'd like to try.

On Becoming a Gardener

It seems to me that I was born with dirt under my fingernails. One of my earliest memories in life is in Grampy's garden, riding in his wooden wheelbarrow, trying to get back to the barn ahead of a thunderstorm. But I realize that many of you were not raised in a garden, or (worse yet) were only there for punishment—perhaps pulling weeds because of that word you didn't quite understand but that your mother overheard and *did* understand. But now if you have your own house, you may be thinking that you should at least *try* gardening. Admittedly, there is so much information about gardening available that it can be overwhelming. Where to begin?

Everyone has their own style of learning. I love reading books, and recommend them as a source of information. If you want to start a vegetable garden, there is a wonderful book called, *The Vegetable Gardener's Bible* by Ed Smith of Cabot, Vermont (Storey Books, 2000, paperback and cloth). His approach to gardening is very much like mine, so of course I like it. The book is straightforward, easy to read, and has lots of great photos. He is an organic gardener, and gets great results using wide raised beds.

If you are planning on developing your overall landscape, I like Sydney Eddison's *The Self-Taught Gardener* (Penguin, 1998). Reading this book is like sitting down with a favorite aunt who knows and loves gardening and who has time for you. She gives good advice like, "If you feel like digging up a circle in the middle of the lawn and planting marigolds, go right ahead." Or "Go out and cut down all those prickly bushes that you hate. In fact, feel free to cut to the ground any straggling shrub that you don't like." And she gives good advice about plants that will look nice and won't easily be killed by the novice.

Then, of course, there is the dreaded World Wide Web. I'm a little skeptical about learning from the Web, but I do go there occasionally for information. I find the Web overwhelming. Go to the search engine Yahoo! and you will find over a thousand sites on gardening.

One hundred and twenty-nine on organic gardening. I get very frustrated on the Web. I don't like all the ads, I don't like the waiting, I don't like somebody or something telling me what I can see. And with a click, you've lost your place. It's a bit like reading in the tub, to me. One oops, and what you're reading is gone.

The other problem I have with information on the Web is that I don't know if it is accurate or not. If I read a book or magazine article, it's probably safe to assume that it has been checked by someone besides the author. On the web any bozo can create a website (and I did) and post whatever they want (and I do). My Web site is www.gardening-guy.com. For example, this morning I went to an organic gardening site that turned out to be from Australia, where it is gardening season. There I read that a 50-50 solution of milk and water will help eradicate mildew on the leaves of peas, pumpkins, and cukes. I have never heard this before, and a quick perusal of my books of organic remedies came up with no mention of this technique. So, is it true? I don't know, but might try it. Most likely I'll just be wasting milk and money, to say nothing of time.

Maybe the best way to learn about gardening is to acquire gardening buddies: people who are passionate about gardening, and who will take time to share information with you. I collect gardening buddies the way some dogs—but not my Emily—attract fleas. Anyone who is interested in gardening knows something that I don't, and I want to learn from them, to talk gardening.

Gardening buddies will invite you to their gardens even though they have weeds. Of course, we all have weeds, but some folks think they are unique in that way, and don't want to let others see them. They are disqualified from the club. The best kind will visit you, talk gardening, and pull a few of your weeds while they do so. And then you can reciprocate. I'm always asking people I think I'm going to like if they are gardeners.

This is the season to take a class in gardening, if you are so inclined, and I highly recommend it. Some greenhouses offer classes or workshops for gardeners, as do some of the county extension services, and some gardening clubs. Sign up for as many as you can afford or have time for. Most gardening clubs have monthly meetings with excellent speakers, and are inexpensive to join. You will always learn something, even if you already are a gardener. And who knows, you might meet a new Gardening Buddy.

Later on, when it is gardening season, you might volunteer to help out at a public garden. Many nonprofit gardens solicit free help. They will offer you the chance to work with experienced gardeners in exchange for some time spent weeding and doing other menial tasks. You will learn the difference between a weed and a flower, and how to "dead head" spent blossoms. If you are lucky, you'll learn the Latin names and the cultural preferences of dozens of plants you might not otherwise encounter. Enquire at your local gardening center, library, or garden club about what opportunities might be available near you for volunteering.

Ultimately, the best way to learn to be a gardener is to, as they say in the ad, "Just do it!" Read, talk, plan this winter, then plunge into it. Start small, don't be afraid to make mistakes, ask questions, and enjoy. For me, gardening is one of life's greatest pleasures.

Beware of Orchids

Reading about orchids and talking to people who grow orchids have made me aware that there is a certain danger involved in buying an orchid. No, they are not carriers of rare tropical diseases, nor will they cause you to break out in a rash on contact. Simply put, they take over the lives of people much the way space aliens take charge of human minds in bad sci-fi movies. During the mid 1800s, orchid mania took hold in Europe, and people paid absurd prices and took extravagant risks to collect rare orchids. Little was known at that time about what was required to make these exotic plants bloom, but that did not deter orchid fanciers.

Even here, in rurual New Hampshire, we have our own orchid fanatics. In 1978 Paul Sawyer was a traffic engineer in Cambridge, Massachusetts, when he bought his first orchid. Three years later he had given up his job, put aside his technical training, and he and his wife opened Sawyer's Exotic Greenhouse in Grafton, New Hampshire. Ten years ago Bob Sullivan of Newport, New Hampshire, was given his first orchid. Today he grows about 250 orchids in his home under a 1,000-watt metal halide lamp in a room whose walls are now lined with a space-age reflective material. Thirty years ago a friend gave Margie Cook of Thetford, Vermont; her first orchid. Today she has a greenhouse attached to her house with about 200 orchids in it. In this season virtually every flat surface in her house has a lovely orchid in bloom on display. So reader, beware: buying an orchid can be addictive.

One deterrent for many people is the fact that most orchids don't have common names. Latin names intimidate many people, even avid gardeners. As a plantsman I have come to appreciate Latin names because they avoid the confusion bred by common names. But we often use simple names. Black-eyed Susan rolls off the tongue much more easily than *Rudbekia hirta* var. *pulcherrima*, for example. There are so many species of orchids and orchid hybrids that common names just are not a practical way of naming them. There is a book that is nine thick volumes long that merely names the orchids. No descriptions, just nine volumes of names. There are over 25,000 species of orchids, and countless registered hybrid crosses.

Many people who grow plants outdoors in summer and enjoy houseplants all year are reluctant to try orchids because they think of orchids as being delicate, expensive, and requiring the environment of a tropical jungle. They are wrong on all three accounts. Granted, there are orchids that fit one or more of those categories, but the majority of orchids sold today do not. In a recent visit to Sawyer's Exotic Greenhouse I found a great selection of gorgeous orchids in the $20 to $30 price range, and many of them are practically "bulletproof."

It is true that years ago orchids were much more finicky than they are today. Orchids that were collected in remote lands still wanted the conditions of home. Today selling orchids is big business, and growers have come a long way toward producing the carefree orchid that will be happy on your windowsill. This is possible because orchids can be crossbred to produce new forms that have characteristics of their parents. Orchids are some of the few living things that can be cross bred even between species with different numbers of chromosomes, which leads to great variety.

Breeders find a plant that is tolerant of low humidity, for example, and cross it with a plant that likes high humidity but has a better looking flower, and the offspring . . . well, if the grower is lucky, they are gorgeous plants that will thrive despite a woodstove in the house.

So what does one need in order to grow an orchid? It varies tremendously, but start off with a sunny windowsill. Some orchids will need supplemental lighting, particularly if they do not receive much direct sunlight. There are many books on orchids that will tell you how much light your plant needs, and most orchid retailers will be more than happy to discuss the particular needs of any orchid *before* you buy it.

Adding humidity in winter will make your orchid happier, although many of us already have humidifiers because we feel better if our environment is not like the Sahara. Placing your plant on a dish of stones and water will increase humidity right around it. Most like to be misted daily, particularly when they are in flower. Flowers have a lot of surface area, and hence lose more water due to evaporation, and the narrow flower stalks can only carry so much water to them each day. Misting will prolong the life of the bloom.

Nearly all orchids in the wild grow attached to trees. They get water when it rains, then dry out completely, then are drenched again. So we grow orchids in bark chips or peat moss to replicate this environment. *Do not overwater your orchid.* Most orchids are not so fragile that forgetting to water them on their weekly schedule will do any harm. Orchids in the wild are often tree dwellers, so they like a breeze, and hate stale air. If you get serious about orchids, you will want to provide them with a fan for air circulation.

Because the potting medium doesn't offer orchids any nutrients, it is important to fertilize them. This is easily done by diluting to one half strength any of a variety of commercially available fertilizers. Water your plant before you fertilize it, letting the water run right through the potting medium.

Talking to successful orchid growers, I learned that the most important season for orchids is the summer. For most it means moving them outside, and giving them extra water and food. Summer is when they do their vegetative growth in order to bloom in the winter. Most will be happy in dappled shade, but some need to move out from shade to full sun. Be careful: Orchids can sunburn as easily as you do, so never put one (or any houseplant) directly in the sun without toughening it up first.

Most, but not all, orchids need some very cool nights outside for a couple of weeks in order to stimulate them to put out flower spikes. Most orchids also like a daily fluctuation of 10 to 15 degrees to stimulate their pores to open and close. Growing them on a windowsill will usually provide this temperature change.

Orchids certainly arouse strong feelings. As one orchid lover said vigorously, "There are dirt plants, and then there are *orchids*." This dirt plant grower has been convinced, I'm ready to try a few more orchids. But I won't get obsessed . . . honest!

Reflections on the Winter Landscape

Winter in New England provides a minimalist's view of the world. Bright colors are largely gone. Flowers and most leaves have disappeared. We have just the "bones" of our gardens to look at. The next sunny day you might enjoy walking around your property to see what permanent features are present, and to think about what you might wish to add. Some gardeners focus just on their flowers, but adding trees, shrubs, stonework, or sculpted embankments can make a garden more interesting, especially in the off-seasons. Now is a good time to do some looking around, and to do some planning.

If your landscape is a barren and flat snowscape, you may wish to think about adding some items next summer to provide winter interest. This could be done in a variety of ways. First, perhaps, ask yourself a few questions.

Are you happy with the ways things look now, and in the other seasons? Do you like spending time in the garden? How do you use your yard? Can you give up a little lawn to add items of visual interest? If you have children, you will not want to use up too much of their play space. But if your lawn is full of crabgrass, dead spots, and dandelions, you might not miss a little grass in order to add some diversity.

What are your needs for privacy? Would it be nice to screen out your yard from the hawklike eyes of a busybody neighbor? This could be accomplished by planting trees or a hedge. Instead of thinking in straight lines, how about something with curves? Imagine a few taller trees in the background, with medium and smaller sized trees or shrubs in front of those. The corner of your lot could become a thicket. A multitextured background is soothing to the eyes, comforting to the soul. Flowering shrubs can provide color, pleasing smells, and berries for birds.

I recommend making a scale drawing of your yard to help you design a major change. It is one thing to add a few petunias, and another thing to spend hundreds of dollars on trees or bulldozer work. Start by measuring the yard, and drawing it on paper. This will take some time, but you don't have to be accurate down to the last inch. Sixty paces by forty paces is good enough.

Make several photocopies of your map so that you can try different designs. Working with a pencil, draw the house and driveway first. Then add existing walkways. Are they satisfactory? If you have several ways to approach the house, the walkway to the door you want used should be bold and direct. Meandering paths through and around flower gardens are fine, but teenagers and FedEx guys want a straight shot. A wide walkway invites use. Although you may enter the house through the garage, visitors generally won't. Draw changes as needed.

Next draw some full-sized trees. Spacing is important, and you might want to visit a neighbor's property or a public park to get an idea of the space a full-sized specimen requires. Look at the trees to see if you like their shape, branching, texture. Get a book from your library and read up on trees that might be candidates for your yard. Note if they are fast or slow growing, and if they have any "bad habits."

For example, the fruit of the female ginkgo tree is quite noxious smelling. Willows (*Salix* spp.) and boxelder (*Acer negundo*) are fragile, with branches easily broken in an ice or wind storm. Norway maples (*Acer platanoides*) are fast growing, but their roots can suck the nutrition out of your soil even at great distances. These are the kinds of problems a wise neighbor or a good book can tell you about.

Then draw in some shrubs. Try to think past evergreen muffins often planted in front of the house. Add them in clusters, perhaps creating islands or peninsulas. Incorporate them in existing flower beds, or in new beds you plan to create. You don't have to choose them all right now; winter is the time for your reading and research. And go look at shrubs others are growing. If they please you, find out what they are. Choose some that look good to you in winter.

Creating terraces and building stone retaining walls can accent plants quite dramatically and be handsome all year long. Stonework in gardens adds texture and a feeling of stability and permanence. Most plants look good in front of stonework. Just as trees stand out well against snow, flowers show up nicely against a backdrop of granite or slate. In order to use stone retaining walls, you may need the help of a bulldozer or backhoe.

Creating mounds or berms by bringing in soil can enhance a landscape by adding a three-dimensional element to a flat landscape, and can create a reason for a stone retaining wall. Bringing in good topsoil can also make starting a new flower bed easier if you have terrible soil.

Boulders or an arrangement of large stones can look wonderful, but need to be incorporated into a larger plan. Dropping one or two boulders on an otherwise empty lot looks funny to my eye. But they can seem natural and pleasing if surrounded by perennials of differing heights and a shrub or two.

Ornamental grasses are becoming popular landscape plants. Now is the time they look best to my eye, perhaps because there is little other plant material in the garden. They flutter in the breeze, creating ballet above the snow. Visit your neighbors to see if they have grasses that look good now, and see how they placed them in the garden.

I was talking to a gardening friend recently who said she likes to go outside in winter to pick a few dried stems of grasses and the sturdy perennials she left standing. I like the concept: the January bouquet. Instead of just planning for spring, Doris is out in her garden looking at the beauty of the winter "soldiers" still standing proudly on duty, and inviting a few indoors to keep her company during afternoon tea.

So have a look around your own gardens. Try to sharpen your skills of observation so that you can take pleasure in what you see, even at this time of year. And do some planning for the spring. But remember, it takes time to transform a landscape, three years or more. Hopefully the planning and anticipation will help you get through the dark days of winter.

A Visit with a Sculptress of Bonsai

Daphne Gratiot is a serious gardener. She grows all kinds of flowers, vegetables, decorative trees and shrubs, and exquisite houseplants. She also creates bonsai, practicing the ancient Japanese art of training miniature trees into living sculpture.

I recently went to visit Daphne Gratiot at her home in Pomfret, Vermont. I wanted to talk gardening and to learn more about bonsai. And I'm always interested to see what serious gardeners do to get through New England winters while maintaining their good humor and keeping their green thumbs dirty.

As a sculptor and cabinetmaker, Daphne Gratiot already had two of the prerequisites for being good at creating bonsai: She has an artist's eye, and capable, practical hands. She also has patience, which is good, because there is no such thing as instant bonsai, not unless you buy one that someone else has already trained and formed. But that gets expensive, and is not nearly as satisfying.

Bonsai requires more than just an understanding of how to grow plants. To do it well, you must be able to see into the future, to be able to envision what a plant can become. Then you must be able to train the plant to fit that ideal. Like a good parent working with a child, you must see the potential.

You need not spend much money on plants and equipment, but you must accept the responsibility of a living being that will depend on you for the rest of its life, or yours. In Japan, bonsai are often passed on from one generation to the next. Yet ignoring the needs (for water) of the plant for just a day in the summer can result in death.

During the winter months deciduous bonsai are dormant, and Daphne's live in an insulated cold box she built for them. If left outside their pottery containers would probably break, so she keeps them indoors in the dark, at 30 to 40°F.

Evergreen bonsai, including her azaleas (which do not lose their leaves in the fall), are chugging along at a slow pace, not dormant, but not growing much. Daphne has a north-facing workshop where she keeps her bonsai in the winter, and she maintains it at around 50°F. Even so, she must water every two or three days. Bonsai have very minimal root systems for their size, and are kept in very small pots with a growing medium that does not hold much water. In the summer she waters every day, even twice a day if it is hot. She keeps her bonsai outdoors in the summer, literally on pedestals, under a shady trellis.

Twelve or thirteen years ago Daphne Gratiot began experimenting with bonsai. She began by using native trees, red maple (*Acer rubrum*), American hornbeam (*Carpinus caroliniana*), hemlocks (*Tsuga canadensis*), and even apples. She read books about bonsai, took a class, and also applied the knowledge she had gained from a lifetime of working with plants. She understood that she had to balance the root size with the top growth, and wasn't afraid to prune either.

Once she decided that bonsai were for her, Daphne bought a few small plants that are popular for their blooms. Her favorites, and the most dramatic, are the azaleas. Most of Daphne's azaleas are a type called Satzuki azaleas, which bloom in May. Despite the diminutive

Reference Books

Here are three books that Daphne Gratiot recommends:

The Beginner's Guide to American Bonsai, by Jerald P. Stowell, Kodanshe International, 1998 (distributed through Harper and Row), paperback.

Bonsai, a Care Manual, by Colin Lewis, Laurel Glen Publishing, 1997, cloth.

Bonsai, Its Art, Science, History and Philosophy, by Deborah R. Koreshoff, Timber Press, 1997. Daphne calls this "the bible of bonsai."

---

size of the trees, the blossoms are full sized, from ¾ to 1½ inches across. They come in a variety of colors, mostly reds and pinks, some of them "shot through" with stripes of a second color. The Japanese have a name for each color combination.

Spring is when bonsai do most of their growth. It also is the time when Daphne wraps certain branches with wire, forcing them to hold the pose she wants. She explained to me that the wires are never permanent; they must be removed after as little as six weeks, depending on how fast the bonsai grow. After her azaleas bloom each spring, Daphne prunes their roots. Although bonsai specialists have guidelines for how a tree should be trained, Daphne follows no formula. "I do what is pleasing for me," she said.

The bonsai in Daphne's simple workshop are not pampered. She is attentive to her plants, and observant, but said very straightforwardly, "If they don't like what I give them, they don't survive in my household." Nor does she believe in spending money unnecessarily. "I do things with what I have. You don't have to have the fanciest tools in the book." So I saw her using things like an ordinary paintbrush and a toothbrush for cleaning up her plants, instead of imported bonsai rakes and brushes.

She starts most of her plants from cuttings she takes off her plants. This allows her to try different techniques with her bonsai without the expense of buying new plants every year. Over the past dozen years Daphne has only purchased perhaps a dozen plants, but has many times that number growing. She grows some forest scenes with eleven to seventeen miniature trees in a single pot.

Daphne showed me an azalea called Tiny Dancer, a name that I thought appropriate. Like many bonsai, it reminds me of a ballet dancer, frozen in place. Maybe that is the allure. One can sculpt these trees, but one can also make them dance, even if our knees and hips and backs keep us from dancing.

Chapter 12

February

Beyond Flowers: A Gardener Enjoys the Winter Landscape

Our winter snows have transformed the landscape for me, and I can see things today that weren't noticeable earlier this winter. Trees and shrubs stand out against a white backdrop just as paintings or sculpture stand out against a pale backdrop in an art gallery. This is an excellent time to take a good look at trees and shrubs in your yard, the "bones" of your garden, so that you can determine if some new plantings need to occur later this year.

Some people enjoy their gardens in spring, fall, and summer, but take no notice of them in winter. Living in New England I think it behooves us to enjoy these cold and snowy months, and to focus on the stark beauty that is—or can be—out there for us to enjoy. If you have never taken time to focus your gaze on the living winter sculpture outdoors, you should. Just as a black-and-white portrait can be hauntingly beautiful, the winter landscape can be glorious in its austere beauty, particularly on a sunny day. Good photography depends on contrasts to make a subject stand out. At this time of year we have excellent contrasts in our gardens outdoors.

For the winter couch potatoes among us I say, look up from your book and study the winter landscape from your windows. Look out windows where you spend some time: from your easy chair, the kitchen sink, the table where you eat, perhaps from your bed. If you don't see any living things that are beautiful and interesting, it is no wonder that you haven't enjoyed the winter landscape. Most of us spend little or no time in the flower garden in winter, but we should be able to enjoy living sculpture from inside the house, and from our cars as we approach the house. We can make some plans now.

If you aren't pleased with what you see from the windows, you need to make some decisions about what you want to see. The best way to figure this out is to observe plantings elsewhere. Visit your neighbors, preferably on foot. When you find something pleasing to your eye, find out what it is and how long it took to get that size. Ask where they got it and how much effort went into making it look like that. I have been known to knock on the doors of strangers to ask questions about plants, and have never been rebuffed. Most gardeners are extremely flattered to be asked about their gardens, and will share their information with you at length. Visit public gardens; notice trees in public places.

It is only in recent years that I trained my eye to appreciate the form of trees and shrubs. As a younger man I focused on colors. I grew flowers, lots of flowers. I used flowers to create moods and spaces. But when winter came I stopped paying attention. It really was only when I learned to prune that I appreciated how beautiful a shrub can be in its "off" season. An unpruned shrub can be as untidy and displeasing as an unmade bed, but a well-trained shrub is a delight. Many people never prune, or don't prune enough, so that their shrubs are cluttered. Our eyes see a mass of twigs, rather than graceful branches that stand out in contrast to the snow. Look at your shrubs: Are there interesting shapes to enjoy, or are they amorphous blobs?

The classic vase-shaped form of an old Pee Gee hydrangea (*Hydrangea paniculata Grandiflora*) still clinging onto some of its snowball-like blossoms pleases my eye. I like the pendulous hanging branches of a weeping crab apple, or a Camperdown elm. I like trellises and garden arches even though the plants themselves may not be noticeable now. The rose trellis reminds me that June will be here before too long, and that red fragrant roses will again entice me into the garden.

Evergreen foundation plantings gave shrubbery a bad name for me. I grew up with unruly muffin-shaped green things that quickly got tall enough to start blocking the windows and, according to my Mom, "giving the burglars a place to hide." So every now and then my mother would instruct me to whack them back, and I did. With a vengeance. Don't have a teenager do your pruning if you want the shrubs to look good.

The absolutely worst way to buy trees and shrubs is to impulse buy. You see a cute little purple-leaved Norway maple, and bring it home. You plunk it in the ground in the front yard, and voila—fifteen years later your yard is shady and nothing else will grow near the tree, including the lawn. Evergreens like mugo pines or cute little blue spruce are snugged up to the foundation of the house, and before the kids are in college you have to hire a backhoe to yank them out. There are many miniature and slow-growing trees and shrubs that can be purchased locally and won't turn into creatures from Jurassic Park. The key is to do your homework, and what better time than now?

Fruit trees are, in my opinion, underutilized as decorative landscape plants. Crabapples are commonly planted and can be a delight. The flowers are pretty, and the fruit is lovely to look at and to feed the winter birds. But there are many apples, plums, pears, and even some peaches that are hardy, handsome, and tasty too! There are dwarf and semidwarf varieties that will start bearing fruit within three to five years of planting, and that will not shade out or dominate your garden. But again I stress, find out how big they will be, and what growing conditions they need. I recommend buying from a knowledgeable local nursery. Chain stores may be cheaper, but you won't usually get good answers to your questions.

Here are a few plants that I like in the winter:

American cranberrybush viburnum (*Viburnum trilobum*) is not related to cranberries, but has lovely red edible berries that persist into the winter. It will do well in either sun or partial shade. Eight to twelve feet tall and wide when mature. There are lots of other nice viburnums available, some of which keep berries into winter.

Common winterberry (*Ilex verticillata*) is another red-berried bush. It is our native holly and in nature it is found in swamps and wet places, often along roadsides. Unlike English holly, it loses its leaves (which are unremarkable) in the fall. You need one male plant for every five females or you won't get the berries. Six to ten feet tall and wide, sometimes more in the wild.

Shadbush or downy serviceberry (*Amelanchier arborea*) is a small tree, growing 15 to 25 feet tall. I like its shape, and its bark in winter, and the fact that it is the first tree to bloom in spring. It needs careful pruning when young to keep it from filling in with too many branches, which mask its nice form.

American beech (*Fagus grandifolia*) will grow into a full sized tree, 50 to 75 feet tall, but is relatively slow growing, gaining 9 to 12 feet in ten years. I particularly like the gray bark as it stands out against the snow, and the delicate branching of young trees. Young trees hold onto some of their light brown leaves throughout most of the winter. It prefers full sun, and will not withstand compacted or wet soils. Not everybody has a place for this magnificent tree, so enjoy them in the woods if you ski. Or you might risk putting one in partial shade. I often observe small ones in the woods, almost as if they are natural bonsai plants when grown in the shade. Certainly they are slower growing in the shade.

Redosier dogwood (*Cornus sericea*) is a multistemmed shrub that has very bright red stems, particularly on new growth, so it needs pruning every year. It is a very tough plant, fast growing, and it will send up shoots from its spreading root system. Winter is its best season. It grows 7 to 9 feet tall and spreads to 10 feet wide.

We can't work in the garden now, but we can certainly dream. I dream about the magnolia (*Magnolia* × *loebneri* "Merrill") that I planted last June. It had but one flower when I bought it, but it was as beautiful as any orchid I have ever seen. I have pampered this young tree and dream of seeing it with dozens of lovely blooms. It won't be so long before that happens, and in the meantime I can see it silhouetted against the snow as I look out the kitchen window, and it gives me great pleasure.

On Growing Houseplants

Winters can be long and drab in New England, and some of my gardening buddies suffer from something I call CLAGS. CLAGS is my acronym for Chronic Lack of Adequate Gardening Syndrome. The symptoms of CLAGS often include, but are not limited to, crankiness, declining sense of humor, and increasing dependence on seed catalogs as a source of entertainment. Severe cases can lead to costly cures involving building of sunrooms or greenhouses, or trips to the tropics. Chocolate may be therapeutic for CLAGS sufferers, but my research on this is not yet complete.

Most of my gardening friends avoid CLAGS by puttering with houseplants, and I recommend it as therapy. There is a portion of the population, however, that resists buying houseplants, thinking that the plants are too much trouble, or that they have "brown thumbs." In my view, houseplants are much cheaper than paying a therapist, and they have been scientifically proven to improve the quality of the air in your house!

There is no reason not to have houseplants in the winter, nice things with blossoms on them. Go to the supermarket, buy something in bloom, and it will probably please you for a week or two, gardener or not. I like cheery little daffodils. Read the tag, follow the directions, and when it stops blooming feel free to put it outside at 20 below. You did not sign up to be its parent for the rest of your life. However, many of the bulb plants like daffodils can be recycled in the spring if you keep them alive till then.

If you want to have something special, go to a florist or garden center, and have a chat with a knowledgeable sales person. There are absolutely splendid plants that you can raise quite easily, depending on your home environment. The questions you need to ask before pulling out your charge card are these: How much light does it need? How much humidity does it want? What temperatures does it require at day, and at night? Then you need to ask yourself if you can provide what it requires.

For example, African violets can be gorgeous. My mother does

Bernie Johnson

My friend Bernice Johnson of Cornish Flat, New Hampshire; grows a lot of houseplants, sometimes keeping more than 100 at any given moment. She propagates them so that she has enough to give away to anyone who could use a pick-me-up. I asked her for advice on houseplants and she gave me this: "Don't fuss with them too much. Give them water when they need it, and don't fertilize too much in the winter." Bernie puts all her houseplants out on the north side of the house for the summer, where they fend for themselves.

Prime among her plants are the Christmas cacti and orchid cacti that she has been growing for more than forty years. To propagate them she cuts off a healthy 4-inch piece and puts it in a sealed plastic bag. She puts the bag in a kitchen drawer and leaves it there till the cutting starts to wither and sends out a shoot. Then she plants it in a pot and it begins to grow.

well with them, but I do not. Why? Her house stays warmer than mine, which cools down to the low sixties at night. African violets don't like temperatures below 65°F, and will even complain if you water them with cold tap water. So I've given up on African violets. I could probably figure out a way to accommodate them, but haven't bothered.

The biggest cause of houseplant failure is bad watering. More is not better. Soggy conditions cause root rot, and sometimes plants can actually drown. So water when the soil is dry to the touch. Small things can be picked up and the weight judged. A dry plant doesn't weigh as much as a moist one. For many things, watering once a week is fine. But learn to really look at your plants, especially when they are new to you, or when the seasons are changing.

If the leaves start to go limp due to dryness, run, do not walk, to the faucet. But be sure that your pot does not end up sitting in a saucer of water, as it may wick the water back up, preventing the pot from ever drying out. Yellowing of the lower leaves is often a sign of overwatering, and may be followed by compete collapse and death.

Some plants do not like water from the faucet that has chlorine. Leave a pitcher of water out overnight before using it, as this allows chlorine to evaporate. Fluoride in the water does not dissipate this way, and some plants will suffer leaf tip die-back because of fluoride in the water. You can either buy jugs of spring water, or choose other plants. Ask a neighbor who is good with houseplants for advice if you are not sure what will do well for you with your tap water.

Be aware that as spring arrives your plants may start a growth spurt. Just like your teenagers, they will require more input when they are growing rapidly. Twice-a-week watering should start for your rosemary plants about now, for example, or you may lose them. Clay pots dry out much faster than plastic pots, and smaller pots more rapidly than big pots.

Plants do best when they have a continuous, even growth pattern. Bursts of sudden green growth stimulated by a shot of soluble nitrogen fertilizer are not as good for your plants as a constant supply of nutrition from an organic fertilizer. I like Neptune's Harvest Liquid Fish. It's not nearly as pretty as the blue stuff, and it *does* smell like fish when you mix it up. But it doesn't make the house smell like fish, nor does it attract cats. It is a nice, slow, gentle fertilizer.

Stop-and-go growth should be avoided, but that is what some fast-acting fertilizers promote, depending on how often you fertilize, and how much you use. Obviously there are people who do just fine with the blue liquid. But if you go that route, remember that more is not better.

How much light your plant needs is also critical. There are plants that will do just fine with ambient light, but these are generally foliage plants. Serious houseplant aficionados usually supplement our feeble winter light with some fluorescent lighting. Plants grown with cool-white fluorescent bulbs will do fine, but probably won't blossom for you. Use one cool-white and one daylight or warm-white tube in a two-tube fixture, and you should get blossoms. You can use cool-white tubes with some added incandescent light and get blooms, I've read.

If you use lights, don't leave them on twenty-four hours a day; plants need their rest, too. Twelve to fourteen hours of light is all they need. Lights will also dry out your plants more quickly.

Most plants like a dip in temperature at night. If you don't set back your thermostat, you can accomplish the same effect by growing them on a windowsill. A drop of 5 to 8 degrees is ideal for most plants.

Unfortunately, the best book I've ever seen on growing houseplants is out of print, though some used bookstores will have it, and most libraries. It is Thalassa Cruso's book *Making Things Grow, A Practical Guide for the Indoor Gardener*. She has a wonderful, chatty style, and the book is full of good advice, good explanations, and useful information about most houseplants.

Although I have lots of houseplants, I'll have to admit that growing them isn't really an adequate substitute for working outside in my *real* gardens. It won't be long before my snowdrops will be blooming, then the crocus, and before long a whole symphony of colors and textures and smells. In the meantime, I'd better go mix up some fish solution, and maybe have a piece of chocolate, just to be on the safe side.

Getting a Gardener through the Winter Blahs

Although I consider myself a serious gardener, I love the winter. According to my definition, winter includes snow, and we have had plenty of it for most of the winter. Snow to cross-country ski on, snow to protect our tender plants, snow to cover up the dog dirt and general griminess. There is something restorative about the quality of light in the late afternoon on a snowy field. But snow or no snow, many gardeners just don't like winter. And by now I am ready for it to go away.

So what's a gardener to do? Commiserate, for starters. On a bright, cold, snowy Saturday recently I got on the phone to friends who are also gardeners to ask them what they were doing about the blahs. "Dreaming about the Bahamas," said one glibly, knowing full well that the Bahamas were not in her budget this year. "But seriously," I countered. "Well, actually I have my catalogs out and I'm drooling over the pictures," she said. "And I'm trying to decide which flowers to get, and how many I can squeeze into the existing beds. You know I never have enough space, but . . ." We talked plants and plans and what this winter will do to our perennial beds, and I felt my lagging spirits pick up.

The next person I called was also planning on spending her Saturday messing about with garden stuff. "I'm going to organize my leftover seeds today. I always keep the seeds I don't use, but then I don't use them the next year. So I'm going to throw out the really old ones, and sort out the good ones. I have this plastic container with little compartments just right for . . ." And so on. We agreed that one- or two-year-old vegetable seeds would be okay to use, and for flowers even the three-year-old seeds would be worth keeping. It is generally considered a crisis if we don't have enough heirloom tomato plants, but less so if the cosmos are a bit sparse.

Last year I found an unopened package of Ma Perkins Sungold Sunflower seeds that were packed in 1943, and although I understood that there was not a snowball's chance in . . . the furnace . . . that they would germinate, I decided that I had to plant them anyway. It's part of the fun of being a gardener. We play in the dirt, we dream, and we are optimists. I hope I never outgrow any of that. They never germinated, but you knew that anyway.

Meanwhile, this is a good time to work on your garden tools if you didn't have time to do that last fall. Bring them into the basement to warm up, and get all of last season's dirt off them. Depending on how much time they spent outside in the sun and rain last summer, they might benefit from some TLC (tender loving care). Are the handles rough and dry? Start by giving them a light sanding with some 100-grit sandpaper until smooth. Then apply a coat of boiled linseed oil to the wood handles, or more than one coat if they really suck it up. Leave them near the furnace, and polish them up after a few days.

Use steel wool to get any rust off your tools, and wipe them with a rag that has been moistened with sewing machine oil. If you are handy with things you might even take a flat file and sharpen the edges of your shovels and hoes. Remember that you are not sharpening a kitchen knife: Don't make them too sharp or they will dull quickly. Check out the angle of a new spade or hoe at the hardware store to get an idea of what angle to use, and how they should look.

It is still way too early to start most seedlings for summer planting, but if you are going a bit squirrely, there are seedlings you could try. Lisianthus, for example, is a lesser-known annual that takes 180 days from planting to flowering. It is a wonderful pastel cut flower that looks good in a vase for up to two weeks. I tried it one year largely because a professional grower told me I'd never succeed. Harumph. I like a challenge.

It takes eighteen days to germinate lisianthus at a constant temperature of 72 degrees, which I took as a good excuse to keep my bathroom warmer than usual. After the seeds germinated, I set up fluorescent lights over the seedlings and stood back, waiting for growth. I watched as these tiny plants sat there and didn't do much for weeks and weeks. They sulked, like a teenager asked to eat a healthy breakfast or put on more appropriate clothing for school. After three months they were the size of week-old radish plants. Very discouraging.

But finally they took off in the warmth of the summer garden, and were worth the effort. Well actually, now I find it easier to buy them from a grower who offers them in small individual pots at a dollar each. I just don't have the dozens I had that summer. Maybe I'll try them again this year.

Artichokes actually do quite well in New England, though you have to play tricks with them. I start mine in February and grow them in a room that is about 65°F for six weeks. Then I move them to a cooler location, growing them at 45° to 50°F for four to six weeks. This makes them think it is winter. When you put them out in the warm sun, they are in their "second summer" and ready to produce artichokes for you.

A gardening friend of mine counts the days till the first of April, which is spring for most of us. Daffodils and crocus should be blooming by then, and the smell of fresh earth will be in the air. It's not so far off, really. But who's counting? I haven't had time to order all my seeds yet.

Gardening Tricks from the Smiths

One clear cold day I tracked down Ed Smith, of Cabot, Vermont, to talk gardening. Ed authored a book, *The Vegetable Gardener's Bible*

(Storey Books, 2000, paperback, and cloth), that I consider one of the best gardening books to come out in years. So I had called him and made arrangements to meet, and to talk about gardening.

Some years ago Ed and his wife, Sylvia, decided that they wanted to live a simple and healthy life. They built their own house, which is not connected to the electrical grid for power. They homeschool their children. They developed gardening systems that work in Vermont and that require no chemical inputs.

The entire family is involved in the gardens, raising and preserving much of their own food. The kids do not view gardening as a chore, but rather as a normal part of life, as part of their responsibilities as members of the family. They have grown up in the garden. Their mulching system works so well that there is little weeding to be done, which eliminates much of the drudgery that often lands on children.

The children are encouraged to experiment in the garden. Last summer Lindsey tried growing a zuchetta, or trumpet zucchini, and won first prize with one in the "Unusual Vegetables" category at the Tunbridge Fair. She said it was very productive, and was great in her zucchini chocolate cake recipe. Nathan tried placing rotting apples underneath his tomato plants to see if the gases released would hasten ripening as he had heard, though the results were ambiguous.

The key to good production, they all agreed, is to build a healthy soil—one that is full of organic matter, earthworms, and other living things. They said it should be a light, loose soil that allows air and water to penetrate and permits roots to travel far and wide. "It's compost, compost, compost," Ed explained. They are strictly organic, using no chemical fertilizers or pesticides.

They also are proponents of wide raised beds, as they know that this makes for good deep loose soil. Compacted soil inhibits root growth. They mulch their walkways heavily with newspapers and straw, which keeps down the weeds and nourishes the soil.

I'm always asking good gardeners about tricks they use to get better results, and the Smiths came up with the following list.

1. Tomatoes. If you start your own plants from seed, pat your seedlings daily, the way you would your dog. This stimulates a production of a hormone (cytokinin) that encourages strong stems and helps prevent legginess. Don't buy plants in six-packs that already have blossoms on them—the blossoms are a response to stress. If you start your own, transplant them into bigger pots if they start to get rootbound. But don't start too early; six-week-old plants are best.

2. Lettuce. Sylvia said she believes it is best to start lettuce seeds in flats, then transplant. People tend to sow lettuce in a row, and the tiny seeds are too close together, so they fight for nutrients. She spaces individual plants 6 to 8 inches apart. Two other tricks: She alternates red-and green-leaved lettuces in her row, as this is visually pleasing. Often she transplants lettuce alongside the peas she has just planted. The lettuce shades the roots of the peas, which benefit from that. The peas fix nitrogen with their roots, which helps the lettuces. She said she only plants lettuces on one side of the peas, the sunnier side.

3. Onions. Onions do best if started in February by seed in the house. Give them a haircut when they are about 6 inches tall, taking off 2 to 3 inches, and the roots will benefit. Seedlings can be purchased by mail order, and these do well, too. And onions love water. Their roots are very shallow, so mulch them well with grass clippings and give supplemental water, even at times your other plants don't ask for it. Plant early for best results.

4. Basil. Prune it early and often, and eat the trimmings.

Cutting it back will make it branch more, and it won't flower as early. Basil turns a little bitter when it flowers, but is still edible, of course.

5. Eggplant. The northern states do not have a climate conducive to growing eggplants. But if you are determined to grow them, do everything you can to provide extra heat. Row covers made of spun agricultural fabric (or Remay) can be used to help contain heat and keep off the potato beetles that love eggplants. Ed suggests making hoops over the eggplants for the Remay, and leaving the fabric on even when the plants are in bloom, as they are not pollinated by insects.

6. Potatoes. If some of last year's potatoes escaped your vigilant eye (and the cookstove) they will start growing earlier than your others. Watch those plants carefully, as the Colorado potato beetles will show up there first. Be sure to pick them off before they start reproducing. Look under the leaves, too, not just on top. The Smiths plant potatoes using a posthole digger, then back fill the hole as the plant grows. They think this is easier than mounding up, or hilling the potatoes.

7. Peppers. "Let your peppers hold hands," Ed told me—which means, plant them close enough that their leaves touch when mature. Peppers need lots of heat, so grow them in a coldframe until they blossom, then remove the coldframe. Otherwise all the flowers will not get pollinated.

8. Cabbages. This is a new trick for me, and I love it! After you harvest your early cabbage, cut a cross in the top of the stem about a quarter of an inch deep. It will produce side shoots just the way broccoli does, often producing four cabbages the size of baseballs!

9. Celery. You can dig up a plant in the fall, put it in a five gallon bucket with drainage holes, and keep it growing and tasty all winter long in a cool dark basement or root cellar, watering occasionally.

10. Carrots. In the fall you can mulch your carrots heavily, and harvest them right out of the ground all winter, according to the Smiths. I've done this with straw, but they get frozen in place. The trick, they said, is a good thick

layer of leaves, then the straw. And cover up well each time after you garner a few. They claim they will stay crisp and tasty all winter long.

Gardening is great fun for us adults, but often it lacks appeal for children. Somehow Sylvia and Ed Smith have created a family where everyone loves to garden. I asked them what the trick is. Sylvia described lots of things they did, but it distilled down to a few basics. Respect your children. Give them meaningful work. Let them experiment. Make things fun, don't hurry. "When your children are young, take time to look at the toads and count the worms," Sylvia said.

Talking about their lifestyle choices, sixteen-year-old Lindsey said to me, "I plan to live this way, too." Ed and Sylvia are doing something right, and it's not just the compost, or the mulch, nor the wide beds and deep fluffy soil.

So Many Seed Catalogs, So Little Time

I like to joke that the spy satellites of the Cold War have all been bought up by the people that sell seeds. That they are up there all summer, seeing who has a garden, and how big. It seems that the bigger my gardens get, the more catalogs arrive each spring.

I'm not complaining, mind you—I love the seed catalogs. They help me get through the winter doldrums, and I do find some wonderful seeds for plants I could never find for sale in a nursery.

Starting plants from seed is not for everyone. But if you don't have a lot of money for gardening, you certainly can save by starting your own plants. One package of tomato seeds that costs me $1.29 will produce all the plants I could want, and still have some left for next year. I grow thirty-six to sixty tomato plants each year, and this would cost me $15 to $25, or more, at a nursery if purchased as seedlings. If you want to grow a lot of cosmos or zinnias, starting seeds is definitely a money saver. Raising a hundred plants started by seed is not much more work than growing a few, and usually each packet of flower seeds has plenty.

I like to grow eight to ten different varieties of tomatoes each year, which is another reason I like to start my own seedlings. I can't necessarily find the types and flavors of tomatoes I want at my local greenhouse. Each year I like to try something new, and I don't like to "put all my eggs in one basket." If my Brandywines don't do well this summer (as was the case last summer), I want some other tomatoes that will produce enough to satisfy my need for home-grown tomatoes. There are hundreds, even thousands of different flowers available by catalog, and I want to try all of them, too. Well, maybe not all this year, but . . .

Starting plants by seed is important to many good cooks. You just can't get everything you want at the grocery store, or even a good farmers' market. Hot peppers are a case in point. There are dozens of varieties available, each with its own Scoville rating of hotness, each with its own distinctive flavor. Squashes, tomatoes, beans, and eggplants are all vegetables with a wide range of flavors, shapes, colors, and textures. Growing your own can add much to the chef's palatte. And every vegetable and herb is so much tastier when it is fresh from the garden.

As you know, I am a proponent of organic gardening. I also believe in supporting family businesses, whether farm stand, bookstore, or seed company. I found two Vermont seed companies that are both organic and family-operated businesses, and as they don't send out glitzy color catalogs to everyone who ever bought seeds from anybody through the mail, I'd like to share their information with you.

High Mowing Seeds is operated by Tom Stearns in Wolcott, Vermont, and can be reached by calling 802-888-1800. This is a certified organic operation specializing in plants that do well in this short season of ours. About a third of the seeds offered are rare or heirloom plants that no one else has for sale.

Tom is a plantsman who is also experimenting with breeding new varieties by cross-pollinating old varieties. He has been working for years trying to get a tomato that will breed true by crossing the Brandywine tomato (my favorite) and an early ripening Czech tomato, the Stupice, but I couldn't talk him out of even a few seeds to try. He is hoping for a truly great tomato: the flavor of the Brandywine combined with the flavor and good qualities of the Stupice, which doesn't split as easily and ripens earlier. But I guess I'll have to wait. Tom said he has grown over 150 varieties of tomatoes to put together the the the list of twenty good ones he sells.

The High Mowing catalog does something I've never seen before: It tells you everything you need to know in order to grow and harvest your own seeds. Will lettuces hybridize (cross-pollinate) if different varieties are planted next to each other? No, according to the catalog, but they may breed with wild lettuces, if any are present. How far apart do you need to plant squashes to prevent unwanted cross-pollination? A quarter of a mile. The catalog tells you this sort of stuff for everything they sell. I'm not sure it is good business, but I suspect Tom Stearns is a seed fanatic who doesn't care so much about the money.

Another source for organically grown seed is Northwind Organic Seeds, run by Thomas Case and Ken Carter in Bakersfield, Vermont. They can be reached at 802-827-6580. Northwind Organic is also one of seven organic farms in Vermont selling seed to High Mowing Seeds.

Some folks (like the two just listed) produce only organically grown seed. But most companies have just a few organically grown varieties. Producing seed commercially is a difficult procedure under the best of conditions, and if a crop gets wiped out, you have nothing to sell next year. I buy most of my seeds from Fedco, a seed cooperative in Maine (call 207-873-7333 for a catalog) that is environmentally conscious and friendly. But even this one needs to buy much of its seed from producers in better climates, and many of those producers are not certified organic.

The same is true for The Cook's Garden, of Londonderry, Vermont (call 1-800-457-9703 for a catalog), which describes itself as the "top supplier of professionally produced, certified organic seed in the USA." The company clearly labels which of its seeds are organic, but half or more of the seeds it sells are not certified organic.

Some seed producers function without pesticides, but for a variety of reasons (economic, philosophical) are not certified. Some use pesticides only in the case of catastrophic "emergency." Being certified as an organic grower in Vermont costs between $150 and $500 for most small operations.

There are a couple of terms you may run across in the catalogs that are good to understand. Seeds are often listed as "treated" or not. You may have bought corn seed that is pink. It is corn that is covered with a chemical to prevent rotting of seeds in the wet soils of early spring. As an organic gardener, I won't buy treated seeds, though many of the seeds I use are not grown organically. As long as I am not importing toxins to my soil, I figure it's okay. I *prefer* to buy organic seeds, but I can't always find what I want. Perhaps I should change my ideas of what I need.

Tomato offerings in catalogs often use the term "determinate" or "indeterminate" to describe them. This is an important distinction. Determinate varieties grow to a certain size, produce one crop of tomatoes, and then no more. Many Roma or paste tomatoes are determinate. Indeterminate tomatoes will keep on growing and producing until Mr. Jack Frost pays a visit. Determinate plants are tidier, but usually produce fewer pounds of tomatoes. On the other hand, they may give you a full harvest, even in years of early frost.

Making selections from seed catalogs can be quite daunting. There are so darn many different offerings, and so little garden space. If only I had more time, more space in the garden, more space in the freezer. . . . But don't get discouraged. Throw out (or pass on to an unsuspecting friend) most of the catalogs. Read one or two, make your choices, write a check, and be done with it. It's still quite a ways till planting time, but I'm already conjuring up the taste of those vine-ripened tomatoes.

Cut Flowers

I love fresh cut flowers. I usually have some that I have grown on my table from March to November. During the winter months I buy cut flowers to bring cheer and remind me that winter doesn't last forever. By now I greatly miss the smells and visual diversity of my flower beds, so I was delighted recently when Lynn Schad of Bloemenwinkel Floral Design Studio in Lebanon, New Hampshire, invited me to go along with her on a buying trip to the Boston Wholesale Flower Market. Here was a chance to be immersed in the smell of flowers, and to learn tricks about flowers from a pro.

We arrived at the market early, having left home at 5 A.M. The market is a big modern building surrounded by parking lots full of trucks and vans, a tall fence, and warning signs that this place is not open to the public. This was going to be an adventure. Lynn comes to the market most weeks, so she is recognized by most of the vendors, and nobody questioned my presence.

I could barely contain my glee when we entered the hall. Back home the temperature would not pass the freezing mark. Here was a room that I later paced off to be a hundred yards long, fifty wide—the size of a football field—filled with summer. Not just spring flowers, but summer. Somewhere in the world it is June, July, and August. There was even one bunch of Festiva Maxima peonies, my favorite of all flowers. In bloom—in late February!

If I had to guess, I'd say I was looking at a million dollars worth of flowers, more packed into one place than I'd ever imagined possible. Things I had never seen. Fantastic roses that cost $9 a stem *wholesale*. Hundreds of roses, packed twenty-five to the bunch in colors only interior designers have names for. When I was growing up, boys only got the packs of crayons with basic colors. Girls got the sixty-four-packs, and learned all the names. Mauve. Burnt sienna. Puce. I'm past fifty and still learning.

Lynn and I first take a quick tour of the market to get a feel for what is special this week. Branches for forcing are what's special, and its not just forsythia and pussy willows. There are 6-foot sprigs of pear, and quince, and then I nearly die. Magnolia. Big branches of magnolias covered with hundreds of deep magenta buds. Each sprig piece is as big as the magnolia tree I planted two or three years ago behind my house. Lynn buys five branches, and I beg and wheedle for a little piece. She agrees.

And nobody is selling us anything. I'm used to African markets where vendors harangue you to buy. Here you pick out what you want, bring it to the counter, pay. Little banter, no hard sell. This is wholesale, they assume you know what you are doing. We spend nearly a thousand dollars on flowers in three hours, loading them onto industrial grade steel carts that argue with me about turning corners.

We buy sweet peas from Italy, which are dreadfully expensive, but so beautiful in look and scent that you shouldn't approach them if you are faint of heart. We get two bunches. Cut daffodils from Ireland, in tight bud, lovely and inexpensive. We buy thirty dozen. One stall has, among other things, three dozen different types of foliage for fillers, everything from cedar to eucalyptus to exotic things I don't know. Lynn gets an armload. This is fun.

The variety in flowers amazed me. Fresh veronica, purple gentians, and other things that don't ever show up at the grocery store, or even in most florist shops. Light lemon-green hellebores and lettuce-green Bells of Ireland. Yellow tulips from France with pastel strokes of color artfully applied to their petals in just the right amount. Little boquets of fresh cut grape hyacinths. Fluffy pink clover. Monkshood.

Lynn taught me some of the tricks she uses for choosing flowers and getting the most out of them. Before buying roses in bud, for example, she squeezes a bud the way you might squeeze a peach to see if it is ripe. If it is not firm, it is old.

The more expensive flowers are, the more the vendors want to sell them, and the less likely they will be to throw them away—even if they are past their prime. This is true in retail, too. Look for mold on stems, and even on blossoms. Look for broken stems in a bunch of ten, or squished flowers. Things get damaged in transport, and by other customers.

I have a frugal streak in me, and have always liked to buy flowers that would last for a week, preferably two. Chrysanthemums, asters, lisianthus, sea lavender last well for me. Roses have usually disapointed me, especially for Valentine's Day. Lynn explained that growers and wholesalers "hold back" their roses before that holiday, accumulating as many as possible for the rush, so they are often well past prime when you buy them.

Lynn challenged me to think about flowers from a different persprective. "Flowers come and flowers go," she said. "Accept that some flowers are just there for a moment, and enjoy them for that. Enjoy your rose in bud, then in full bloom. Enjoy the petals when they fall." It is true that some of the most wonderful flowers are ephemeral, which is part of what makes them special.

When we got back to Lebanon with a rent-a-van full of flowers there was still lots of work "conditioning" our purchases, and you should do this when you bring yours home. First we cut off half an inch with sharp scissors; then we placed them in warm water, not cold. If something looks very sad, submerge it completely, stem, flower, and all.

Woody stems like the magnolias or forsythia need to be split and crushed. Lynn handed me a hammer for mashing them. I also found that my big pocket knife was good to help split the stems the recommended 3 inches, though it wouldn't be difficult to slash a finger doing this, so be careful. Then they need to be placed in your hottest tap water.

Lynn explained that flowers last best if you put them in a clean glass vase, and that metal vases like Grandma's silver one will shorten their lives a little. I still like silver, and will use it anyway. Bacteria or fungus in the water is a real detriment to longevity, so she recommends adding about a teaspoon of Chlorox to each quart of water. And you can prolong flower life by recutting the stems and changing the water every couple of days, or when the water gets murky.

My own experiments with cut flowers this winter taught me that those little white packets of powder you get with cut flowers really do double the life of many flowers. I tried adding sugar to the water, as I'd heard it helped, but it grew gray fuzzy stuff on the stems instead. I heard gin worked, but didn't have or want any. Maybe it works on the Chlorox principle. Or maybe it's an excuse to buy gin.

Putting three pennies in the water with tulips in tight bud helps them keep from opening. Lynn pointed out that flowers in hot places or in the direct sun would not last as long as flowers in cool places. I knew that, and in winter I often move my flowers into the 40-degree mudroom at night to prolong their beauty. The fridge would work, too, I suppose. It's what the wholesalers in Boston do every night.

I was amazed at how much work it is to keep fine cut flowers in a shop, and how little they cost, especially since it is accepted in the business that you will end up throwing away about one third of what you buy. And if someone complains about flowers not doing well, most florists replace them to keep you coming back, even if you put the vase next to the woodstove.

The tip that pleased me the most was this: If you are having a party and want some drop-dead gorgeous flowers for tonight only, talk to your florist. Ask for flowers "on their way out." These are flowers that are past the prime and headed for the dumpster, but that still have one last gorgeous gasp left. You can buy them at a greatly reduced cost, and the florist will be happy to let you do so. It gives some flowers one last chance to show off, and they deserve that.

The Perfect New England Window Box

I love driving by those nice white New England farmhouses, the ones with a neatly mowed lawn, a lilac or two, and a big flower bed with all the flowers my grandmother grew. As likely as not, the house will also have window boxes full of plants in bloom all summer. Window boxes are the icing on the cake, that extra touch that says, "A gardener lives here." This is a good time to build one for your house.

I have built and bought a couple of different types of window boxes. When my boy Josh was little, we built window boxes for his mother out of plywood. We ended up using them as planters on the deck because they were heavy and not sturdy enough to hang out front. Then I bought a plastic window box and the associated hardware. The plants baked on hot days, their tender roots cooking next to a thin layer of plastic. The hardware for hanging a 36-inch box of plants was flimsy, and I ended up jerry-rigging ugly guy wires.

I was delighted when my friend Jim Phelps, an architect in Windsor, Vermont, came up with the perfect design, and let me copy it. Although I can drive a nail without bending it over, I am not a carpenter, but this design was pretty easy for me.

I built my window box out of cedar, because pressure treated pine is heavier and full of toxins (which make it necessary to wear a mask when sawing it into pieces). The materials cost me about twenty-five dollars.

This window box has a good, sturdy design, and it can be taken off the window simply by lifting it from its hanging hardware. When

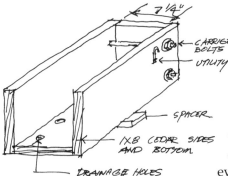

7 1/4"

CARRIGE BOLTS

UTILITY HOOK

SPACER

1X8 CEDAR SIDES AND BOTTOM

DRAINAGE HOLES

EYE

UTILITY HOOK.

I go away for a week, I just lift it off and leave it in a shady place. The wood is a good insulator to protect plant roots from the hot afternoon sun. The cedar itself holds a little water, helping to keep roots cool. It hangs from two screw eyes, which do not protrude much from the surface of the house and are not very noticeable during the winter when the window box is stored in the barn.

Since I don't have a table saw, I asked the guys at my local building supply center to use their "chop saw" to cut my cedar to size, thus assuring it would be cut perfectly. I asked for two pieces 36 inches long, one piece 34½ inches long, and two pieces 7¼ inches square (8-inch lumber comes 7¼ inches wide). If the length of yours will be different, just be sure you have two of one length, and another 1½ inches shorter.

I used a ⅜-inch drill bit to drill holes for the carriage bolts. To get them to line up perfectly, stack your two long boards together and drill through both at the same time. The holes for the bolts should be 2 inches from the top and bottom, and 1½ inches from the ends. I clamped the two boards together so they wouldn't move while I was drilling.

Next put together a bottomless box. I stood up the four sides on a flat surface with the end pieces in between the sides. I did this with the bolts running through the two sides and the nuts loosely attached. Then I used a wrench to snug up the nuts, pulling it all together.

Then I nailed the end blocks in place. Keep the nails away from the corners to avoid cracking the wood. It is important to drive your nails through carefully, so they don't veer off at an angle.

Finally, I installed the bottom of the box using six nails on each side.

A window box needs drainage holes. I used a ⅝-inch paddle

To make a 36-inch window box, you need to buy the following:

~ One 12-foot long cedar board, 1 × 8 inches;

~ Four 10-inch carriage bolts, ⅜ inch in diameter, with washers and nuts;

~ Two utility hooks resembling the letter J, each 2 inches long and protruding 1½ inches;

~ Two sturdy screw eyes (the eye should be about 1 inch in diameter, and the screw 4 to 6 inches long, or long enough to lag into something solid on your house);

~ Twenty-four 2-inch stainless steel ring nails (#6);

~ One scrap of wood 6 inches long, 2½ inches wide, and ¾ inch thick (strapping is fine); and

~ Two 1¼-inch galvanized Phillips head screws.

bit to drill a series of holes about 2 inches apart. Keep the holes toward the front of the box so that excess water won't drip on you house. Be sure to avoid the nails, which extend in 1¼ inches into the wood.

The screw eyes need to be screwed into something solid. There should be solid wood right below the window sill. Pre-drill small holes, then screw in the eyes. For my 36-inch box, I separated the screw eyes by 30 inches.

Mount your utility hooks on the back of the box so they are about an inch from the top. Use a square to draw lines that are perpendicular.

Now mount your box by placing the hooks into the eyes. You will see that the box will swing down until it hits the side of your house. Don't despair! This is easily fixed with a 6-inch scrap of board to serve as a brace or spacer. Tip the window box back up until it is almost level, then attach the brace to the bottom of the box. A screw gun will allow you to do this in place, using 1¼-inch screws. A slight downward angle at the front will cause any excess water to drain to the front, where you have drilled the drainage holes.

Your window box is now ready for planting. I put a piece of weed mat (made of synthetic woven fibers) in the bottom to keep dirt from washing out through the drainage holes. I then added a 2-inch layer of styrofoam peanuts to provide drainage while minimizing weight.

I made my own soil mix of 3 parts compost, 2 parts garden soil, 1½ parts perlite, and 1 part sand. I mixed about ½ cup Pro-Gro organic fertilizer into the soil in this window box. When the plants were in and watered, the whole thing weighed about 40 pounds.

My lawn and gardens will probably never be perfect. I'm just too busy. But when I walk up to the front door and see the bright faces of my window box plants smiling at me, I smile back. So dust off your hammer, and give this a try.

Index

This index lists all plants by common name, even though Latin names are given for most plants in the book. My thought is that, if you know the Latin name, you probably also know the common name, but the reverse is not always true. A few Latin names *are* listed, in cases where most gardeners normally use the Latin. Hostas, for example, are called Hostas, as no one I know calls them Fragrant Plantain–Lily, which is what most books cite as their common name.

References to illustrations are printed in **bold**.